# 2nd Edition

# TEN STEPS
## ★ ★ ★ ★ ★ ★ ★ ★ ★ TO A ★ ★ ★ ★ ★ ★ ★ ★ ★
# FEDERAL JOB

## How to Land a Job in the Obama Administration

### Kathryn Troutman

D0752047

The Resume Place, Inc.
Federal Career Training Institute

Published by The Resume Place, Inc.
Baltimore, MD
Phone: (888) 480-8265
www.resume-place.com

**Published by The Resume Place, Inc.**
**Baltimore, MD**
**Phone: (888) 480-8265**
**www.resume-place.com**
**Email: resume@resume-place.com**

Copyright © 2009
Printed in the United States of America

ISBN: 978-0-9647025-9-2

**AUTHOR'S NOTE:**
Sample case studies are real, but fictionalized.
All federal applicants have given permission for their job application information
to be used as samples for this publication. Privacy policy is strictly enforced.

**PUBLICATION TEAM:**
Interior Page Designer: Paulina Chen, LivingWaterDesigns, LLC
Cover and CD-ROM Designer: Brian Moore
Developmental Editor/Technical Researcher: Paulina Chen
Samples Editor: Carla M. Waskiewicz
CD-ROM Production: Mark Hoyer
Proofreader: Young H. Chung
Indexer: L. Pilar Wyman
Contributing Technical Researchers/Writers:
Emily K. Troutman, Sarah Blazucki, and Elizabeth Juge

**REAL STORY FEDERAL RESUME STORY CONTRIBUTORS:**
Carla Waskiewicz, Elizabeth Juge, Diane Burns, Nancy Segal,
Michael Ottensmeyer, Mary Carroll-Mason, Dottie Hendricks, Sarah Blazucki,
and Rita Chambers.

**PHOTO CREDITS:**
Patsy Lynch and Emily Troutman

# Table of Contents

# Case Studies Table of Contents

The following list of 24 case studies are from real life federal job search experiences. Fictionalized names are used, but the other information is actual data. Many of these studies are printed in the book; all of the studies are included on the CD-ROM and can be used as templates for writing your resume.

# Acknowledgements

This book is a team project from The Resume Place, Inc. Based on our experiences since 2003, just after 9/11 and the first edition of the book, we have helped thousands of private industry jobseekers begin their federal careers. Here at The Resume Place, our expert, trained Certified Federal Resume Writers and Coaches have analyzed transferrable skills and possibilities for federal careers from all walks of private industry life. I would like to sincerely thank Carla Waskiewicz, Elizabeth Juge, Diane Burns, Nancy Segal, Michael Ottensmeyer, Mary Carroll-Mason, Dottie Hendricks, Sarah Blazucki, and Rita Chambers for their incredible before & after, private industry to federal real stories in this book.

A very special thanks to Senior Federal Resume Writer and Analyst, Carla Waskiewicz, who was the Sample Real Story Case Manager who researched some of the best private industry to federal resume samples for your study and review. Carla is also our firm's senior consultant in converting private industry to federal resumes. She is an expert in analyzing the "skills or mission match" between a private industry career and a federal agency career.

Elizabeth Juge provided editorial direction and insight into Chapter 7 regarding KSA writing with her expertise in story-telling KSAs. Elizabeth Juge and Craig Taylor developed the latest "how to apply" builders and web addresses for the amazing Federal Resume Builder Chart in Step 8. Sarah Blazucki provided a technical review of the most complex chapter—*Master the Federal and Electronic Resume*—to make sure the step-by-step instructions are easy to follow for a federal resume writer.

This book could never have been so beautiful or clearly presented without the clear, critical thinking, knowledge of federal application processes, editorial expertise, and print book design skills contributed by Paulina Chen, a former federal employee of the Environmental Protection Agency. Her attention to detail, logic, and graphic design makes this book readable and understandable, even though it is a complex process for first-time federal job applicants. Paulina also did the interior page design for the first edition of this book (2002), which won the Best Careers Book of the Year.

Brian Moore designed the cover of the 1st edition (contributing to the Best Careers Book of the Year recognition as well) and now the 2nd edition. His creative presentation of the steps for the first-time applicant sets the tone for the book.

I would also like to thank Young Chung for her detailed proofreading of this entire manuscript and case studies and Mark Hoyer, as the producer of the CD-ROM.

Private industry to federal resume stories from real people who contributed their resumes to this book include: Lisa Ford, Natalie Wood-Smith, Martin Frazier, Julie Kubiak, Cathy Sampson, Stephanie Gallahan, KeRita Anakoro, Jeff Clopein, Gary Bills, David Matthews, Philip Loftus, John Leszczynski, and Charlie McCoy. Thank you so much for sharing your before and after resumes and federal job search stories. Your stories will result in successes for thousands of jobseekers.

If I had $1 (U.S., of course) for each time that a reader of my long-running careers column has asked me about the adventure of capturing a federal civil service job for his or her very own, the author of this guide and I could afford to cruise around the world on the Queen Mary II. No such luck, but the questions keep floating in.

In bad times and good, I receive queries from new graduates seeking to invest their youth in doing something meaningful for their country, and from transitioning military members who've already done something meaningful for their country and, after earning bonus points for their service, are headed to the front of the line for fine federal jobs.

I hear questions from midcareer switchers seeking greater employment stability than they've found in private industry, and from prime-timers who are discovering that Uncle Sam's one of the nation's best-paying employers, as well as one who looks at abilities rather than birthdays.

Enormous interest in government merit jobs is not surprising. Federal employees are a microcosm of the country's workforce—virtually every kind of work found in the private sector is mirrored in the federal. While headquarters for federal civilian workplaces are typically located in Washington or nearby, 80 percent of federal jobs are found in other parts of the country and the world.

So what's the catch? Is government employment one big bureaucratic yawn? Not at all, says this book's author, Kathryn Troutman: "I speak with federal employees almost every day. The majority like what they do and feel that their work matters."

I met Kathryn a few years ago when she came to Southern California on a book tour promoting another of her excellent how-to books on government employment. Impressed with the depth of her knowledge, I took the unusual step of inviting her to lunch. I was rewarded with the confirmation that Kathryn is an authentic expert on the specialty of federal employment. Since that meeting, Kathryn Troutman is the first source I tap when readers ask me federal job questions that I can't answer.

I expect that the questions will continue nonstop. Countless job seekers are intensely interested in learning all about the reality of rewards and challenges in federal employment – and especially they ask: "How can I get hired sooner rather than later?"

This guidebook holds the answers.

*Joyce Lain Kennedy*
Syndicated careers columnist
Tribune Media Services

This book, *Ten Steps to a Federal Job, Second Edition,* is the culmination of my years of teaching, coaching, writing, and editing for anxious federal jobseekers who are applying for Competitive positions in the federal government. The subtitle—*How to Land a Job in the Obama Administration*—is NEW. If you follow the Ten Steps you CAN land a Civil Service job in an exciting new government with new leadership and new purpose. The book and CD-ROM also contains a collection of 23 successful private industry to federal resumes created by the expert Certified Federal Resume Writers and Coaches of The Resume Place, Inc. who have written the best federal resumes that resulted in being referred to a job, selected for an interview, and hired.

Recently, with the development of the 2nd edition of this book, I realized that through my many years of training federal resume & KSA writing, I have developed a simple 5-point writing method, which I now call the "Troutman Method." I was thrilled to realize that the techniques I have honed over the last 15 years have come together into one awesome application approach to getting hired by the federal government.

According to dictionary.com, the definition of the word "method" is "a procedure, technique, or way of doing something, esp. in accordance with a definite plan."

This book is a clear introduction to the successful Troutman Method, which has been proven by thousands of individuals who have been referred for jobs, selected for interviews, and hired into federal careers.

*Why is the Troutman Method so special?*

- **It really works.** The success of the Troutman Method is demonstrated by all of the True Stories of the samples in this book. Real people volunteered their true federal job search stories for this book to help you break into government.

- **It is simple.** I have figured out how to explain this complicated process to jobseekers, every step of the way, with tools, tips, and formatting techniques that are clear and helpful.

- **It is complete.** Applying for a federal job is a job search campaign, not simply a job application as in private industry. I have covered ALL of the steps needed to successfully navigate the maze of requirements.

- **It is well tested.** The Ten Step curriculum is also a training program that has been taught in military bases around the world by military transition counselors. More than 10,000 people per year learn about the Ten Step method. I also teach this curriculum in a popular half-day course to federal employees all over the U.S. *The Steps to a Federal Job* is focused on the transition from private industry to federal jobs, but the Troutman Method also works for federal employees seeking promotions.

*Five Main Lessons from the Troutman Method*

- ACCOMPLISHMENTS. Writing, remembering, and sharing accomplishments for your resume, KSAs, and preparation for Behavior Based Interviews (Step 3 – Target Your Top Accomplishments)

- VACANCY ANNOUNCEMENTS. Researching and interpreting vacancy announcements for keywords to be included in the federal resume and KSAs (Step 4 – Find the Perfect Job Announcement)

- KEYWORDS. Learning about the new Outline Format with Keywords and Headlines for USAJOBS and CPOL Resume Builders (Step 5 – Identify your Keywords)

- OUTLINE FORMAT. Learning how to write your Outline Format for USAJOBS Resume Builder (Step 6 – Master the Federal and Electronic Resume)

- KSAS WITH THE CCAR. Learning how to write KSAs that are impressive using the Context-Challenge-Action-Results formula, and how to cover the KSAs in the resume when that is required! (Step 7 – Conquer the KSAs and Questionnaires)

In this book, Steps 1 and 2 are critical research steps about federal jobs to gain the information you need to write the resume and KSA. When you get to Step 3 through 7, you will be writing your federal resume and KSA and following the Troutman Method.

The Ten Steps to a Federal Job Campaign and the Troutman Method for Applying for Federal Jobs are presented in this book in the most colorful, clear, and simplified way that I could dream up this year. Follow the directions and you could land the career of a lifetime that will last for the remainder of your career!

Finally, remember to send your federal job success story to me at Kathryn@resume-place.com.

Sincerely,
***Kathryn Troutman***
Author, Trainer, and President
The Resume Place, Inc.

**Quote**

" Things have changed and there are going to be lots of smart, established, really poised and terrific people OUT-OF-WORK.  If you just put on the TV you'll see the folks who are supposed to be economic advisors, captains-of-industry, top of the class, front-of-the-line folks clamoring for their footing in an unfamiliar economic setting, -- you'll understand nobody knows what to do.  The only way to begin to find out what to do is to find out what works. And your tips work. I got my first paycheck…just in time as the banks and the market are collapsing.  A number of people were surprised I got hired as the City and State have hiring freezes... but the Feds keep hiring. "

*Karen Rosenberger, PP, AICP*
*Intermodal Transportation Coordinator*
*with the Federal Highway Administration*

*Photo: Patsy Lynch, 2008*

**Do you want to be a part of the change** in government, the economy, jobs, and improved service to the American Public?

Do you want a stable, quality public service job where you can make a difference?

There are many good reasons why a person would want to work for the government. The federal government closely monitors employee satisfaction on factors such as pay, perks, location, infrastructure, training, supervision, fairness, and contribution to the agency's mission. The proof that most federal employees are satisfied with their jobs is the very high retention rate. Most feds *stay* feds.

However, the process of getting hired is a key drawback. But remember that this book—*Ten Steps to a Federal Job*—and The Resume Place, Inc. can help make this process much easier for you.

This chapter will help you weigh these pros and cons to make the right decision about whether or not to pursue a government job.

## Pros: Working for the Federal Government

### ✪ Job Security and Career Stability

The federal government is widely regarded as one of the most stable and reliable employers, especially in turbulent economic times. Federal employees have more job protection than their private sector counterparts, who may be fired at any time for any reason (or for no reason). Though occasionally "reductions in force," (RIFs) are instituted, outright termination is rare. Attrition and voluntary retirement incentives are usually the first line of action for any necessary "downsizing" before firings or layoffs. Once the employee's probationary period (usually a year) is over, most employees can be fired only for "cause," i.e., a performance or discipline-related issue. Review bodies such as the Merit Systems Protection Board, union membership, clear expectations, regular performance appraisals, and other mechanisms all help to ensure fairness in employment decisions.

### ✪ Competitive Pay

It is frequently thought that federal service pays less than the private sector. This assumption is not true in many of the cases we have seen when people made the jump from private industry to federal employment. Furthermore, if a person took a job with less annual salary (though not necessarily less in hourly pay when you consider the hours that some work in private industry), federal service is almost always still competitive with private industry jobs when you take into account the many benefits of federal employment. Some benefits can be assigned a dollar value, such as health benefits, family leave, vacation time, and holidays, while others are less tangible, but often equally important, such as job stability, lower levels of job stress, and flexible hours. Instead of competing against your co-workers for raises, salary increases in the federal government are generally awarded on a set schedule. An employee under the General Schedule usually receives annual increases for the first three years, followed by several biannual increases, and then increases every three years. Employees work their way up a scale of known salary hikes, and this system allows the employee to plan ahead. Federal employees also receive cost of living adjustments (COLAs) nearly every year, ranging from about 1.8% to 3.9%.

### ✪ Public Service / Mission-Oriented

According to the U.S. Merit Systems Protection Board, *Merit Principles Survey 2005*, "Results show that Federal employees are committed public servants."

• 94% believe that their agency's mission is important

• 92% understand how their work contributes to the agency's overall mission

• 86% find the work they do to be meaningful

Recently, there has been more focus in the federal government on "linking" the work of each employee with specific aspects of the agency's mission. In this way, each employee understands what he or she contributes to the overall purpose of the agency, instead of feeling like just a cog in the wheel.

## ✪ Prestige, Pride, and History

Despite the notion that federal employees are just bureaucrats, most federal employees have a sense of pride in serving their government. To be a part, large or small, of the United States Government is an honor. To know that you are representing your country, can be very satisfying!

## ✪ Opportunity to Fight Terrorism

In the post-9/11 world, terrorism is no longer a far-away concept we see on the nightly news, unfolding in distant countries. Federal employment offers many opportunities to fight terrorism right here at home to keep America safe. These opportunities can be found not only in the armed forces or law enforcement agencies. For example, the U.S. Postal Service is on the front lines of ensuring that mail is not used to effectuate terrorist attacks.

## ✪ Transfers and Promotions

It is often said that the key to federal employment is to "get your foot in the door." In many cases, this is sage advice. For example, an attorney may give up a salary of $75,000 for a federal salary of $64,000, then get promoted in the next year or two, ending up with a salary of around $100,000. Thus, getting your foot in the door— getting a federal job in the first place—can position you for other opportunities such as promotions or transfers. Also, many agencies are generous in allowing voluntary or hardship transfers. The federal government has offices practically everywhere in America (and abroad), and this could be an important benefit if you should find yourself needing to relocate to take care of an elderly or sick relative, or if your spouse got a great job offer in another town.

## ✪ Freedom from Discrimination

In the private sector, hiring and promotion decisions are supposed to be made free from unlawful discrimination on the basis of race, color, religion, sex, national origin, age, or disability. The federal sector takes this requirement very seriously, and aspires to be the example for the American workforce. If you suspect that the private sector has been turning you down for jobs on the basis of age or disability, or other unlawful basis, consider trying the federal sector.

## ✪ Disaster Assistance and Employee Assistance Programs (EAP)

The federal government demonstrates a real commitment to the safety, health, and well-being of its employees. During recent disasters such as Hurricane Katrina, the federal government allowed many of its employees to remain on payroll even when offices were closed. Agencies also invited their employees to take advantage of counseling and other services to enable employees to deal with the emotional, logistical, and financial fallout from such disasters. Agencies were flexible in allowing employees time off or modified schedules to deal with housing issues, contractors, insurance adjusters, and other disaster-related issues.

## ✪ Training Opportunities

Many agencies have a special budget for training, which not only better prepares employees for their current jobs, but positions them for advancement. Some training is online and can be conducted right from your desk. This training improves the employee's skills and their resume!

## ✪ Excellent Benefits

Federal benefits are among the best available anywhere, including vacation days, sick leave, leave donation programs, and retirement benefits. The health coverage is equal to or better than almost anything else around, and you can contribute your premiums in pre-tax dollars. Coverage for the employee and his or her family is very competitive! There are no medical examination requirements, age restrictions, exclusions for preexisting conditions, or waiting periods for benefits to begin.

The federal government also offers excellent life insurance and long-term disability insurance options.

The Flexible Spending Account (FSA) program reimburses employees for many non-covered medical expenditures and dependent-care costs. FSAs are effective financial management tools that can stretch the disposable incomes and ensure that funds are available, when needed, to pay for out-of-pocket medical costs or dependent-care expenses of a child or parent.

Check out this link for a great overview of federal job benefits: http://www.usajobs.gov/ei61.asp.

## ✪ Family and Medical Leave

The Family and Medical Leave Act (FMLA) requires covered employers to provide eligible employees up to 12 weeks of unpaid leave for the birth and care of the newborn child of the employee; for placement with the employee of a son or daughter through adoption or foster care; to care for an immediate family member (spouse, child, or parent) with a serious health condition; or to take medical leave when the employee is unable to work because of a serious health condition. Federal employees also enjoy "family-friendly leave policies," such as paid time off to serve as an organ donor or bone marrow donor, along with leave-sharing programs for sick employees who have used up their sick leave, and other benefits. Find out more at: http://www.opm.gov/oca/leave/index.asp.

## ✪ 401(k)-type Match Program

The Thrift Savings Program, similar to a 401(k), lets you save money in pre-tax dollars with substantial federal matching. Many experts consider it the best savings/investment program around. There are several options to choose from, including government funds that are considered very safe in economically turbulent times, and various funds geared to different retirement goals. Employees can also borrow against the TSP account. Find out more at www.tsp.gov.

## ✪ Flexible Work Schedules and Telecommuting

Most agencies allow flexible work hours that enable employees to take an extra day or two off every pay period. Flexible schedules can take the form of nine 9-hour days in a two-week period, with an extra day off in that period, or four 10-hour days with one day off every week.

Employees may also be able to opt for flexiplace. Employees on flexiplace, also called telecommuting, typically work at home, but can work at other agency-approved locations. For example, some agencies have telecommuting centers established in metropolitan areas for federal employees who would otherwise commute long distances between home and work. Telecommuting centers are furnished with the necessary office supplies and equipment.

## ✪ Transit Subsidy (in the Washington, DC metropolitan area)

This program can pay for most or all of the cost of public transit. In the DC area, subway transit is excellent. Save the wear and tear on your car, or go even greener and skip the car payment altogether!

## ✪ 10 Federal Holidays Each Year

How many people do you know in the private sector who is off for Columbus Day? Efficient and self-starting workers can get all their work done, earn an honest day's pay, and still have quite a lot of leisure time given the holidays, the flexible work hours, and the generous leave policies. Because the President ordains these holidays, you can enjoy these holidays off without guilt, and your boss will not frown—he or she will be off too! Stress-free time off from work is a major benefit of federal service.

The holidays are:
- New Year's Day
- Martin Luther King, Jr.'s Birthday
- Washington's Birthday
- Memorial Day
- Independence Day
- Labor Day
- Columbus Day
- Veterans Day
- Thanksgiving Day
- Christmas Day

## ✪ 13-26 Days of Leave Each Year (depending on years in government)

The longer you serve, the more leave time you receive each year. By combining flexible work hours and leave, most federal employees work fewer hours per week than their private-sector counterparts. As long as your work gets done, many supervisors are very flexible about how you plan your time. Also, your boss will almost never make you give up your vacation plans for a last-minute emergency project, which is all too common in the private sector!

## ✪ Government Rates

Many public airline carriers and hotels provide government rates. In some cases, you are not required to be on official duty to take advantage of the government rate; simply show your federal ID.

## ✪ Generosity

It is not widely known, but federal employees are among the most generous givers in America. The Combined Federal Campaign, a coordinated program of charitable giving, collects hundreds of thousands of dollars a year for important charities, such as helping the blind, conducting life-saving research, assisting veterans, among many others. In 2007, federal employees donated $273.1 million to thousands of organizations. Donations of any size can be made in lump sums or through relatively painless payroll deductions, and all donations are tax deductible. Sharing in this sense of community outreach and improvement of America through charitable giving is a meaningful benefit to federal employment.

## ✪ Other Benefits

Some agencies also offer tuition assistance, tuition reimbursement, extra pay for difficult-to-fill positions, relocation reimbursement, awards, bonuses, and other benefits. The website of each agency usually lists the benefits available. Specific benefits are also often listed in the vacancy announcement for each position.

## Cons: The Federal Job Search

- The government as an employer is huge and intimidating; it is a challenge to understand how to "get in."
- The federal job application process is significantly different from the private sector; it will require substantial time and commitment to learn and execute the steps to landing a federal job.
- Novice federal jobseekers using materials they have prepared for the private sector usually do not get too far in their federal job search.
- Federal resumes are more detailed and complex to prepare. The average private industry resume is 2 pages. The average federal resume is 3-4 pages, and many applications require additional written responses to essay questions.
- A response to your federal application can take months. The government is working on an initiative to make a job offer within 45 days from the vacancy announcement closing date. This is a vast improvement from the past.

"Supervisors and upper level new employees believed that the hiring process was too complex and took too long. About a third of the new hires did not apply for other Federal jobs they were interested in because they would have had to write new essays or revise their existing essays describing their knowledge, skills and abilities; while about a fourth did not apply because they would have needed to rewrite or reformat their résumé." (U.S. Merit Systems Protection

Board, *In Search of Highly Skilled Workers; A Study on the Hiring of Upper Level Employees from Outside the Federal Government*, February 2008)

## Good News: Job Growth in the Federal Government

The good news for those of you who still want to pursue a federal job—the jobs are out there. The following statistics demonstrate one of the reasons why the government will be hiring more from outside sources in the next 10 years.

- In September 2006, 40% of permanent full-time federal employees were 50 years of age or older.
- About 60% of the federal government's white-collar employees and 90% of the members of the Senior Executive Service will become eligible to retire within the next 10 years. (U.S. Merit Systems Protection Board, *Issues of Merit*, July 2007)

Besides hiring to backfill an aging workforce, the government must also hire to meet changing missions.

"Over the next two years, our largest federal agencies project that they will hire nearly 193,000 new workers for "mission-critical" jobs. While there are other federal jobs that will be filled during this time, including those in clerical and support positions, the jobs listed in this report constitute the bulk of our federal government's hiring needs. These jobs cover almost every occupational field, will be available across the country and all of them advance the interests of the American people. This report confirms that no matter what your area of expertise, or where you live, if you are looking for a job where you can develop your professional skills and make a difference in the lives of others, the federal government has a job for you."
(Partnership for Public Service, *Where the Jobs Are: Mission Critical Opportunities for America*, July 2007, http://ourpublicservice.org/OPS/publications/viewcontentdetails.php?id=118)

## Federal Job Search Decision Questions

The following questions may help you determine whether or not a federal job search is right for you:

1, Do you need a good job with good pay, benefits, career growth opportunities, and stability?
*Yes or no*

2  Can you handle a job search that might take two to six months?
*Yes or no*

3. Can you spend one to three hours per day researching job announcements, mission statements, agency programs, preparing applications, and updating your application list?
*Yes or no*

4. Are you organized and efficient in preparing and saving your applications and announcements?
*Yes or no*

5. Are you determined to persevere at searching for a career-type position?
*Yes or no*

6. Do you want a job where you can make a difference for many people?
*Yes or no*

If you have answered yes to four out of the six questions above, then you should begin your federal job search now.

## Case Studies of Successful Federal Job Campaigns

In this book, you will find federal resume case studies for 12 types of positions in government. The case studies showcase real people who are employed by the government, and each case study contains before/after resumes and their success stories. Many of these employees received a raise shortly after hiring and were promoted the following year. Keep these success stories in mind to stay motivated and to MAKE THIS HAPPEN!

## Strategy Tip

Throughout this book, we will provide you with key strategy tips. Our first one is simple: *Always keep your objective visible during your federal job search. At times, you may become frustrated with the process. Keep your goal clear and persevere!*

## Summary

To remind you about your reasons for starting a federal job search, fill in the following:

✪ The date you started your federal job search campaign:

✪ Your personal reasons for pursuing a federal job:

✪ Your goals (for example, what type of job, location, or time frame for getting hired):

## Quote

**"** I have been officially selected for and offered the position of Program Analyst, SV-0343-I (GS-13 equiv) with the Dept of Homeland Security, Transportation Security Admin. My background check was completed last week and I started my new position on June 22, 20xx. I submitted 43 applications in all; 35 online and 8 by mail. I received 27 responses indicating that I was considered qualified for the applied position. Most of these are at the GS-9 to GS-12 level. I officially interviewed for 5 positions. Thank you again for your fantastic "wordmanship" and assembly of my resume. **"**

*Private Sector to Federal Job Seeker*
*Inventory Specialist*
*to Management & Program Analyst (GS-13)*

# STEP ONE
## Focus Your Federal Job Search

You probably already know that the federal government is the largest employer worldwide. But what else can we learn about the federal government? This step is about researching valuable information to give you a head start towards a successful job search. You should also be aware that the information presented here is just the tip of the iceberg; the government has a vast amount of research and statistics available to the general public on the internet. Go ahead and take advantage of it!

## Overview

Federal Job Statistics

How Much Time Will A Typical Federal Application Take to Prepare?

Do I Have to be a U.S. Citizen to Apply for a Federal Job?

Top Reasons Why Federal Managers Hire Outside Applicants

Do You Have the Skills the Government is Looking For?

Which Occupations is the Government Hiring From the Outside?

Backgrounds of Outside Hires

Types of Federal Jobs

Decide on Agencies

Review Job Titles and Occupational Series

Matching Qualifications

Federal Grade and Pay Structure

Senior Executive Service

## Federal Job Statistics

| | |
|---|---|
| Full-time federal civilian employees (excluding U.S. Postal Service and foreign nationals employed overseas) | 1.85 million |
| Average age | 46.8 |
| Average length of service | 16.6 |
| Men | 56% |
| Women | 44% |
| Total minorities | 31.4% |
| College degreed | 42% |
| Average salary | $61,714 |
| Average salary, DC metropolitan area | $79,695 |
| White collar | 89% |
| Largest Agency – Department of Defense | 35% |
| Homeland Security | 13% |

U.S. Office of Personnel Management, *Federal Civilian Workforce Statistics Fact Book*, 2005 Edition.

*Translation*

On any given day, there are more than 30,000 jobs posted on USAJOBS. In order to be successful, you need to focus your federal job search. You will need to narrow down which of the these jobs you will invest your time applying for. To narrow your focus, you will need to take into account your interests, your qualifications, and the current hiring needs of the federal government.

"Supervisors and upper level new employees believed that the hiring process was too complex and took too long. About a third of the new hires did not apply for other Federal jobs they were interested in because they would have had to write new essays or revise their existing essays describing their knowledge, skills and abilities; while about a fourth did not apply because they would have needed to rewrite or reformat their résumé."
(U.S. Merit Systems Protection Board, *In Search of Highly Skilled Workers; A Study on the Hiring of Upper Level Employees from Outside the Federal Government*, February 2008)

## How Much Time Will a Typical Federal Application Take to Prepare?

Keep in mind that professional resume writers at The Resume Place spend roughly 8 – 10 hours preparing your first job application package without KSAs (Knowledge, Skills, and Abilities essays), and up to 15 hours preparing your first job application package with KSAs. Additional job applications require nearly 2 hours to research the vacancy announcements and edit your resume, and another 3-5 hours for KSAs and questionnaires. Of course, if you are new to the federal job search process, the application packages could take you longer to prepare on your own.

Searching for appropriate vacancy announcements could take an hour per day if you are serious about your federal job search campaign, but keep in mind that this investment could pay off tremendously for you.

### Strategy Tip
Your best time saver will be to carefully select the vacancy announcements that you are most interested in and most qualified for.

## Do I Have to be a U.S. Citizen To Apply For a Federal Job?

As a general rule, only U.S. citizens or nationals are eligible for competitive jobs in the civil service. This restriction was established by an executive order. In addition, Congress annually imposes a ban on using appropriated funds to hire noncitizens within the United States (certain groups of noncitizens are not included in this ban). Further, immigration law limits public and private sector hiring to only individuals who are 1) U.S. citizens or nationals; 2) aliens assigned by the U.S. Citizenship and Immigration Services (CIS) to a class of immigrants authorized to be employed (the largest group in this class is aliens lawfully admitted for permanent U.S. residence); or 3) an individual alien expressly authorized by the CIS to be employed.

Despite all of these limitations and restrictions, it is possible for noncitizens to obtain federal jobs in the U.S. For example, an agency may hire a qualified noncitizen in the excepted service or the Senior Executive Service if it is permitted to do so by the annual appropriations act and immigration law. And, if agencies cannot find qualified citizens to fill jobs in the competitive service, they may then hire noncitizens for those jobs. However, noncitizens may only be given an excepted appointment and will never acquire status. They may not be promoted or reassigned to another civil service job except in situations where qualified citizens are not available.

## Top Reasons Why Federal Managers Hire Outside Applicants

What would make a supervisor hire you over someone who is already working in the government? A recent government survey asked just that question of supervisors who hired new employees from outside the federal government. Here is their answer:

"With 95 percent of supervisors having hired the candidate they believed to be the best qualified, it is not surprising that a majority of these supervisors (67 percent) indicated that the overall quality of the external applicant they hired was better than that of other Federal employees they knew in similar positions. Furthermore, an overwhelming majority of supervisors (95 percent) indicated that the individual they hired had the talent they needed to accomplish their mission."

| Reasons Given by Supervisors for Hiring External Candidates | |
| --- | --- |
| This particular applicant was clearly better qualified than the others, including internal applicants | 68% |
| To fill a skill gap | 64% |
| To improve the quality of my workforce | 47% |
| I have previously observed the employee perform on the job | 34% |
| There were no, or very few, well-qualified internal applicants | 32% |
| To get someone with new or fresh perspective | 19% |
| To improve the diversity of my workforce | 17% |
| To meet succesion planning goals | 15% |
| Felt pressured by higher management | 0.3% |

U.S. Merit Systems Protection Board, *In Search of Highly Skilled Workers: A Study on the Hiring of Upper Level Employees from Outside the Federal Government*, February 2008.

### Strategy Tip

Make sure you are highly qualified for the job opening. In fact, it may be to your advantage to apply for a job that is at a lower level than your qualifications, so that you can get hired by the federal government and move to a higher level later.

## Do You Have the Skills the Government is Looking For?

You will greatly improve your chances of getting hired if you apply for jobs in the career field that the government is currently hiring. If you are applying for a job not listed on these tables, you could still find the job that you are looking for, but it may take you longer to get hired if there are only a few available openings. We will look at three current measures.

### New Hires by Occupation, FY 2007

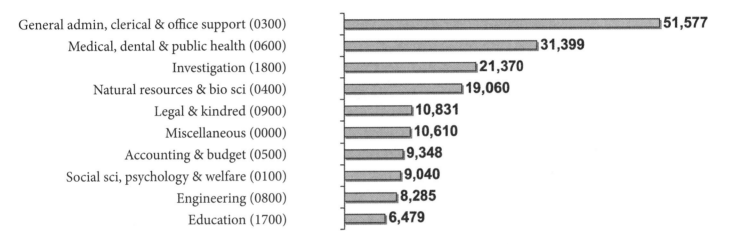

| Occupation | New Hires |
|---|---|
| General admin, clerical & office support (0300) | 51,577 |
| Medical, dental & public health (0600) | 31,399 |
| Investigation (1800) | 21,370 |
| Natural resources & bio sci (0400) | 19,060 |
| Legal & kindred (0900) | 10,831 |
| Miscellaneous (0000) | 10,610 |
| Accounting & budget (0500) | 9,348 |
| Social sci, psychology & welfare (0100) | 9,040 |
| Engineering (0800) | 8,285 |
| Education (1700) | 6,479 |

U.S. Office of Personnel Management, *Table 18—Accessions by type, branch, and selected agecy, all areas,* December 2006 and January 2007, http://www.opm.gov/feddata/html/2007/january/table18.asp.

**Top 10 Occupations Posted on USAJOBS** (as of September 5, 2008)

- ✪ Administration & Program Management, GS-0301
- ✪ Office Clerk/Assistant, GS-0303
- ✪ Management & Program Analyst, GS-0343
- ✪ Information Technology, GS-2200
- ✪ HR Specialist, GS-0201
- ✪ Business/Industry, GS-1101
- ✪ Training & Education Tech, GS-1702
- ✪ Education & Training Spec, GS-1701
- ✪ Training Instructor, GS-1712
- ✪ Health Aid/Technician, GS-0640

To find the latest information on the top jobs being posted on USAJOBS, go to http://www.usajobs.gov/infocenter/topOccupations.asp.

**Top 10 Areas Where the Government Is/Will Be Hiring, FY 2007-2009**

| Career Field | Projected Hires |
|---|---|
| Security & Protection | 35,620 |
| Medical & Public Health | 35,350 |
| Compliance & Enforcement | 27,243 |
| Administration/Program Management | 14,305 |
| Information Technology | 11,562 |
| Business & Industry | 11,407 |
| Engineering | 10,712 |
| Accounting & Budget | 9,841 |
| Legal | 9,691 |
| Social Sciences | 4,151 |

Partnership for Public Service, *Where the Jobs Are: Mission Critical Opportunities for America*, July 2007, http://ourpublicservice.org/OPS/publications/viewcontentdetails.php?id=118.

## Which Occupations is the Government Hiring From the Outside?

The data below is split between upper level new hires (in the GS-12 through 15 range or similar) and entry-level new hires (GS-5 through 9 range or similar).

| Percent of Upper Level New Hires by Occupation, FY 2005 | |
|---|---|
| Information Technology Management | 12.4% |
| General Management & Administration | 9.0% |
| Medical Officer | 7.1% |
| Program and Management Analysis | 6.1% |
| Attorney | 5.4% |
| Intelligence | 4.4% |
| Security Administration | 2.6% |
| Logistics Management | 2.4% |
| General Engineering | 2.2% |
| Internal Revenue Agent | 1.6% |

U.S. Merit Systems Protection Board, *In Search of Highly Skilled Workers: A Study on the Hiring of Upper Level Employees from Outside the Federal Government*, February 2008.

| Top 10 Occupations for Which the Government Hired Professional and Administrative Entry-Level New Hires, FY 2005 | | |
|---|---|---|
| *Job Title* | *Occupational Series* | *Percent of New Hires* |
| Social Insurance Administration | 0105 | 13.5% |
| Customs and Border Protection Officer | 1895 | 6.1% |
| Miscellaneous Administration | 0301 | 5.5% |
| Contracting | 1102 | 4.7% |
| Auditing | 0511 | 4.3% |
| Information Technology Management | 2210 | 3.6% |
| Natural Resources/Biological Sciences | 0401 | 3.4% |
| Nurse | 0610 | 3.3% |
| Criminal Investigator | 1811 | 3.0% |
| Management/Program Analyst | 0343 | 2.6% |

U.S. Merit Systems Protection Board, *Attracting the Next Generation: A Look at Federal Entry-Level New Hires*, January 2008.

## Backgrounds of Outside Hires

**Upper Level Hires' Work Background (GS-12 through 15 or similar)**

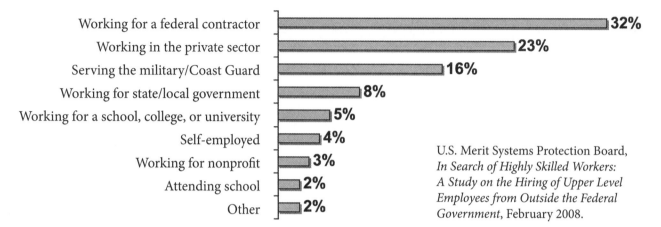

| Background | Percent |
|---|---|
| Working for a federal contractor | 32% |
| Working in the private sector | 23% |
| Serving the military/Coast Guard | 16% |
| Working for state/local government | 8% |
| Working for a school, college, or university | 5% |
| Self-employed | 4% |
| Working for nonprofit | 3% |
| Attending school | 2% |
| Other | 2% |

U.S. Merit Systems Protection Board, *In Search of Highly Skilled Workers: A Study on the Hiring of Upper Level Employees from Outside the Federal Government*, February 2008.

According to this chart, about half of the new upper-level (GS 12 – 15) hires responding to this survey had some government-related experience either as federal contractors or military personnel. This type of work experience gives these applicants some advantages, such as:

- Networking contacts with people with information about job vacancies
- Better understanding of the agency culture
- More knowledge of the federal hiring process
- Knowing the hiring officials

### Strategy Tip
If you are having difficulty landing a federal job, you could first try to get a job as a federal contractor to better position yourself among your competition.

For entry-level (GS 5-9 or similar) hires, regardless of whether you have been working or just completed school, you have roughly the same chance of being hired into the federal government. (U.S. Merit Systems Protection Board, *Attracting the Next Generation: A Look at Federal Entry-Level New Hires*, January 2008)

## Types of Federal Jobs

### Job Classification

The different classes of jobs in the federal government each have different hiring practices. This information is important for you to strategize your application depending on the job type you are applying for. Ligaya Fernandez, retired Senior Personnel Policy Analyst, had this to say about the Occupational Families and Groups: "The government likes to create groups and categorize everything, so that we can analyze information, create reports and statistics." The government has neatly organized Job Families and Job Titles according to skill sets. This can help you find the job you are qualified for and stay organized in your federal job search.

### Competitive Service Jobs

Competitive Service jobs are under U.S. Office of Personnel Management's (OPM) jurisdiction and follow laws to ensure that applicants and employees receive fair and equal treatment in the hiring process. Selecting officials have broad authority to review more than one applicant source before determining the best-qualified candidate based on job-related criteria. A basic principle of federal employment is that all candidates must meet the qualification requirements for the position for which they receive an appointment.

- ✪ Positions are open to the public. For positions lasting more than 120 days, vacancies must be announced and posted on USAJOBS, the federal government's central repository of job information.

- ✪ Applicants are rated against set criteria.

- ✪ Veterans' preference rules are applied.

- ✪ Candidates are ranked and referred in order, i.e., highest scoring candidates or candidates in the highest quality group are referred first for selection. However, compensable disabled veterans "float" to the top, except for scientific and professional upper-level positions.

In filling competitive service jobs, agencies can generally choose from among three groups of candidates:

*Competitive list of eligibles,* also known as the Cert List. This record lists the applicants (in rank order) who meet the qualification requirements for a specific vacancy announcement. Your primary objective is to get on the cert list, which means you will be referred to a supervisor for further consideration.

*Eligibles with civil service status.* This list consists of applicants who are already working for the federal government and are eligible for noncompetitive movement within the competitive service. They can receive an appointment by promotion, reassignment, transfer, or reinstatement.

*Special noncompetitive eligibles.* Examples of special noncompetitive appointing authorities include the Veterans' Readjustment Appointment (VRA), the special authority for 30% or more disabled veterans, and the Peace Corps.

### Excepted Service Jobs

Excepted Service jobs are the jobs with agencies that set their own qualification requirements and are not subject to the appointment, pay, and classification rules in Title 5, United States Code. These excepted agencies are able to be more flexible with recruitment incentives, salaries, promotions, and other personnel matters. They are also subject to veterans' preference. Positions may be in the excepted service by law, executive order, or action of OPM.

Some federal agencies, such as the Federal Bureau of Investigations (FBI) and the Central Intelligence Agency (CIA), have only excepted service positions. In other cases, certain organizations within an agency or even specific jobs may be excepted from civil service procedures.

Excepted service jobs are not required to be posted on USAJOBS. To learn about their job opportunities you must go to the specific agency websites.

See a list of Excepted Service Positions and Excepted Service Agencies on the CD-ROM included with this book.

### Direct Hire

Agencies use direct hiring when there is a shortage of qualified candidates, or when an agency has a critical hiring need, such as one caused by an emergency or unanticipated events, or changed mission requirements.

Direct hire provides a quick way to hire individuals in the competitive service. Although it requires agencies to publicly post their vacancies on USAJOBS, they do not need to apply veterans' preference or rate and rank qualified candidates. Once a qualified candidate is found, agencies may offer the job on the spot and may appoint the candidate immediately.

OPM has allowed government-wide use of direct hire for the following occupations:
- Information technology management related to security
- X-ray technicians
- Medical officers, nurses, and pharmacists
- Positions involved in Iraqi reconstruction efforts requiring fluency in Arabic

### Strategy Tips

If you qualify for and apply to a direct hire position, you will encounter less-than-normal competition for these jobs.

You will find the competitive service and direct hire job openings on USAJOBS, but you may need to check with agency websites to locate excepted service job announcements.

Many of the Direct Hire positions are offered at federal job fairs. Be sure to bring a good resume, because it is possible you could get hired on the spot for a position if you are qualified.

### Federal Career Intern Program (FCIP)

The Federal Career Intern Program is designed to help agencies recruit and attract exceptional individuals into a variety of occupations. This program is NOT intended for students only. Anyone can apply.

In general, individuals are appointed to a two-year excepted service internship. Upon successful completion of the internships, the interns may be eligible for permanent placement within an agency.

It is intended for positions at grade levels GS-5, 7, and 9. This program requires agencies to train and develop the interns.

Individuals interested in Career Intern opportunities must contact specific agencies directly. FCIP vacancies are not required to post on USAJOBS. The applicant must meet OPM's qualification requirements in order to be hired, and veterans' preference rules apply.

(Based on Government data and reports, including U.S. Merit Systems Protection Board, *Building a High-Quality Workforce: The Federal Career Intern Program*, September 2005)

> **❝** This past year, I made the conscious decision to focus less on the PMF (Presidential Management Fellows Program) and more on FCIP positions. My reasoning is that since the PMF represents maybe 400-450 new hires in the fed. govt., and **FCIPs now number close to 17,000**, it would be better to focus there. The PMF is like an FCIP too, so that makes it easier to incorporate information on the PMF into my presentation. **❞**

*Paul Binkley, Director of Career Development Services, Trachtenberg School of Public Policy and Public Administration at The George Washington University, October 6, 2008*

### Strategy Tip
The FCIP program is open to anyone. If you qualify for an entry-level GS position, then you may want to look into this program at the agencies you are interested in.

| New Hires by Authority or Program (full-time non-temporary Professional, Administrative, and Technical positions at the GS-5/6/7/8/9 levels) FY2004 | |
|---|---|
| Competitive Examining | 11,473 |
| Veterans Employment Opportunity Authority | 2,557 |
| Direct Hire | 433 |
| Outstanding Scholar Program | 1,060 |
| Bilingual/Bicultural Program | 92 |
| Federal Career Intern Program | 7,017 |
| Presidential Management Fellows Program | 256 |
| Veterans Recruitment Appointment | 1,943 |
| Student Career Experience Program | 79 |
| All Other | 13,365 |
| TOTAL | 38,275 |

## Strategy Tip
Find out if you qualify for one of the programs listed above.

## Decide on Agencies

To select an agency of interest to you, follow these steps:
1) Conduct a mission statement match
2) Determine location(s)
3) Consider job availability

### Mission Statement Match

Your choice to pursue a career in public service gives you the opportunity to choose an agency whose mission matches yours. Mission statements are often a practical guide and contain valuable information about each agency's goals, structure, and culture. Federal agencies are diverse and provide various services and missions for the American public. Reading the agency's mission statements is an important part of your federal job search. If you do not understand or know the agency's mission, you might not be successful with your application. To find mission statements, visit the homepage of any federal agency. You can also find a discussion to help you gain this knowledge of the missions of the various government agencies at http://www.firstgov.gov/featured/usgresponse2.html#agencies.

### Location, Location, Location

Contrary to popular belief, most federal jobs are NOT located only in Washington, DC. In fact, only 12% of the federal civilian workforce is located in the Washington, DC metropolitan area (U.S. Office of Personnel Management, *Federal Civilian Workforce Statistics Fact Book*, 2005 Edition). Federal government employment is available throughout the United States and overseas as well. You should ask yourself whether you are willing and able to relocate in order to expand your job search.

### Job Availability

For job-seeking purposes, you can divide federal agencies into two categories—classic and hot. You can count on certain classic agencies to continually hire people with your skill set. For example, if you come from a business background, you might find jobs in agencies specializing in business services, such as the General Services Administration, the Small Business Administration, and the Department of Commerce. But remember, every federal agency has at least some employees who provide basic business services!

Some federal agencies simply hire more employees than others based on how much money is available and our nation's current employment focus. Such agencies are considered hot. As this book is written, the Department of Homeland Security (DHS) is definitely hot. As a result of recent national events, the new department was created and is experiencing significant hiring increases.

Let us take a look at which agencies are doing the most hiring:

### Top Hiring Agencies from Partnership for Public Service

*Where the Jobs Are: Mission Critical Opportunities for America,* July 2007,
http://ourpublicservice.org/OPS/publications/viewcontentdetails.php?id=118.

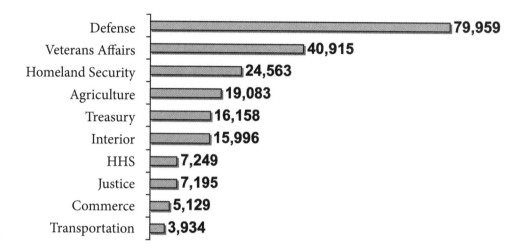

| Agency | Number |
| --- | --- |
| Defense | 79,959 |
| Veterans Affairs | 40,915 |
| Homeland Security | 24,563 |
| Agriculture | 19,083 |
| Treasury | 16,158 |
| Interior | 15,996 |
| HHS | 7,249 |
| Justice | 7,195 |
| Commerce | 5,129 |
| Transportation | 3,934 |

### TOP 10 Agencies with the Most Openings on USAJOBS (as of September 5, 2008)

- USAF
- Navy Field Offices
- VA – Veterans Health Administration
- Army Corps of Engineers
- Army Medical Command
- National Park Service
- Office of the Secretary of the Navy
- Army Installation Management
- Citizenship & Immigration
- Transportation Security Administration

## Top Hiring Agencies for Upper Level New Hires (GS-12 through 15 or similar) and Upper Level Workforce by Agency, FY 2005

| Agency | New Hires | Upper Level Workforce |
|---|---|---|
| Department of the Army | 18.2% | 12.2% |
| Department of the Navy | 12.2% | 12.0% |
| Department of the Air Force | 10.9% | 7.1% |
| Department of Veterans Affairs | 10.1% | 6.2% |
| Department of Health and Human Services | 8.0% | 4.8% |
| Department of Homeland Security | 5.3% | 1.9% |
| Department of Defense (Other) | 5.2% | 5.3% |
| Department of Treasury | 3.9% | 8.2% |
| Social Security Administration | 3.1% | 2.3% |
| Department of Agriculture | 2.9% | 4.8% |
| All others | 20.2% | 35.2% |

U.S. Merit Systems Protection Board, *In Search of Highly Skilled Workers: A Study on the Hiring of Upper Level Employees from Outside the Federal Government*, February 2008.

## Top Hiring Agencies for Professional and Administrative Entry-Level Hires (GS-5 through 9), FY2005

| Agency | New Hires |
|---|---|
| Social Security Administration | 16.2% |
| Department of the Army | 15.0% |
| Department of Homeland Security | 10.9% |
| Department of the Air Force | 7.6% |
| Department of the Navy | 7.4% |
| Department of Veterans Affairs | 6.7% |
| Department of Defense | 6.1% |
| Department of the Treasury | 5.2% |
| Department of Commerce | 3.2% |
| Departments of Justice and Agriculture | 3.0% |

U.S. Merit Systems Protection Board, *Attracting the Next Generation: A Look at Federal Entry-Level New Hires*, January 2008.

## AGENCY LIST

### A

Administration for Children and Families
Administration on Aging (AOA)
Administrative Office of the U.S. Courts
Advisory Council on Historic Preservation
Agency for Healthcare Research and Quality
Agency for International Development
Agency for Toxic Substances and Disease Registry
Agricultural Marketing Service
Agricultural Research Service
Air Force, Department of
AMTRAK (National Railroad Passenger Corporation)
Animal and Plant Health Inspection Service
Appalachian Regional Commission
Architect of the Capitol
Armed Forces Retirement Home
Arms Control and International Security, Under Secretary for
Army, Department of
Army Corps of Engineers (USACE)

### B

Botanic Garden (USBG)
Broadcasting Board of Governors (BBG), (Voice of America, Radio/TV Marti and more)
Bureau of Alcohol, Tobacco, Firearms, and Explosives (ATF)
Bureau of Economic Analysis
Bureau of Engraving and Printing
Bureau of Indian Affairs
Bureau of Industry and Security
Bureau of International Labor Affairs
Bureau of Labor Statistics
Bureau of Land Management
Bureau of Public Debt
Bureau of Reclamation
Bureau of Transportation Statistics

### C

Census Bureau
Center for Nutrition Policy and Promotion
Centers for Disease Control and Prevention (CDC)
Centers for Medicare & Medicaid Services
Central Intelligence Agency (CIA)
Citizenship and Immigration Services Bureau (USCIS)
Civilian Radioactive Waste Management
Coast Guard (USCG)
Commission on Civil Rights
Community Oriented Policing Services
Community Planning and Development
Comptroller of the Currency, Office of the
Congressional Budget Office
Consumer Product Safety Commission (CPSC)
Cooperative State Research, Education and Extension Service

Corporation for National and Community Service
Council of Economic Advisers
Council on Environmental Quality
Court of Appeals for the Armed Forces
Court of Appeals for the Federal Circuit
Court of Appeals for Veterans Claims
Court of Federal Claims
Court of International Trade
Customs and Border Protection

### D

Defense Advanced Research Projects Agency
Defense Commissary Agency
Defense Contract Audit Agency
Defense Contract Management Agency
Defense Finance and Accounting Service
Defense Information Systems Agency
Defense Intelligence Agency (DIA)
Defense Legal Services Agency
Defense Logistics Agency
Defense Nuclear Facilities Safety Board
Defense Security Cooperation Agency
Defense Security Service
Defense Threat Reduction Agency
Department of Agriculture (USDA)
Department of Commerce (DOC)
Department of Defense (DOD)
Department of Education (ED)
Department of Energy (DOE)
Department of Health and Human Services (HHS)
Department of Homeland Security (DHS)
Department of Housing and Urban Development (HUD)
Department of the Interior (DOI)
Department of Justice (DOJ)
Department of Labor (DOL)
Department of State (DOS)
Department of Transportation (DOT)
Department of the Treasury
Department of Veterans Affairs (VA)
Disability Employment Policy, Office of
Drug Enforcement Administration (DEA)

### E

Economic and Statistics Administration
Economic, Business and Agricultural Affairs
Economic Development Administration
Economic Research Service
Elementary and Secondary Education, Office of
Employee Benefits Security Administration
Employment and Training Administration
Employment Standards Administration
Energy Efficiency and Renewable Energy
Energy Information Administration
Environmental Management
Environmental Protection Agency (EPA)

Equal Employment Opportunity Commission (EEOC)
Executive Office for Immigration Review

**F**

Fair Housing and Equal Opportunity, Office of
Faith-Based and Community Initiatives Office
Farm Service Agency (FSA)
Federal Aviation Administration
Federal Bureau of Investigation (FBI)
Federal Bureau of Prisons
Federal Communications Commission (FCC)
Federal Deposit Insurance Corporation (FDIC)
Federal Election Commission (FEC)
Federal Emergency Management Agency (FEMA)
Federal Financing Bank
Federal Highway Administration
Federal Housing Enterprise Oversight
Federal Housing Finance Board
Federal Judicial Center
Federal Labor Relations Authority
Federal Law Enforcement Training Center
Federal Mediation and Conciliation Service
Federal Motor Carrier Safety Administration
Federal Railroad Administration
Federal Reserve System
Federal Trade Commission (FTC)
Federal Transit Administration
Financial Management Service
Fish and Wildlife Service
Food and Drug Administration (FDA)
Food and Nutrition Service
Food Safety and Inspection Service
Foreign Agricultural Service
Forest Service
Fossil Energy

**G**

Government Accountability Office (GAO)
General Services Administration
Geological Survey (USGS)
Global Affairs
Government National Mortgage Association
Government Printing Office
Grain Inspection, Packers and Stockyards Administration

**H**

Health Resources and Services Administration
Holocaust Memorial Museum
House of Representatives
House Office of Inspector General
House Office of the Clerk
House Organizations, Commissions and Task Forces

**I**

Indian Health Service
Industrial College of the Armed Forces
Information Resource Management College
Institute of Museum and Library Services
Internal Revenue Service (IRS)
International Broadcasting Bureau (IBB)
International Trade Administration (ITA)

**J**

Joint Chiefs of Staff
Joint Forces Staff College
Judicial Circuit Courts of Appeal by Geographic Location
    and Circuit

**L**

Lead Hazard Control
Legal Services Corporation
Library of Congress

**M**

Marine Corps
Maritime Administration
Marketing and Regulatory Programs
Marshals Service
Merit Systems Protection Board
Mine Safety and Health Administration
Mineral Management Service
Minority Business Development Agency
Mint
Missile Defense Agency
Multifamily Housing Office

**N**

National Aeronautics and Space Administration (NASA)
National Agricultural Statistics Service
National Archives and Records Administration (NARA)
National Capital Planning Commission
National Cemetery Administration
National Commission on Terrorist Attacks Upon the United
    States (9-11 Commission)
National Communications System
National Council on Disability
National Credit Union Administration
National Defense University
National Drug Intelligence Center
National Endowment for the Arts
National Endowment for the Humanities
National Guard Bureau
National Highway Traffic Safety Administration
National Institute of Standards and Technology (NIST)
National Institutes of Health (NIH)
National Labor Relations Board
National Laboratories

## Agency List Continued

National Marine Fisheries
National Mediation Board
National Nuclear Security Administration
National Oceanic and Atmospheric Administration (NOAA)
National Park Service
National Science Foundation
National Security Agency/Central Security Service
National Technical Information Service
National Telecommunications and Information
    Administration
National Transportation Safety Board (NTSB)
National War College
National Weather Service
Natural Resources Conservation Service
Navy, Department of the
Nuclear Energy, Science and Technology
Nuclear Regulatory Commission
Nuclear Waste Technical Review Board

### O

Occupational Safety & Health Administration (OSHA)
Office of Government Ethics
Office of Management and Budget (OMB)
Office of National Drug Control Policy (ONDCP)
Office of Personnel Management
Office of Science and Technology Policy
Office of Special Counsel
Office of Thrift Supervision
Overseas Private Investment Corporation

### P

Pardon Attorney Office
Parole Commission
Patent and Trademark Office
Peace Corps
Pension Benefit Guaranty Corporation
Policy Development and Research
Political Affairs
Postal Rate Commission
Postal Service (USPS)
Postsecondary Education, Office of
Power Marketing Administrations
Presidio Trust
Public Diplomacy and Public Affairs
Public and Indian Housing

### R

Radio and TV Marti (Español)
Radio Free Asia (RFA)
Radio Free Europe/Radio Liberty (RFE/RL)
Railroad Retirement Board
Regulatory Information Service Center

Research and Special Programs Administration
Research, Education and Economics
Risk Management Agency
Rural Business-Cooperative Service
Rural Development
Rural Housing Service
Rural Utilities Service

### S

Science Office
Secret Service
Securities and Exchange Commission (SEC)
Selective Service System
Senate
Small Business Administration (SBA)
Smithsonian Institution
Social Security Administration (SSA)
Social Security Advisory Board
Special Education and Rehabilitative Services
Stennis Center for Public Service
Student Financial Assistance Programs
Substance Abuse and Mental Health Services Administration
Supreme Court of the United States
Surface Mining, Reclamation and Enforcement
Surface Transportation Board

### T

Tax Court
Technology Administration
Tennessee Valley Authority
Trade and Development Agency
Transportation Security Administration
Trustee Program

### U

U.S. International Trade Commission
U.S. Mission to the United Nations
U.S. National Central Bureau – Interpol
U.S. Trade Representative
Unified Combatant Commands
Uniformed Services University of the Health Sciences

### V

Veterans Benefits Administration
Veterans Employment and Training Service
Veterans Health Administration
Voice of America (VOA)

### W

White House
White House Office of Administration
Women's Bureau

# Review Job Titles and Occupational Series

The job titles are not the same in government as in private industry.

Before you can find vacancy announcements that are appropriate for your experience, education, and skills, you will need to know what the job titles entail. Some federal job titles mean something entirely different than in the private industry. For instance, if you are a university researcher and writer, you could very well be qualified for a Management or Program Analyst position in government yet, how would you know this if you did not know the federal government's job title scheme?

You can find the Handbook of Occupational Groups and Families, 2008 edition at https://www.opm.gov/fedclass/gshbkocc.pdf to learn more about how the federal government organizes job categories.

## Program Analysts and Management Analysts

These are popular job titles in federal agencies. Employees in these titles conduct analyses and advise management on the effectiveness of government programs and operations, or on the productivity and efficiency of agency management, or both. These jobs require knowledge of the substantive nature of agency programs and activities, knowledge of agency missions, policies, and objectives, management principles and processes, and analytical and evaluative techniques and methods. These jobs require skill in applying fact-finding and investigative techniques, oral and written communications, and development of presentations and reports. They do not require specialized subject-matter expertise in a specialized line of work.

## Some Elusive Job Titles

Some job titles that seem familiar and carry a promise of exciting careers include Special Agent and Researcher, especially when the latter is used in medical or scientific settings such as the National Institutes of Health (NIH) or the Center for Disease Control (CDC). But when we search for these titles, we do not find them. Why? Typically, these are working titles rather than official titles. As a result, they may not be used in vacancy announcements. So exercise your analytical and investigative skills and think investigator rather than special agent, especially criminal investigator (the government also has general investigators), for example.

On the following pages is a list of Occupational Groups and Series and Families that could provide you with some clues to your job title and series number for your job search. Two of the occupational groups are difficult to understand, but are important for private industry applicants. The 300-General Administrative and the 1100-Business and Industry Group series have a number of positions that equate well to private industry job experience.

## OCCUPATIONAL GROUPS AND SERIES
## FIND YOUR JOB TITLES

### HANDBOOK OF OCCUPATIONAL GROUPS AND SERIES
**U.S. Office of Personnel Management Office of Classification; Washington, DC**

#### GS-000 – MISCELLANEOUS OCCUPATIONS GROUP (NOT ELSEWHERE CLASSIFIED)

This group includes all classes of positions the duties of which are to administer, supervise, or perform work, which cannot be included in other occupational groups either because the duties are unique, or because they are complex and come in part under various groups.

Series in this group are:
GS-006 - Correctional Institution Administration Series
GS-007 - Correctional Officer Series
GS-011 - Bond Sales Promotion Series
GS-018 - Safety and Occupational Health Management Series
GS-019 - Safety Technician Series
GS-020 - Community Planning Series
GS-021 - Community Planning Technician Series
GS-023 - Outdoor Recreation Planning Series
GS-025 - Park Ranger Series
GS-028 - Environmental Protection Specialist Series
GS-029 - Environmental Protection Assistant Series
GS-030 - Sports Specialist Series
GS-050 - Funeral Directing Series
GS-060 - Chaplain Series
GS-062 - Clothing Design Series
GS-072 - Fingerprint Identification Series
GS-080 - Security Administration Series
GS-081 - Fire Protection and Prevention Series
GS-082 - United States Marshal Series
GS-083 - Police Series
GS-084 - Nuclear Materials Courier Series
GS-085 - Security Guard Series
GS-086 - Security Clerical and Assistance Series
GS-090 - Guide Series
GS-095 - Foreign Law Specialist Series
GS-099 - General Student Trainee Series

#### GS-100 – SOCIAL SCIENCE, PSYCHOLOGY, AND WELFARE GROUP

This group includes all classes of positions the duties of which are to advise on, administer, supervise, or perform research or other professional and scientific work, subordinate technical work, or related clerical work in one or more of the social sciences; in psychology; in social work; in recreational activities; or in the administration of public welfare and insurance programs.

Series in this group are:
GS-101 - Social Science Series
GS-102 - Social Science Aid and Technician Series
GS-105 - Social Insurance Administration Series
GS-106 - Unemployment Insurance Series
GS-107 - Health Insurance Administration Series
GS-110 - Economist Series
GS-119 - Economics Assistant Series
GS-130 - Foreign Affairs Series
GS-131 - International Relations Series
GS-132 - Intelligence Series
GS-134 - Intelligence Aid and Clerk Series
GS-135 - Foreign Agricultural Affairs Series
GS-136 - International Cooperation Series
GS-140 - Manpower Research and Analysis Series
GS-142 - Manpower Development Series
GS-150 - Geography Series
GS-160 - Civil Rights Analysis Series
GS-170 - History Series
GS-180 - Psychology Series
GS-181 - Psychology Aid and Technician Series
GS-184 - Sociology Series
GS-185 - Social Work Series
GS-186 - Social Services Aid and Assistant Series
GS-187 - Social Services Series
GS-188 - Recreation Specialist Series
GS-189 - Recreation Aid and Assistant Series
GS-190 - General Anthropology Series
GS-193 - Archeology Series
GS-199 - Social Science Student Trainee Series

#### GS-200 – HUMAN RESOURCES MANAGEMENT GROUP

This group includes all classes of positions the duties of which are to advise on, administer, supervise, or perform work involved in the various phases of human resources management.

Series in this group are:
GS-201 - Human Resources Management Series
GS-203 - Human Resources Assistance Series
GS-241 - Mediation Series
GS-243 - Apprenticeship and Training Series
GS-244 - Labor Management Relations Examining Series
GS-260 - Equal Employment Opportunity Series
GS-299 - Human Resources Management Student Trainee Series

#### GS-300 – GENERAL ADMINISTRATIVE, CLERICAL, AND OFFICE SERVICES GROUP

This group includes all classes of positions the duties of which are to administer, supervise, or perform work involved in management analysis; stenography, typing, correspondence, and secretarial work; mail and file work; the operation of office appliances; the operation of communications equipment, use of codes and ciphers, and procurement of the most effective and efficient communications services; the operation of microform equipment, peripheral equipment, mail processing equipment, duplicating equipment, and copier/duplicating equipment; and other work of a general clerical and administrative nature.

Series in this group are:
GS-301 - Miscellaneous Administration and Program Series
GS-302 - Messenger Series
GS-303 - Miscellaneous Clerk and Assistant Series
GS-304 - Information Receptionist Series
GS-305 - Mail and File Series
GS-309 - Correspondence Clerk Series
GS-312 - Clerk-Stenographer and Reporter Series
GS-313 - Work Unit Supervising Series
GS-318 - Secretary Series
GS-319 - Closed Microphone Reporting Series
GS-322 - Clerk-Typist Series
GS-326 - Office Automation Clerical and Assistance Series
GS-332 - Computer Operation Series
GS-335 - Computer Clerk and Assistant Series
GS-340 - Program Management Series
GS-341 - Administrative Officer Series
GS-342 - Support Services Administration Series
GS-343 - Management and Program Analysis Series
GS-344 - Management and Program Clerical and Assistance Series
GS-346 - Logistics Management Series
GS-350 - Equipment Operator Series
GS-356 - Data Transcriber Series
GS-357 - Coding Series
GS-360 - Equal Opportunity Compliance Series
GS-361 - Equal Opportunity Assistance Series
GS-382 - Telephone Operating Series
GS-390 - Telecommunications Processing Series
GS-391 - Telecommunications Series
GS-392 - General Telecommunications Series
GS-394 - Communications Clerical Series
GS-399 - Administration and Office Support Student Trainee Series

## GS-400 – NATURAL RESOURCES MANAGEMENT AND BIOLOGICAL SCIENCES GROUP

This group includes all classes of positions the duties of which are to advise on, administer, supervise, or perform research or other professional and scientific work or subordinate technical work in any of the fields of science concerned with living organisms, their distribution, characteristics, life processes, and adaptations and relations to the environment; the soil, its properties and distribution, and the living organisms growing in or on the soil, and the management, conservation, or utilization thereof for particular purposes or uses.

Series in this group are:
GS-401 - General Natural Resources Management and Biological Sciences Series
GS-403 - Microbiology Series
GS-404 - Biological Science Technician Series
GS-405 - Pharmacology Series
GS-408 - Ecology Series
GS-410 - Zoology Series
GS-413 - Physiology Series
GS-414 - Entomology Series
GS-415 - Toxicology Series
GS-421 - Plant Protection Technician Series
GS-430 - Botany Series
GS-434 - Plant Pathology Series
GS-435 - Plant Physiology Series
GS-437 - Horticulture Series
GS-440 - Genetics Series
GS-454 - Rangeland Management Series
GS-455 - Range Technician Series
GS-457 - Soil Conservation Series
GS-458 - Soil Conservation Technician Series
GS-459 - Irrigation System Operation Series
GS-460 - Forestry Series
GS-462 - Forestry Technician Series
GS-470 - Soil Science Series
GS-471 - Agronomy Series
GS-480 - Fish and Wildlife Administration Series
GS-482 - Fish Biology Series
GS-485 - Wildlife Refuge Management Series
GS-486 - Wildlife Biology Series
GS-487 - Animal Science Series
GS-499 - Biological Science Student Trainee Series

## GS-500 – ACCOUNTING AND BUDGET GROUP

This group includes all classes of positions the duties of which are to advise on, administer, supervise, or perform professional, technical, or related clerical work of an accounting, budget administration, related financial management or similar nature.

Series in this group are:
GS-501 - Financial Administration and Program Series
GS-503 - Financial Clerical and Technician Series
GS-505 - Financial Management Series
GS-510 - Accounting Series
GS-511 - Auditing Series

GS-512 - Internal Revenue Agent Series
GS-525 - Accounting Technician Series
GS-526 - Tax Specialist Series
GS-530 - Cash Processing Series
GS-540 - Voucher Examining Series
GS-544 - Civilian Pay Series
GS-545 - Military Pay Series
GS-560 - Budget Analysis Series
GS-561 - Budget Clerical and Assistance Series
GS-592 - Tax Examining Series
GS-593 - Insurance Accounts Series
GS-599 - Financial Management Student Trainee Series

## GS-600 – MEDICAL, HOSPITAL, DENTAL, AND PUBLIC HEALTH GROUP

This group includes all classes of positions the duties of which are to advise on, administer, supervise or perform research or other professional and scientific work, subordinate technical work, or related clerical work in the several branches of medicine, surgery, and dentistry or in related patient care services such as dietetics, nursing, occupational therapy, physical therapy, pharmacy, and others.

Series in this group are:
GS-601 - General Health Science Series
GS-602 - Medical Officer Series
GS-603 - Physician's Assistant Series
GS-610 - Nurse Series
GS-620 - Practical Nurse Series
GS-621 - Nursing Assistant Series
GS-622 - Medical Supply Aide and Technician Series
GS-625 - Autopsy Assistant Series
GS-630 - Dietitian and Nutritionist Series
GS-631 - Occupational Therapist Series
GS-633 - Physical Therapist Series
GS-635 - Kinesiotherapy Series
GS-636 - Rehabilitation Therapy Assistant Series
GS-637 - Manual Arts Therapist Series
GS-638 - Recreation/Creative Arts Therapist Series
GS-639 - Educational Therapist Series
GS-640 - Health Aid and Technician Series
GS-642 - Nuclear Medicine Technician Series
GS-644 - Medical Technologist Series
GS-645 - Medical Technician Series
GS-646 - Pathology Technician Series
GS-647 - Diagnostic Radiologic Technologist Series
GS-648 - Therapeutic Radiologic Technologist Series
GS-649 - Medical Instrument Technician Series
GS-650 - Medical Technical Assistant Series
GS-651 - Respiratory Therapist Series
GS-660 - Pharmacist Series
GS-661 - Pharmacy Technician Series
GS-662 - Optometrist Series
GS-664 - Restoration Technician Series

GS-665 - Speech Pathology and Audiology Series
GS-667 - Orthotist and Prosthetist Series
GS-668 - Podiatrist Series
GS-669 - Medical Records Administration Series
GS-670 - Health System Administration Series
GS-671 - Health System Specialist Series
GS-672 - Prosthetic Representative Series
GS-673 - Hospital Housekeeping Management Series
GS-675 - Medical Records Technician Series
GS-679 - Medical Support Assistance Series
GS-680 - Dental Officer Series
GS-681 - Dental Assistant Series
GS-682 - Dental Hygiene Series
GS-683 - Dental Laboratory Aid and Technician Series
GS-685 - Public Health Program Specialist Series
GS-688 - Sanitarian Series
GS-690 - Industrial Hygiene Series
GS-696 - Consumer Safety Series
GS-698 - Environmental Health Technician Series
GS-699 - Medical and Health Student Trainee Series

## GS-700 - VETERINARY MEDICAL SCIENCE GROUP

This group includes positions that advise on, administer, supervise, or perform professional or technical support work in the various branches of veterinary medical science.

Series in this group are:
GS-701 - Veterinary Medical Science Series
GS-704 - Animal Health Technician Series
GS-799 - Veterinary Student Trainee Series

## GS-800 – ENGINEERING AND ARCHITECTURE GROUP

This group includes all classes of positions the duties of which are to advise on, administer, supervise, or perform professional, scientific, or technical work concerned with engineering or architectural projects, facilities, structures, systems, processes, equipment, devices, materials or methods. Positions in this group require knowledge of the science or art, or both, by which materials, natural resources, and power are made useful.

Series in this group are:
GS-801 - General Engineering Series
GS-802 - Engineering Technician Series
GS-803 - Safety Engineering Series
GS-804 - Fire Protection Engineering Series
GS-806 - Materials Engineering Series
GS-807 - Landscape Architecture Series
GS-808 - Architecture Series
GS-809 - Construction Control Technical Series
GS-810 - Civil Engineering Series
GS-817 - Survey Technical Series

GS-819 - Environmental Engineering Series
GS-828 - Construction Analyst Series
GS-830 - Mechanical Engineering Series
GS-840 - Nuclear Engineering Series
GS-850 - Electrical Engineering Series
GS-854 - Computer Engineering Series
GS-855 - Electronics Engineering Series
GS-856 - Electronics Technical Series
GS-858 - Biomedical Engineering Series
GS-861 - Aerospace Engineering Series
GS-871 - Naval Architecture Series
GS-873 - Marine Survey Technical Series
GS-880 - Mining Engineering Series
GS-881 - Petroleum Engineering Series
GS-890 - Agricultural Engineering Series
GS-892 - Ceramic Engineering Series
GS-893 - Chemical Engineering Series
GS-894 - Welding Engineering Series
GS-895 - Industrial Engineering Technical Series
GS-896 - Industrial Engineering Series
GS-899 - Engineering and Architecture Student
         Trainee Series

## GS-900 – LEGAL AND KINDRED GROUP

This group includes all positions that advise on, administer, supervise, or perform work of a legal or kindred nature.

Series in this group are:
GS-901 - General Legal and Kindred Administration Series
GS-904 - Law Clerk Series
GS-905 - General Attorney Series
GS-920 - Estate Tax Examining Series
GS-930 - Hearings and Appeals Series
GS-945 - Clerk of Court Series
GS-950 - Paralegal Specialist Series
GS-958 - Employee Benefits Law Series
GS-962 - Contact Representative Series
GS-963 - Legal Instruments Examining Series
GS-965 - Land Law Examining Series
GS-967 - Passport and Visa Examining Series
GS-986 - Legal Assistance Series
GS-987 - Tax Law Specialist Series
GS-991 - Workers' Compensation Claims Examining Series
GS-993 - Railroad Retirement Claims Examining Series
GS-996 - Veterans Claims Examining Series
GS-998 - Claims Assistance and Examining Series
GS-999 - Legal Occupations Student Trainee Series

## GS-1000 – INFORMATION AND ARTS GROUP

This group includes positions which involve professional, artistic, technical, or clerical work in (1) the communication of information and ideas through verbal, visual, or pictorial means, (2) the collection, custody, presentation, display, and interpretation of art works, cultural objects, and other artifacts, or (3) a branch of fine or applied arts such as industrial design, interior design, or musical composition. Positions in this group require writing, editing, and language ability; artistic skill and ability; knowledge of foreign languages; the ability to evaluate and interpret informational and cultural materials; or the practical application of technical or esthetic principles combined with manual skill and dexterity; or related clerical skills.

Series in this group are:
GS-1001 - General Arts and Information Series
GS-1008 - Interior Design Series
GS-1010 - Exhibits Specialist Series
GS-1015 - Museum Curator Series
GS-1016 - Museum Specialist and Technician Series
GS-1020 - Illustrating Series
GS-1021 - Office Drafting Series
GS-1035 - Public Affairs Series
GS-1040 - Language Specialist Series
GS-1046 - Language Clerical Series
GS-1051 - Music Specialist Series
GS-1054 - Theater Specialist Series
GS-1056 - Art Specialist Series
GS-1060 - Photography Series
GS-1071 - Audiovisual Production Series
GS-1082 - Writing and Editing Series
GS-1083 - Technical Writing and Editing Series
GS-1084 - Visual Information Series
GS-1087 - Editorial Assistance Series
GS-1099 - Information and Arts Student Trainee Series

## GS-1100 – BUSINESS AND INDUSTRY GROUP

This group includes all classes of positions the duties of which are to advise on, administer, supervise, or perform work pertaining to and requiring a knowledge of business and trade practices, characteristics and use of equipment, products, or property, or industrial production methods and processes, including the conduct of investigations and studies; the collection, analysis, and dissemination of information; the establishment and maintenance of contacts with industry and commerce; the provision of advisory services; the examination and appraisal of merchandise or property; and the administration of regulatory provisions and controls.

Series in this group are:
GS-1101 - General Business and Industry Series
GS-1102 - Contracting Series
GS-1103 - Industrial Property Management Series
GS-1104 - Property Disposal Series
GS-1105 - Purchasing Series
GS-1106 - Procurement Clerical and Technician Series
GS-1107 - Property Disposal Clerical and Technician Series

GS-1130 - Public Utilities Specialist Series
GS-1140 - Trade Specialist Series
GS-1144 - Commissary Management Series
GS-1145 - Agricultural Program Specialist Series
GS-1146 - Agricultural Marketing Series
GS-1147 - Agricultural Market Reporting Series
GS-1150 - Industrial Specialist Series
GS-1152 - Production Control Series
GS-1160 - Financial Analysis Series
GS-1163 - Insurance Examining Series
GS-1165 - Loan Specialist Series
GS-1169 - Internal Revenue Officer Series
GS-1170 - Realty Series
GS-1171 - Appraising Series
GS-1173 - Housing Management Series
GS-1176 - Building Management Series
GS-1199 - Business and Industry Student Trainee Series

## GS-1200 – COPYRIGHT, PATENT, AND TRADEMARK GROUP

This group includes all classes of positions the duties of which are to advise on, administer, supervise, or perform professional scientific, technical, and legal work involved in the cataloging and registration of copyrights, in the classification and issuance of patents, in the registration of trademarks, in the prosecution of applications for patents before the Patent Office, and in the giving of advice to Government officials on patent matters.

Series in this group are:
GS-1202 - Patent Technician Series
GS-1210 - Copyright Series
GS-1220 - Patent Administration Series
GS-1221 - Patent Adviser Series
GS-1222 - Patent Attorney Series
GS-1223 - Patent Classifying Series
GS-1224 - Patent Examining Series
GS-1226 - Design Patent Examining Series
GS-1299 - Copyright and Patent Student Trainee Series

## GS-1300 – PHYSICAL SCIENCES GROUP

This group includes all classes of positions the duties of which are to advise on, administer, supervise, or perform research or other professional and scientific work or subordinate technical work in any of the fields of science concerned with matter, energy, physical space, time, nature of physical measurement, and fundamental structural particles; and the nature of the physical environment.

Series in this group are:
GS-1301 - General Physical Science Series
GS-1306 - Health Physics Series
GS-1310 - Physics Series

GS-1311 - Physical Science Technician Series
GS-1313 - Geophysics Series
GS-1315 - Hydrology Series
GS-1316 - Hydrologic Technician Series
GS-1320 - Chemistry Series
GS-1321 - Metallurgy Series
GS-1330 - Astronomy and Space Science Series
GS-1340 - Meteorology Series
GS-1341 - Meteorological Technician Series
GS-1350 - Geology Series
GS-1360 - Oceanography Series
GS-1361 - Navigational Information Series
GS-1370 - Cartography Series
GS-1371 - Cartographic Technician Series
GS-1372 - Geodesy Series
GS-1373 - Land Surveying Series
GS-1374 - Geodetic Technician Series
GS-1380 - Forest Products Technology Series
GS-1382 - Food Technology Series
GS-1384 - Textile Technology Series
GS-1386 - Photographic Technology Series
GS-1397 - Document Analysis Series
GS-1399 - Physical Science Student Trainee Series

## GS-1400 – LIBRARY AND ARCHIVES GROUP

This group includes all classes of positions the duties of which are to advise on, administer, supervise, or perform professional and scientific work or subordinate technical work in the various phases of library and archival science.

Series in this group are:
GS-1410 - Librarian Series
GS-1411 - Library Technician Series
GS-1412 - Technical Information Services Series
GS-1420 - Archivist Series
GS-1421 - Archives Technician Series
GS-1499 - Library and Archives Student Trainee Series

## GS-1500 – MATHEMATICS AND STATISTICS GROUP

This group includes all classes of positions the duties of which are to advise on, administer, supervise, or perform professional and scientific work or related clerical work in basic mathematical principles, methods, procedures, or relationships, including the development and application of mathematical methods for the investigation and solution of problems; the development and application of statistical theory in the selection, collection, classification, adjustment, analysis, and interpretation of data; the development and application of mathematical, statistical, and financial principles to programs or problems involving life and property risks; and any other professional and scientific or related clerical work requiring primarily and mainly the understanding and use of mathematical theories, methods, and operations.

Series in this group are:
GS-1501 - General Mathematics and Statistics Series
GS-1510 - Actuarial Science Series
GS-1515 - Operations Research Series
GS-1520 - Mathematics Series
GS-1521 - Mathematics Technician Series
GS-1529 - Mathematical Statistics Series
GS-1530 - Statistics Series
GS-1531 - Statistical Assistant Series
GS-1540 - Cryptography Series
GS-1541 - Cryptanalysis Series
GS-1550 - Computer Science Series
GS-1599 - Mathematics and Statistics Student Trainee Series

## GS-1600 – EQUIPMENT, FACILITIES, AND SERVICES GROUP

This group includes positions the duties of which are to advise on, manage, or provide instructions and information concerning the operation, maintenance, and use of equipment, shops, buildings, laundries, printing plants, power plants, cemeteries, or other Government facilities, or other work involving services provided predominantly by persons in trades, group require technical or managerial knowledge and ability, plus a practical knowledge of trades, crafts, or manual labor operations.

Series in this group are:
GS-1601 - Equipment, Facilities, and Services Series
GS-1603 - Equipment, Facilities, and Services Assistance Series
GS-1630 - Cemetery Administration Services Series
GS-1640 - Facility Operations Services Series
GS-1654 - Printing Services Series
GS-1658 - Laundry Operations Services Series
GS-1667 - Food Services Series
GS-1670 - Equipment Services Series
GS-1699 – Equipment, Facilities, and Services Student Trainee Series

## GS-1700 – EDUCATION GROUP

This group includes positions that involve administering, managing, supervising, performing, or supporting education or training work when the paramount requirement of the position is knowledge of, or skill in, education, training, or instruction processes.

Series in this group are:
GS-1701 - General Education and Training Series
GS-1702 - Education and Training Technician Series
GS-1710 - Education and Vocational Training Series
GS-1712 - Training Instruction Series
GS-1715 - Vocational Rehabilitation Series
GS-1720 - Education Program Series

GS-1725 - Public Health Educator Series
GS-1730 - Education Research Series
GS-1740 - Education Services Series
GS-1750 - Instructional Systems Series
GS-1799 - Education Student Trainee Series

## GS-1800 – INVESTIGATION GROUP

This group includes all classes of positions the duties of which are to advise on, administer, supervise, or perform investigation, inspection, or enforcement work primarily concerned with alleged or suspected offenses against the laws of the United States, or such work primarily concerned with determining compliance with laws and regulations.

Series in this group are:
GS-1801 - General Inspection, Investigation, and Compliance Series
GS-1802 - Compliance Inspection and Support Series
GS-1810 - General Investigating Series
GS-1811 - Criminal Investigating Series
GS-1812 - Game Law Enforcement Series
GS-1815 - Air Safety Investigating Series
GS-1816 - Immigration Inspection Series
GS-1822 - Mine Safety and Health Series
GS-1825 - Aviation Safety Series
GS-1831 - Securities Compliance Examining Series
GS-1850 - Agricultural Commodity Warehouse Examining Series
GS-1854 - Alcohol, Tobacco and Firearms Inspection Series
GS-1862 - Consumer Safety Inspection Series
GS-1863 - Food Inspection Series
GS-1864 - Public Health Quarantine Inspection Series
GS-1881 - Customs and Border Protection Interdiction Series
GS-1884 - Customs Patrol Officer Series
GS-1889 - Import Specialist Series
GS-1890 - Customs Inspection Series
GS-1894 - Customs Entry and Liquidating Series
GS-1895 - Customs and Border Protection Series
GS-1896 - Border Patrol Agent Series
GS-1897 - Customs Aid Series
GS-1899 - Investigation Student Trainee Series

**GS-1900 – QUALITY ASSURANCE, INSPECTION, AND GRADING GROUP**

This group includes all classes of positions the duties of which are advise on, supervise, or perform administrative or technical work primarily concerned with the quality assurance or inspection of material, facilities, and processes; or with the grading of commodities under official standards.

Series in this group are:
GS-1910 - Quality Assurance Series
GS-1980 - Agricultural Commodity Grading Series
GS-1981 - Agricultural Commodity Aid Series
GS-1999 - Quality Inspection Student Trainee Series

**GS-2000 – SUPPLY GROUP**

This group includes positions that involve work concerned with furnishing all types of supplies, equipment, material, property (except real estate), and certain services to components of the Federal Government, industrial, or other concerns under contract to the Government, or receiving supplies from the Federal Government. Included are positions concerned with one or more aspects of supply activities from initial planning, including requirements analysis and determination, through acquisition, cataloging, storage, distribution, utilization to ultimate issues for consumption or disposal. The work requires a knowledge of one or more elements or parts of a supply system, and/or supply methods, policies, or procedures.

Series in this group are:
GS-2001 - General Supply Series
GS-2003 - Supply Program Management Series
GS-2005 - Supply Clerical and Technician Series
GS-2010 - Inventory Management Series
GS-2030 - Distribution Facilities and Storage Management Series
GS-2032 - Packaging Series
GS-2050 - Supply Cataloging Series
GS-2091 - Sales Store Clerical Series
GS-2099 - Supply Student Trainee Series

**GS-2100 – TRANSPORTATION GROUP**

This group includes all classes of positions the duties of which are to advise on, administer, supervise, or perform clerical, administrative, or technical work involved in the provision of transportation service to the Government, the regulation of transportation utilities by the Government, or the management of Government-funded transportation programs, including transportation research and development projects.

Series in this group are:
GS-2101 - Transportation Specialist Series
GS-2102 - Transportation Clerk and Assistant Series
GS-2110 - Transportation Industry Analysis Series
GS-2121 - Railroad Safety Series
GS-2123 - Motor Carrier Safety Series
GS-2125 - Highway Safety Series
GS-2130 - Traffic Management Series
GS-2131 - Freight Rate Series
GS-2135 - Transportation Loss and Damage Claims Examining Series
GS-2144 - Cargo Scheduling Series
GS-2150 - Transportation Operations Series
GS-2151 - Dispatching Series
GS-2152 - Air Traffic Control Series
GS-2154 - Air Traffic Assistance Series
GS-2161 - Marine Cargo Series
GS-2181 - Aircraft Operation Series
GS-2183 - Air Navigation Series
GS-2185 - Aircrew Technician Series
Gs-2199 - Transportation Student Trainee Series

**GS-2200 – INFORMATION TECHNOLOGY GROUP**

Series in this group are:
GS-2210 - Information Technology Management Series
GS-2299 - Information Technology Student Trainee

# Matching Qualifications

Trying to figure out which positions you can apply for given your private industry work experience? The chart below has some of the private sector job title/federal skills matchings for the top ten career groups that the federal government is currently hiring for. The examples in this chart come from our real life case studies that are included in the back of the book and and on the CD-ROM.

| Federal Career Group | Private Sector Job Title | Federal Skills Match | Case Study |
|---|---|---|---|
| Accounting and Budget | Wall Street Financial Consultant | Senior Finance | Frank Mason |
| | Credit Union Area Manager | Banking / Compliance | Barbara Kelly |
| | Senior Accountant | Senior Accounting | Edward Williams |
| Admin/Program Mgmt | Inventory Spec/Operations Manager | Analysis / Programs | Benjamin Gaston |
| | Customer Service Rep | Customer Services | Susan Curtis |
| | Financial Solutions Consultant | Administration / Solutions | Grace Stanford |
| | Real Estate Office Manager | Administration | Patricia Richards |
| | Sous Chef | Analyst / Interpersonal | John Wallstone |
| Business and Industry | Warehouse Supervisor | Logistics / Material | Margaret Chaplin |
| | Consumer Loan Officer | Loans / Cust. Serv. | Eleanor Washington |
| Compliance & Enforcement | Material Damage Appraiser | Investigations | Lionel Richmond |
| Engineering | VP of Risk Management | Risk Mgmt | Janna Johnson |
| Information and Arts | Clinical Director (Fed. Contractor) | Health Information | Linda Sussex |
| Information Technology | Senior IT Consultant | IT Specialist | Tom Danson |
| | IT | IT Specialist | Jane Addams |
| Iraq Jobs | Real Estate Developer | Economic Development | Michael Drummer |
| Legal | Teacher | Communications / Documents | Katrina Jackson |
| | Legal Assistant | Legal Assistant | Constance Jenkins |
| | Attorney | Attorney | Lionel Timmons |
| Medical/Public Health | Program Analyst, Govt Contractor | Public Health | Stephanie Monroe |
| Security and Protection | Special Investigator | Security Investigation | Alice Paul |
| | Security Interviewer | Security Investigation | Harold Denton |
| Social Sciences | State Voc. Rehab. Spec. Super. | Voc Rehab | Chad Jones |
| | State Voc. Rehab. | Voc Rehab | Anne Kilmer |

## Federal Grade and Pay Structure

The federal civil service has different grading and pay structures for its professional and trade workforces. In this book, we will focus on the professional jobs that the government categorizes in a system called PATCO (Professional, Administrative, Technical, Clerical, and Other). See definitions on the next page.

In many agencies, the professional jobs are organized into one of 15 grades in a system called the General Schedule. General Schedule grades represent levels of difficulty and responsibility that are in fact defined by law. They are identified by the letters GS, followed by numbers, such as GS-1 (the lowest grade) to GS-15 (the highest). A recent graduate with a bachelor's degree would usually qualify for a GS-5 or 7.

Each GS grade has an associated base pay range that includes a minimum and a maximum rate of pay. There are ten pay rates between the base minimum and maximum. Base pay ranges are approximate (usually lower) than actual salary, because a locality pay is added depending on the city of employment, (i.e. New York includes a locality pay). Both the base pay and locality pay are subject to adjustments each year, generally upward.

### The GS Pay System

The ten rates for each GS grade are called steps. Movement through steps of a grade recognizes increased skill and knowledge level in the job. This contrasts with movement between grades, which really is a promotion involving taking on new, greater duties and responsibilities and getting paid more for doing so. Movement among steps is faster at the lower end of the scale, when people are learning more about their jobs. See the general schedule pay scale on page 40.

Certain administrative and managerial positions have minimum requirements for education and experience based on the GS grade. The criteria involve either the education or experience minimums in combination or equivalency:

- **GS-5**: a four-year course of study above high school leading to a bachelor's degree; three years of general experience, with one year equivalent to GS-4

- **GS-7**: one full academic year of graduate-level education or superior academic achievement (college graduates in the upper third of their graduating class, with a minimum 3.0 GPA, or a member of a national scholastic honor society); one year of specialized experience at least equivalent to GS-5

- **GS-9**: two full academic years of graduate-level education or a master's degree; one year of specialized experience at least equivalent to GS-7

- **GS-11**: three full academic years of graduate-level education or a Ph.D.; one year of specialized experience at least equivalent to GS-9

- **GS-12**: one year of specialized experience at least equivalent to next lower grade level; no education requirements, as experience is considered the primary factor

## PATCO

Federal jobs are made up of the following basic categories, titles, and grades:

### PROFESSIONAL – GS-5 through 15

The professional positions have a POSITIVE EDUCATIONAL REQUIREMENT, including such occupations as chemist, accountant, doctor, engineer, social worker, or psychologist. Where there is an educational requirement, the education must meet standards set by the profession involved.

### ADMINISTRATIVE – GS-5 through 15

These jobs usually have the title of ANALYST or SPECIALIST. You can qualify for these jobs solely on the basis of experience, but below GS-12 education can be substituted for the required experience. If you have no experience, then you will need a degree to qualify for entry-level (GS-5 through 7) administrative positions. Certain law enforcement investigative and inspection positions are in this category: Special Agent, Border Patrol, Customs Inspector, and Immigration Inspector.

### TECHNICAL – GS-6 through 9

These jobs are the TECHNICIAN or ASSISTANT positions, such as Accounting Technician or Assistant. Although a two- or four-year degree may be required in some fields (especially medical technician occupations), the primary qualifications requirement is experience. The Federal Aviation Administration Electronics Technician can be classified as high as a GS-12. Bachelor's degree graduates can qualify for Technician or Assistant positions starting at GS-7 with superior academic achievement.

### CLERICAL – GS-1 through 5

These are the CLERK positions. There is no college degree requirement. An Associate of Arts degree graduate or two-year certification program will qualify for GS-3 or 4 positions.

### OTHER

This category includes jobs that do not fit other categories. It includes many law enforcement occupations, including security guard, police, ranger, park ranger, and U.S. Marshall, but does not include criminal investigators (special agent). Research psychologists and social scientists are also among the occupations in this category. The grades for this Other category can range from GS-3 to GS-15.

## U.S. Office of Personnel Management, Salary Table 2009-GS

Effective January 2009
http://www.opm.gov/oca/09tables/pdf/gs.pdf

| Grade | Step 1 | Step 2 | Step 3 | Step 4 | Step 5 | Step 6 | Step 7 | Step 8 | Step 9 | Step 10 | Within Grade Amounts |
|-------|--------|--------|--------|--------|--------|--------|--------|--------|--------|---------|----------------------|
| 1 | 17,540 | 18,126 | 18,709 | 19,290 | 19,873 | 20,216 | 20,792 | 21,373 | 21,396 | 21,944 | VARIES |
| 2 | 19,721 | 20,190 | 20,842 | 21,396 | 21,635 | 22,271 | 22,907 | 23,543 | 24,179 | 24,815 | VARIES |
| 3 | 21,517 | 22,234 | 22,951 | 23,668 | 24,385 | 25,102 | 25,819 | 26,536 | 27,253 | 27,970 | 717 |
| 4 | 24,156 | 24,961 | 25,766 | 26,571 | 27,376 | 28,181 | 28,986 | 29,791 | 30,596 | 31,401 | 805 |
| 5 | 27,026 | 27,927 | 28,828 | 29,729 | 30,630 | 31,531 | 32,432 | 33,333 | 34,234 | 35,135 | 901 |
| 6 | 30,125 | 31,129 | 32,133 | 33,137 | 34,141 | 35,145 | 36,149 | 37,153 | 38,157 | 39,161 | 1004 |
| 7 | 33,477 | 34,593 | 35,709 | 36,825 | 37,941 | 39,057 | 40,173 | 41,289 | 42,405 | 43,521 | 1116 |
| 8 | 37,075 | 38,311 | 39,547 | 40,783 | 42,019 | 43,255 | 44,491 | 45,727 | 46,963 | 48,199 | 1236 |
| 9 | 40,949 | 42,314 | 43,679 | 45,044 | 46,409 | 47,774 | 49,139 | 50,504 | 51,869 | 53,234 | 1365 |
| 10 | 45,095 | 46,598 | 48,101 | 49,604 | 51,107 | 52,610 | 54,113 | 55,616 | 57,119 | 58,622 | 1503 |
| 11 | 49,544 | 51,195 | 52,846 | 54,497 | 56,148 | 57,799 | 59,450 | 61,101 | 62,752 | 64,403 | 1651 |
| 12 | 59,383 | 61,362 | 63,341 | 65,320 | 67,299 | 69,278 | 71,257 | 73,236 | 75,215 | 77,194 | 1979 |
| 13 | 70,615 | 72,969 | 75,323 | 77,677 | 80,031 | 82,385 | 84,739 | 87,093 | 89,447 | 91,801 | 2354 |
| 14 | 83,445 | 86,227 | 89,009 | 91,791 | 94,573 | 97,355 | 100,137 | 102,919 | 105,701 | 108,483 | 2782 |
| 15 | 98,156 | 101,428 | 104,700 | 107,972 | 111,244 | 114,516 | 117,788 | 121,060 | 124,332 | 127,604 | 3272 |

**Strategy Tip**
If you are qualified for a certain grade, you can negotiate your step.

## Pay Banding Pay Schedules

Now that we have covered the basic general schedule grade and pay system, we must tell you that not every agency follows this pay system anymore. Pay banding, which allows an organization to combine two or more grades into a wider band, is an increasingly popular alternative to the traditional GS system. The grade information for jobs in agencies using pay banding will have a different look, and that look may be specific to a particular agency. Do not be surprised to see something as odd as ZP-1 or NO-2 in place of GS-5 or GS-7. Focus rather on the duties, the salary, your qualifications for the job, and whether you want to pursue it. Remember, the federal government is large, and needs a way to increase flexibility of pay based on performance. Pay bands are their answer.

## Examples of Pay Band Salaries

Department of Commerce, National Institute of Standards and Technology Pay Bands

| | GS 1 | GS 2 | GS 3 | GS 4 | GS 5 | GS 6 | GS 7 | GS 8 | GS 9 | GS 10 | GS 11 | GS 12 | GS 13 | GS 14 | GS 15 |
|---|---|---|---|---|---|---|---|---|---|---|---|---|---|---|---|
| ZA Administrative | | | 1 | | | | | | 2 | | | 3 | | 4 | 5 |
| ZP Professional | | | 1 | | | | | | 2 | | | 3 | | 4 | 5 |
| ZS Support | 1 | | 2 | | 3 | | 4 | | 5 | | | | | | |
| ZT Technical | | | 1 | | | | 2 | | | 3 | | 4 | 5 | | |

Navy Research Lab

| | GS 1 | GS 2 | GS 3 | GS 4 | GS 5 | GS 6 | GS 7 | GS 8 | GS 9 | GS 10 | GS 11 | GS 12 | GS 13 | GS 14 | GS 15 | GS 16+ |
|---|---|---|---|---|---|---|---|---|---|---|---|---|---|---|---|---|
| NP Scientist & Engineer Professional | | I | | | | | II | | | | | III | | | IV | V |
| NR Scientist & Engineer Technical | | I | | | | II | | | III | | IV | V | | | | |
| NO Administrative Specialist/Prof. | | I | | | | | II | | | | | III | IV | V | | |
| NC Administrative Support | | I | | | | II | | | III | | | | | | | |

## Senior Executive Service (SES)

The SES administers public programs at the top levels of the federal government. Positions are primarily managerial and supervisory. The SES is a tiered system in which salary is linked to individual performance, not position. Basic annual salaries range from $114,468 to $172,200, not including locality pay. Some positions include additional recruitment incentives. In setting pay rates, agencies consider such factors as qualifications, performance, duties, and responsibilities of the position, and private sector pay.

Total compensation (including salary, cash awards for top performance, relocation, recruitment, or retention allowances) may not exceed the pay for Executive Level I ($191,300 in 2008).

More information about SES can be found at https://www.opm.gov/ses.

## Additional Resources

For more information, be sure check out our additional resources listed in the Appendix.

## Summary

To capture what you have learned in this step, fill in the following:

Agency(ies) I want to apply to:

Job title(s) I am interested in:

Grade level(s) I qualify for:

*Great! Now you are ready to get started in finding job openings that fit your focus.*

## Quote

" Research the agency's website and get hold of contact information and organizational structure of that agency to "network" your contacts. Make contact with program managers within the organization you are applying to and send your resume indicating you have applied for this job and are very interested in working for the agency. Know the agency that you are applying to as far as mission and type of work they perform that matches your job skills and expertise.  Another point is to network with people you know who may be your neighbor, classmate, or a former colleague who used to work with you and is now working for the federal agency that you are pursuing so they can assist with getting your name to the hiring manager and getting the word out too. "

*Jeff Clopein*
*State Government to VR Program Specialist*
*U.S. Department of Education/RSA*

# STEP TWO
## Networking Success

Some people think that the only way you can apply for a federal job is through a posted vacancy announcement at www.usajobs.opm.gov or other federal job-posting sites.

You do not have to wait for your USAJOBS results; you can take some control with networking and the new email job search campaign approach that can help move your job search forward.

## Overview

Networking Works

Government Networking—Getting Started with Self-Marketing

Identify Your Network

Are You LinkedIn? Web Networking

Federal Job Fairs

New! The 1-2 Federal Networking/Application Campaign

When to Use the 1-2 Approach

Email Introduction Sample

## Networking Works

If you doubt that networking can help you land a job in the federal government, read this statistic:

"Some 45 percent of the new hires had first learned about their new Federal job from their friends and relatives (17 percent), their new Federal supervisors (15 percent), or their new Federal co-workers (13 percent). In comparison, only about a quarter (23 percent) of our respondents first learned about their Federal job through USAJOBS. Even fewer new hires first learned about their jobs through newspaper, journal, or magazine ads (2 percent) or from a Federal recruiter (1 percent). Friends and relatives were especially useful to new hires who previously were self-employed, unemployed, or working for a nonprofit or private company." U.S. Merit Systems Protection Board, *In Search of Highly Skilled Workers; A Study on the Hiring of Upper Level Employees from Outside the Federal Government*, February 2008.

Your contacts probably will not be able to get you a Federal job, but they can give you the information you need to know what is going on in an agency and when they might be hiring. Even with an electronic resume writing application where you post your resume to a database, it helps to know people in the agency who know what jobs are coming up.

## Government Networking - Getting Started with Self-Marketing

### Be Bold
Start with people you know. Do not be embarrassed to cash in favors from family and friends. Send your Intro Email to all of your friends and family members so they know what you have been doing for the last five years. Tell them what you are looking for, geographic locations you are open to, and the skills that you hope to use. Be enthusiastic, professional, and informative.

### Do Your Research
Get to know people, missions, and agencies. Federal employees and managers are often more than happy to speak with potential candidates about their jobs, if you can find them online.

*Government Executive Magazine* – www.govexec.com – Read about federal employees and managers. You can read about the Top 10 CEOs, CIOs, CFOs, and CHRMs at www.govexec.com. You can read about their background, agencies, missions, and objectives.

*Partnership for Public Service* – www.ourpublicservice.org – You can read about The Best Agencies To Work For, Where the Jobs Are, and Mission Critical Areas and people who won the award for Best Federal Employee of the Year.

*Agency Websites* – My favorite pages include public affairs pages where you can read the latest press releases (what is totally new today/yesterday), mission statements, programs, customers, problems, offices, agencies, people who manage, and new initiatives. You can probably also find an organizational chart with names and titles in the website. This is a goldmine of information about people who run programs and who need talented employees like you to help them.

### Do Not Expect a Miracle

Try to remember that a network is an opportunity to learn, but in the end the federal government cares about what you know, not who you know. In an online job search you have to handle rejection well. You have to be determined to make this work, follow-up, and look for another contact. Determination, perseverance, and initiative are critical core competencies for federal jobseekers.

### Master the Email Informational Interview

In the old days, you might talk by phone or meet in person. The new informational interview is by email. The new online informational interview is simply an email to introduce oneself and ask one or two questions.

*Suggested Questions to Ask in an Email Informational Interview*

✪ What is your organization's mission?

✪ Is your organization growing or changing? If so, how?

✪ What qualifications are you seeking for any new hire?

✪ Will you be posting announcements in the near future?

✪ What are the top skills or attributes that you look for in a candidate in your organization?

✪ What other agencies do you work with?

## Strategy Tip

Remember to ask questions about the organization rather than the supervisor's particular job.

## Identify Your Network – Friends and Family

Nearly everyone knows a federal employee or someone else who does. Do not be hesitant to introduce yourself to connections you are less familiar with. Simply introduce yourself and tell them that you have decided to begin your federal job search. Indicate that you know they work for the government, and that you would appreciate ten minutes of their time to talk about their job and their agency at their convenience. It is advisable to first inquire about their job before asking for ideas about how you could fit into their agency and information about whether their organization is hiring in the near future. Remember also to check with organizations you belong to. Locate your alumni membership list and look it over carefully. Who works for the government? Send them an email introduction as though they could be your next possible supervisor.

## Are You LinkedIn? Web Networking

Linkedin.com is an online network of more than 25 million professionals from around the world, representing 150 industries. When you join, you create a profile that summarizes your professional accomplishments. Your profile helps you find and be found by former colleagues, clients, and partners. You can add more connections by inviting trusted contacts to join LinkedIn and connect to you. This website is a great way to manage your network, keep your resume up-to-date, collect testimonials, broadcast your comings and goings professionally, and stay in touch professionally.

## Federal Job Fairs

Government job fairs are increasing in number and are valuable opportunities to network. You may locate possible job leads, meet federal supervisors, and human resources staff to get a sense of your audience, and see some of your competition. Do not go to the job fair as a spectator, but plan a strategy for a successful and informative job fair experience. Think of attending a job fair as walking into a mini-interview. You could be talking to the actual people who are making hiring decisions, so it is important for you to make a good first impression as an informed, credible, and motivated jobseeker.

Before you go to the job fair, do your research so that you know who to talk to and what to say.

- ✪ Go to the job fair website and find the list of attending federal agencies or government contractors.
- ✪ Select five or ten of these to focus on.
- ✪ Research these organizations online, finding out critical background information such as their mission and their main office locations.
- ✪ Decide which of these agencies you will approach at the job fair.
- ✪ Look up each agency in USAJOBS to see how many jobs they have listed currently.
- ✪ Get familiar with the job titles on the current announcements.

### Job Fair Script
Review your resume and be prepared to make a short presentation to a job fair recruiter on the following key points:
- ✪ Your name
- ✪ Where you are from
- ✪ Where you last worked
- ✪ Your last job title
- ✪ Your top qualifications
- ✪ What you are seeking now
- ✪ Your availability
- ✪ Your message

# New! The 1-2 Federal Networking/Application Campaign

The 1-2 Federal Networking/Application campaign is a new online job search system adapted for current times that is similar to the cold call job search approach from the 1960s through 1980s. In those days the cold call was very effective. A candidate would walk in the door, smile, say hi, leave a resume, develop a connection with a person in the office, and maybe even get an impromptu opportunity to meet the hiring supervisor.

Today, with stringent security measures at government agencies, the in-person cold call is not an option. Instead, there is another way to network: the government version of Web 2.0 networking. The new cold call campaign for government consists of an email introduction to your job application. By simply making email contact before you submit your application, you are taking a more proactive approach that is friendly, while adding a human element to your job search campaign. You will also connect with people in government.

### Possible Results

With the 1-2 Federal Networking/Application campaign, the old adage definitely applies: it cannot hurt to try. On the other hand, going that extra mile could improve your chances of landing your target federal position.

When the supervisor receives your email, he or she might:

✪ Delete your email without responding.

✪ Look at the subject line and glance at your email, which should be impressive and short.

✪ Be looking for someone with your background and level of experience and write back to you regarding one of the following possible scenarios:

- To start a dialogue about your background and the agency's mission.
- To refer you to human resources who would advise you of forthcoming position openings.
- To refer you to another program manager in the office, who might be interested in your background.
- To advise you about upcoming job openings or announcements.

When an announcement that fits your background is posted in that agency and office, you could have already gained some tangible benefits by having sent an introductory email and standing out from the rest of the applicants. For example:

✪ When the supervisor receives the Certified List of Eligibles, he or she may already know your name, background, and education and might look for your name, knowing that you are interested in this type of position.

✪ When the supervisor reviews your resume, he or she will already know that you are interested, determined, personable, skilled, ready to work, and dedicated to the mission.

## When to Use the 1-2 Approach

*Open Inventory Announcements* - These announcements have a long-term closing date and are basically resume collection vehicles. This database might be searched once a week just to see the submissions. The 1-2 Approach will let the supervisor know that you have put your resume into the Open Inventory Announcement, and that you will apply if there is a position that matches your qualifications. Examples of agencies that use the Open Inventory Announcements are the U.S. Navy, U.S. Marine Corps, and FBI.

*Mission Specific* - If you have a particular agency, office, and mission in mind for your federal career, then you should research this office and its manager. Learn their name and write to them directly by email.

*Geographic Preference* – If you are relocating, or if you want to relocate to a certain city, state, or country, find agencies and offices in those locations. Locate the supervisors' names and departments, and write to them directly to introduce your background and interests.

*Meet and Greet Anyone* – If you want to introduce yourself to a certain supervisor (by email), just write about your interests and specialized background and see what happens.

Keep in mind that this approach might not work for Intelligence Agencies, because you may not be able to find names of managers or staff in these agencies. Networking for intelligence jobs will have to come through people you already know.

### Strategy Tip

Be sure to include the following in your email introduction: a short summary of your specialized knowledge, skills, education, and experience; the title of the position and the announcement number you are targeting so they can find you in the system; and an indication that you will also be submitting your resume into the "Open Inventory" Announcement process, if applicable.

# Email Introduction Sample

**Tom Danson**
Past Position: Senior IT Consultant, Fortune 500 Company
Target Position: Supervisory IT Specialist (Product Assurance); GS-2210-14

SUBJECT: Request for Informational Interview for Tom Danson on Supervisory IT Specialist position

Dear Sir or Madam:

My name is Tom Danson and I am inquiring about the Supervisory Information Technology Specialist position with the Office of the Chief Information Officer currently advertised on USAJOBS. Throughout my career, I have built extensive experience in the skills and competencies requested in this announcement as a supervisor, government contract manager, and subject matter expert for information technology with particular expertise in conducting systems analysis and managing software life cycle processes.

Most recently, I have served as a Senior Consultant with the Sentry Corporation, developing strategic and technical approaches to foster new business opportunities within the public sector. In this capacity, I have served as a program manager for large-scale federal government contracts, identifying information technology requirements to support agency business systems. As an IT subject matter expert, I conducted systems analysis and managed life cycle processes such as quality assurance, product testing, and configuration management in order to ensure complete customer satisfaction. My accomplishments have included:

- Serving as competition and pricing strategist for Sentry's bid for the Alliant GWAC for the GSA. Regarded as the premier next generation GWACs for GSA, this broad, ten-year, multiple-award, indefinite Delivery/Indefinite Quantity (MAIDIQ) contract for IT solutions for federal departments and agencies is due for award in FY0x and will represent a $50 billion opportunity.

- Technical Lead and on-site project coordinator for the NGA Re-engineering and Implementation Support Initiative. Analyzed the legacy system infrastructure and developed engineering requirements for a Commercial-of-the-Shelf (COTS) Enterprise Resource Planning (ERP) solution, fully compliant with the Joint Financial Management Improvement Program (JFMIP).

- Completing a security analysis of the Federal Technical Data Solution (FedTeDS) to determine its compliance with federal security directives, including the DOD Information Technology Security Certification and Accreditation Process (DITSCAP), the National Information Assurance Certification and Accreditation Process (NIACAP), and the National Institute of Standards and Technology (NIST) security standards.

I have formally applied to this position using the directions outlined in the USAJOBS announcement, but would like to communicate with you further to determine if this position would be a good fit. I would be more than happy to meet with you in person if it would be helpful. Thank you for your time and I hope to hear from you soon.

Sincerely,
Tom Danson

## Quote

"My previous job was as an IT project manager in the private sector – 20 years experience, I am 58 years old. I used the *Ten Steps* book to apply for a job with the Office of the Inspector General for a HIPAA Compliance officer.

I spent at least 8 hours preparing my resume and application for the announcement, probably more, and used all 30 days of the open period to tweak everything. I made sure I told the truth every step of the way, and I carefully applied your principles to my application. Between November 4th 2007 and early Feb 2008 I applied for the other 8 jobs.

I also browsed the web to read blogs and postings from other applicants, and read story after story of frustrated individuals that applied for dozens of federal jobs and never even got a sniff of positive feedback. Some of these people are experienced attorneys trying to get a federal job. In all cases it seemed they applied by sending their "basic resume", and that they did not understand how the announcement process works.

I purchased your *Ten Steps* book and companion CD in 2003. Your material helped me understand how the process works. In total, I applied for 10 jobs, was best qualified on all 10, and received 2 interviews. I am now working for the federal government. There is no question in my mind that the key techniques you provided had a material impact on my getting hired."

*Victor Voldish*
*Private sector to Project Manager*
*Bureau of Alcohol Tobacco Firearms and Explosives*

# STEP THREE
## Target Your Top Accomplishments

The hiring supervisor will be looking for accomplishments that demonstrate your skills and performance levels and give an indication of what your future performance will be in the job. Outstanding achievements can help your resume get noticed and land an interview.

The qualifications page of the job announcement will provide you a roadmap to understand what the hiring officials are looking for. Remember that to be considered for the position, you must have at least one year of specialized experience aligned with the skills and experience outlined in the qualifications page. Furthermore, in order to be selected as the Best Qualified candidate, you need to demonstrate that you are outstanding in those same areas through—you guessed it—your accomplishments.

## Overview

Troutman Method Lesson 1: What Are Your Top Accomplishments?

What Can Be Considered An Accomplishment?

How Many Accomplishments Should I List?

What Kind Of Format Should I Use?

What Will I Do With This List?

Examples of Top Accomplishments – Short Format

Example of Top Accomplishments – Long Format

Exercise: Top Accomplishments

## Troutman Method Lesson 1: What Are Your Top Accomplishments?

After the federal job decision-making we have completed in the first two steps, we are now ready to get down to the task of creating an outstanding federal resume. It is time to think about YOU.

I find that many people have a difficult time getting started on writing their resumes, because they are either intimidated or bogged down with the daunting task of generating all the details that go into their resume, especially their federal resume.

My solution for easing into resume writing is to start first with the easiest—and most important—piece: your top accomplishments. Your top accomplishments will be the vital sound bites that you want to make sure are communicated to the people reviewing your job application.

Your top accomplishments will be used in the federal application process THREE TIMES:

✪ A short version of your accomplishments will be included in your federal resume (Step 6);

✪ A longer version will be drafted for the Knowledge, Skills, and Abilities narratives or essays that are required by the application questionnaires (Step 7); and

✪ You will review these accomplishments once again when you prepare for your Behavior-Based interview (Step 10).

This step is critical to your success throughout your federal job campaign.

### Strategy Tip
Supervisors are more easily impressed by accomplishments than duties. Sell yourself with your outstanding accomplishments.

## What Can Be Considered An Accomplishment?

Start with these basic questions when you are thinking about your accomplishments:

• What did you actually accomplish in your current job or previous job?
• What did you do that was outstanding – above average?
• Did you achieve something new or better?
• Did you save money for the organization?
• Did you come up with a new idea that saved time or improved customer service?

There are generally two types of accomplishments: *significant accomplishments* and *tangible results*.

Let's start with *significant accomplishments*. Some examples are:
- Projects or teams you lead
- High profile situations
- Controversial or otherwise difficult situations / projects
- Unusually large projects
- Projects subject to very short deadlines
- Big problems you solved
- Important customer service solutions
- New training you implemented
- First time assignments or those requiring creativity to address
- Events or duties you performed that went far beyond your usual expected duties

In some cases, your particular line of work may not have provided you the opportunity to engage in activities resulting in significant accomplishments. Instead, you might need to consider listing tangible results, otherwise known as bean counting. It may be difficult to quantify these numbers after the fact, but remember that demonstrating your accomplishments with numbers could greatly boost the impact of an accomplishment on your resume.

Examples of *tangible results*:
- Number of phone calls you answer in a day or week
- Number of emails you answer in a day or week
- Number of phone calls and emails you receive in a day or week
- Email management strategies created to improve the organization
- Number of times you update the budget in a week or month
- Number of invoices you process in a week or month
- Dollars you spend or handle in a week or month
- Number of appointments you make in a week or month for supervisors
- New Excel files you designed or managed each week or month

**Develop a Project List with Results**
A very useful regular work habit is to develop and track a list of accomplishments and projects. This information is invaluable for future job applications as well as during evaluation time. Here is a suggested basic outline for your project or accomplishment list:
- Title of Project/Program
- Budget (if relevant)
- Role you played
- Mission, objective, purpose of project
- Customer/vendor
- Who you communicated or worked with to complete project
- Major challenge(s) or problem(s) during project
- Results (i.e., cost savings, increased efficiency, improved service to customers)

## How Many Accomplishments Should I List?

Aim for a list of five to ten accomplishments.

## What Kind of Format Should I Use?

There are two recommended formats for writing your top accomplishments:

### Short Format
Write one or two sentences to summarize your best accomplishments for your resume. We have included seven samples of the short format.

### Longer Format: Top Ten List of Accomplishments
The Top Ten format is a full story about the accomplishment, so that you have a narrative to use in a KSA, essay, Executive Core Qualification narrative (ECQ for Senior Executive Service positions), or to prepare for a job interview.

## What Will I Do With This List?

Your top accomplishments will be the starting point for writing by helping you target the key messages in your resume and KSAs. You will improve on your accomplishments by adding keywords from the job announcements and the core competencies (see Step 5), and you will learn how to transform your list into your resume (see Step 6) and your KSAs (see Step 7).

## Examples of Top Accomplishments – Short Format

**Example #1**
**Target Job: PARALEGAL**
**Top 3 Accomplishments**

LEGAL ASSISTANT to General Counsel, SVP    xx/20xx – xx/20xx [6 years]
1. Acquired a good working knowledge of the Sarbanes-Oxley Act 2002 and other securities laws in order to better facilitate in the **filing of financial statements**.
2. Effectively handled many aspects of a **compliance position** after the attorney in charge left the Company.
3. Prepared approximately $30 million dollars in Company stock certificates for senior officers of the Company.

**Example #2**
**Target Job: PERSONNEL SECURITY SPECIALIST**
**Top 7 Accomplishments**

AS A SPECIAL INVESTIGATOR:

1. For efficient, thorough, and focused work, selected for temporary duty assignments in high volume areas (e.g., Washington, DC) to reduce the backlog.

2. Regularly accepted and completed **high priority / short turnaround** cases. Recently received five priority cases on Tuesday and completed all by the mandated Friday deadline (three-day turnaround).

3. Expanded investigations in order to obtain information after being told that witnesses were not going to be honest because of personal fear of retaliation.

4. Awarded Investigator of the Quarter 20xx.

5. Chosen by case manager to mentor new investigator based on my extensive experience, February 20xx.

AS A CHILD PROTECTIVE SERVICES SPECIALIST:

1. ON TIGHT DEADLINES, INVESTIGATED SOME 30-50 SIMULTANEOUS CASES, all with a turnaround of only a few weeks. Made literally life-and-death decisions daily to protect children from abuse, neglect, and sexual offenses. Demonstrated ability to work well and calmly under great pressure.

2. IMPORTANT CASE: First and most challenging CPS investigation resulted in the removal of a child from the mother. The new mother received a positive drug test report. Upon my arrival at the hospital to meet with the mother, she initially denied that her drug use resulted in her child testing positive for methamphetamine. For the next several hours, I persisted in a six-hour interview until she admitted to the drug use. Over the next few days, I interviewed the mother's friends and family members. I worked with the family to provide services and weekly visits with the child. I testified in court to support the removal as being in the best interest of the child. The court upheld the removal under one of the highest standards of proof in civil litigation.

**Example #3**
**Target Job: INVENTORY SPECIALIST**
**Top 13 Accomplishments**

INVENTORY SPECIALIST, xx/xxxx – Present [2 years}
Home Store Building Supply Co.

1.  MANAGED AND CONTROLLED $14-$18 MILLION IN INVENTORIES.

2.  TRACKED INVENTORIES AT 27 WAREHOUSES using Distribution Management Software.

3.  Revitalized underperforming inventory operations by implementing new inventory management and purchasing procedures and processes, including reducing inventory losses using cycle counts and additional training and mentoring for location personnel on proper ordering and receipt of products.

4.  Developed a new monthly report to track metrics on unsold products, which improved the accuracy of inventory audit reporting and enhanced management decision-making.

5.  Through accurate monitoring of inventory levels, minimized lead times, depleted $550,000 in "non-performing" inventory, and improved inventory accuracy.

CORPORATE CREDIT MANAGER, xx/xxxx – xx/xxxx [20 years]
Home Store Building Supply Co.

1.  Implemented E-business and cross-training initiatives, that saved up to $150K annually in payroll costs.

2.  Automated a cash application process reducing processing time and improving accuracy.

3.  Reduced annual overhead by $250K through effective contract negotiations.

4.  Negotiated a contract with a financial service provider that generated a $400K cost savings.

5.  Reduced bad debts to 0.75% of sales and increased recoveries by 75% through strict adherence to policy, employee training, and new collection procedures.

6.  Automated the credit application and payroll systems, driving improvements in information accuracy, speed, and completeness while reducing overall costs.

7.  Championed the implementation of company credit cards, which successfully lowered overall credit exposure while building sales and customer loyalty.

8.  Instrumental in coordinating a seamless assimilation of customer accounts, technology, and personnel following an acquisition of three competitors.

## Example #4
## Target Job: LOAN SPECIALIST
## Top 8 Accomplishments

Branch Operations Coordinator, September 20xx – Present [3 years]
State Officer Credit Union, Baton Rouge, LA and Statewide

1.  Managed and directed the operations of 8 branches state-wide.

2.  Supervised, developed, and monitored the performance of 29 employees.

3.  Continuity of operations planning: member of disaster recovery team

4.  Regulatory oversight: assistant Compliance Officer in charge of compliance

5.  Oversaw the build out and opening activities of the last four branches.

6.  Developed and updated policy manuals for tellers, branch managers, member service reps, lending, personnel, ATM policy, internal security, and first IT policy.

7.  Developed training materials and standard operating procedures for lending, tellers, and member services.

8.  Reduced staff and expenses by utilizing web-based online loan and new account applications; promoted online banking and bill pay services.

## Example #5
## Target Job: VOCATIONAL REHABILITATION SPECIALIST
## Top 5 Accomplishments

Pennsylvania Department of Education-Division of Rehabilitation Services (DORS)
9/19xx - Present

1.  Instrumental in achieving a placement success rate of 70% and a customer service satisfaction rate of 86%. Achieved or exceeded federal and state performance standards throughout 16-year career.

2.  Orchestrated and led a successful vocational rehabilitation placement for a challenging client with immediate employment needs. Assembled a team to expedite assessment and training, and arranged employer interviews and community resources. By expediting the case management process, client was able to secure a new temporary job within weeks and subsequently secured a permanent position.

3.  Drove increases in employment outcomes for the disabled through networking, teamwork, and positive, open communication with community groups and employers.

4.  Developed and implemented best organizational and time management practices to improve the delivery of services and staff efficiencies, including utilizing a tickler system (activity due) to address timelines and projects due; and prioritize and implement service importance according to client's needs. Implemented a new organizational/filing system that improved management of paper documents.

5.  Frequently requested as a presenter by workforce partners and employers because of reputation for clarity and quality of communications on disability issues and depth and breadth of vocational rehabilitation knowledge.

**Example #6**
**Target Job: CONSUMER LOAN OFFICER**
**Top 6 Accomplishments**

Consumer Loan Officer                                                    xx/20xx to Present

1. Procured and processed an average of 25 to 30 automobile loans monthly for a diverse client base for financing division of international lending institution.

2. **Customer Service And Advisor**: Managed 50 or more inbound and outbound call traffic per day.

3. **Loan Officer**: Procured and closed on 25 to 30 auto loans monthly.

4. Nominated as Acting Vice President for African American Heritage Committee Smith Bank Auto Finance Consumer Loans.

5. Coordinated and titled "Credit & You" lunch and learn training seminar.

6. Awarded bonus ten out of twelve months as Consumer Loan Officer for customer service, business decision, and 16 Step application detail quality.


**Example #7**
**Target Job: PROGRAM ANALYST**
**Top 7 Accomplishments**

Government House, State of Maryland    06/19xx to Present [8 years]
SOUS CHEF

1. Served as second in command of kitchen staff for First Family of Maryland. Managed kitchen operations and directed staff to ensure efficient business processes and customer satisfaction.

2. Operations Management: Directed daily operations of full-service kitchen, planning, coordinating, and preparing formal and informal meals and events for up to 3,000 people

3. Planned, coordinated, and executed breakfast, lunch, dinner for First Family and other events, including seated dinners and open houses for up to 4,000, with usually 3-5 events per week, as many as 2 per day.

4. Instituted process changes to increase efficiency and change mind-set from reactive to proactive. Created plan to work one meal ahead, allowing time to respond to last minute requests, changes, and events.

5. Received letter of appreciation from the White House for organizing luncheon attended by President Bill Clinton with less than 24-hour notice.

6. Implemented industrial production system, automated systems, and information management for production, scheduling, and cost control.

7. Actively built team mindset and morale and implemented employee incentive program, stressing interdepartmental cooperation and employees' role in organizational success. Resulted in improved attendance and performance.

## Example of Top Accomplishments – Long Format

The longer version will be a first draft for a Knowledge, Skills, and Abilities narrative, a Questionnaire Essay, or an Executive Core Qualification Narrative. If you have many excellent accomplishments, you should write your Top Ten List with some details.

**Top Ten Career Accomplishments**

1. **Obtained permission from the Vice Admiral, Deputy Chief of Naval Operations, to implement a capital planning and investment control (CPIC) process for the Navy for all Navy commands.** Championed the CPIC effort because not only is it required by statute, it is the right thing to do. Although the Clinger-Cohen Act of 1996 requires all federal agencies to develop and implement a capital planning and investment control process by which to analyze, select, control, and evaluate its information technology investments, Navy had not done so until now. Overcame a Navy culture of fierce agency independence and intense competition for funds.

Navy is beginning to realize significant financial benefits with the CPIC process, as well as increased IT system interoperability, increased Federal Information System Management Act compliance rate, and a faster rate of elimination of legacy software. Developed the governance structure and policy for implementing the capital planning and investment control process.

2. **Created the Navy CIO Council (federated council of 26 CIOs from major Navy commands, world-wide).** The Council is the chief governance vehicle for the Navy CIOs, as well as the lead policy vetting and enforcement body. Created targeted "Centers of Governance" for Architecture and Standards; Cyber Security; Investment Management; Human Capital Management; eGovernment; and Data Management. These Centers of Governance provide focal points for Navy-wide convergences of experts. The Capital Planning and Investment Control process utilizes the Centers to assign health ratings to proposed and current systems that are under development or deployed. For the first time, Navy has coordinated efforts of all its IT policy experts and has broken the many stovepipes. This required substantial effort to break the culture barrier of "that's not the way we do things" mentality.

3. **Founded and managed Precision Systems, Incorporated, to provide custom software and systems integration, installation, and to support commercial markets nation-wide.** Developed and executed strategic and tactical business plans, including policies focused to meet company goals and objectives. Grew a client base of 600 firms (impressive) by creating focused marketing and sales strategies. Managed and directed all business operations, making resource allocations, developing budgets, managing expenditures, and determining all business operation decisions.

Managed and led technical direction of organization, including determining changes in product offerings, services, and determining direction in development and delivery of new products and services. Managed numerous IT projects for clients. Selected target architecture though which all corporate software would be evaluated. Prepared and executed client-focused deployment schedules for new software product releases and implementations. Introduced transformational and innovative technologies to target markets. Provided leadership and direction to staff in implementing client requests for products and services, with successful use of multi-project teams.

4. **Provided essential support to the Department of the Navy IM/IT Strategic Plan** resulting in strategic focus on network operations security, capital planning and investment control, mission operations of the Navy, human resources development and leadership, and performance measurement. Crafted goals and measures for both the Navy and Marine Corps. The Plan was used as a focal point and performance benchmark for two fiscal years. Presently providing input to the next version (fiscal years 20xx-20xx).

Shaped key components of Department of Navy IM/IT policies and governance resulting in significant advances in scare resource utilization and performance, while simultaneously improving the security posture of Navy IT systems and data and reducing overall operating costs. The Navy spends about $10 billion annually on IM/IT services and products. The recommended changes in policy and governance will reduce the expenditures by 20% within two years. Results have already begun and are on track to achieve the target reductions.

Developed the manpower and staffing plan for the USMC Enterprise Information Technology Service. The service supplies secure and networked server services to the Marine Corps worldwide.

5. **Improved contracting services, valued at $500 million annually, to over 100 Navy commands** in the Washington DC area as the Officer-in-Charge of the Fleet Industrial Supply Center Washington while conducting operations during a period of extreme stress on the ethnically-diverse workforce of 150 persons. Customers included the Chief of Naval Operations and the Vice President of the United States. Shortly after being assigned as Officer-in-Charge, the command was designated for significant reductions in the workforce, resulting in over a 50% decrease in employees. Personally interviewed each impacted employee to ensure they had maximum opportunities for reassignment throughout the Government acquisition workforce or retirement on favorable terms. Concurrently, increased the level of contracting service through negotiating terms of assistance from other contracting offices including Philadelphia, PA and Norfolk, VA.

6. **Consolidated, within six months, seven major Navy installations into one as the Naval District Washington Regional Supply Manager.** Services provided by the Region, covering installations over 150 miles apart, included business, contracting, postal, transportation, and anthrax screening of mail. This duty was conducted simultaneously with the Officer-in-Charge position of the Fleet Industrial Supply Center Washington. Responsible for preparing, justifying, and presenting business financial analysis projects, cost analysis, performance metrics for long range and short range initiatives, providing oversight, preparation of operating budgets, conducting audits, and resolving problems including IAIP. Worked with the NDW leadership to develop regional business partnerships and initiatives. Was responsible for strategic business planning, communicating organizational vision, and achieving objectives

on time and on budget. Responsible for resource management, including determining requirements and committing resources to meet organizational goals and objectives. Created and implemented workforce policies covering a full range of personnel issues that included administration and management issues, productivity and effectiveness, performance management, and development of the workforce.

7. **As Deputy Director, Management Analysis Group for the Assistant Secretary of the Navy for Personnel and Reserve Affairs** led the Manpower and Personnel Process/Function Board of the Business Initiatives Council for the Secretary of the Defense. The position was a Senior Executive Service level. Served as Assistant Deputy for the transformational Naval Personnel Task Force, which impacted the recruiting, retention, and training of the 500,000 members of the military and civilian workforce. Assisted in the creation of the military officer Information Professional cadre within the Department of the Navy, as a joint effort with the Chief Information Officer. Participated in HQ-level panels to develop policies related to recruitment, compensation, education, training, and performance management. Reviewed and assessed Navy-wide Enterprise Resource Planning (ERP), enterprise portal, information assurance vulnerabilities and precautions, and web-enabling efforts for the purpose of developing recommendations to the Secretary of the Navy regarding best use of limited resources, protecting its assets, and eliminating redundancy in the information systems field.

8. **Managed challenging, complex business process reengineering, performance-based programs,** using business metrics and return on investment analyses, targeting increased customer service, and improved financial performance, at less cost, while serving as Senior Project Manager for Science Applications International Corporation. Workforce planning tasks included the analysis of software systems, personnel productivity and effectiveness, facilities, equipment, and material costs evaluation. Organizations engaged had operating budgets in excess of $40,000,000 per year. Responsible for preparing, justifying, and presenting financial analysis projects, performing resource allocation and management, providing oversight, preparing operating budgets, conducting audits, and resolving problems. Prepared the economic analysis for the Lawrence Livermore National Laboratory's National Ignition (Laser) System.

9. **Demonstrated superlative leadership skills by being competitively selected and serving as Commanding Officer of four Naval reserve commands.** Each successive selection as Commanding Officer was achieved under ever-increasing competition. While serving as Commanding Officer of the Navy Regional Contracting Center Washington, the unit was selected as "Best Unit" from a highly competitive field of 99 units. Other commands were the Naval Supply Systems Headquarters, Defense Contracts Management Command Atlanta, and the unit representing the Assistant Secretary of the Navy for Acquisition, Research, and Development. Retired from the Naval Reserves October 20xx.

10. **During 20xx-20xx, earned Masters of Science in Computer Science degree, Chief Information Officer, and Information Assurance Security Program Certificates from the National Defense University** with emphasis on federal Chief Information Officer roles and responsibilities. Wrote a thesis for the Masters Degree with a focus on Enterprise Resource Planning. Also, earned an Oracle Database Administration diploma.

# Quote

" I received 30 resumes for 30 applicants for an accounting position.
Only one resume included accomplishments. I interviewed that person,
and I hired that person. Kathryn's idea about the Top Ten List and
separating accomplishments in your work experience section is critical
and can help the resume to stand out on the supervisor's desk. "

*Supervisor*
*Federal High Administration, DOT*
*Lakeland, Denver, Colorado*

# STEP FOUR
# Find the Perfect Job Announcement

This step is active, involved, and mandatory for your federal job search. The federal government does NOT use only one website and resume builder. Researching vacancy announcements is essentially a part-time job requiring about five hours per week to search multiple websites, set up your profiles (at least an hour each), and submit your resume for matching announcements.

## Overview
Types of Job Announcements
A Systematic Federal Job Search
Federal Job Websites
    USAJOBS
    Application Manager
    Avue Central Recruiting System
    Resumix
Agency Job Listing Websites
Excepted Agencies
Other Websites Worth Checking
Troutman Method Lesson 2: Interpreting A Vacancy Announcement

## Types of Job Announcements

*Job Announcements with Specific Closing Dates:*
These announcements are for positions that are being recruited for specifically. Timing for response could be as little as two weeks or as long as several weeks. Agencies set these dates based on their experience with the relevant job markets.

*Job Announcements with Cut-offs; Multiple / Rolling Deadlines:*
You might see an announcement with a closing date of three months from today and have cut-off dates in addition to the final deadline. The human resources specialists will not close the collection of resumes until the final deadline. They will check their resumes in the database at the cut-off-dates, but they will wait until the end of the time period to review all resumes for consideration.

*Open Inventory – Standing Registers – Database Announcements:*
These are announcements for jobs that are continually being recruited for or when a future need for candidates is anticipated. The closing dates could be far into the future, or there may be none. The names of qualified applicants are stored in a database, and the HR staff will search the database when a supervisor requests a person meeting the job's requirements. Timing for filling jobs covered by this kind of announcement is unknown, so you may be in for a long wait if you respond to one.

**Strategy Tip**
Apply to all types of job announcements listed here.

## Example of Announcement with Specific Closing Date

## Example of an Open Inventory Announcement

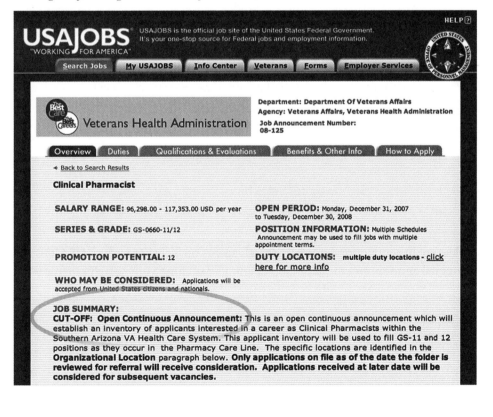

## A Systematic Federal Job Search

In Step 1, you focused your job search. In this step, you will need to further specify the key agencies hiring the job types you are seeking, and identify how each agency advertises their job openings. The table on pages 170-171 shows which websites and builders the major agencies currently use. This table should give you a starting point, but make sure to verify that the information for your agencies of interest are up-to-date.

How often you check the websites for new announcements depends in large part on how much time you have available to dedicate to your job search. In general, you should be prepared to check announcements at least weekly in order to ensure that you do not miss a potentially matching job announcement.

Set up your accounts and profiles on the websites serving the agencies you are targeting, such as:
- ✪ www.usajobs.gov
- ✪ www.applicationmanager.gov
- ✪ www.avuecentral.com
- ✪ www.cpol.army.mil
- ✪ https://chart.donhr.navy.mil

When you create your profile(s), check that you will accept Term, Temporary, and Career Conditional positions. With a change in administration, many positions will be posted as term or temporary positions. These positions provide an opportunity for you to get into the federal government, and you can later apply for a status position. As a term or temporary employee, you will receive many of the same benefits as your full-time status counterparts.

Write down your vacancy announcement search plan and, if necessary, schedule it as a regular activity.

### Strategy Tip
To save time, make sure to sign up for automatic search agents on websites such as USAJOBS to receive regular email announcements about job openings matching your search criteria.

Here are some example plans:

### Plan 1 – USAJOBS Only

USAJOBS "All Search" weekly check
Set up and read automatic search agent emails

### Plan 2 – More Comprehensive Search

USAJOBS "All Search" weekly check
Set up and read automatic search agent emails
Agency listings weekly check
Check other websites weekly, such as www.avuecentral.com, www.indeed.com,
or www.washingtonpost.com/wl/jobs/home.

### Plan 3 – Focus on Army positions

Search on www.cpol.army.mil – all of the Army positions are posted here
USAJOBS search weekly for positions other than Army
Set up and read automatic search agent emails on USAJOBS

## Strategy Tip

Sometimes jobseekers will update a resume on USAJOBS when they are really applying for
a job with the Army – which would be the CPOL site. Remember that if you are applying for
an Army position, you will need to submit your resume to the Army resume builder and self-
nominate at the Army's recruitment website, www.cpol.army.mil. If you want to apply for a
Navy position, make sure to take the same steps on the Navy's website. If you want to apply for
a position at the Department of Interior, apply to USAJOBS and submit answers to questions
at www.applicationmanager.gov.

## Federal Job Websites

### USAJOBS
www.usajobs.gov

This is the Office of Personnel Management's main website for federal jobs. It is free of charge and very easy to use.

### Quick Start: Search ALL JOBS

This is the No. 1 search strategy on USAJOBS, as recommended by OPM's USAJOBS' managers and website developer.

*Quick Search Instructions:*

- Go to www.usajobs.gov
- Click on SEARCH JOBS
- Leave the "Keyword Search" box empty
- Choose your geographic preference
- Choose "Select All" in the Job Category Search box
- Choose your salary range and pay grade, or leave blank
- Click on Yes if you have military or other preference
- Click SEARCH FOR JOBS

**Strategy Tip**
Do the ALL SEARCH on a weekly basis AND set up your job search agents as well.

This search will present all of the job titles in this geographic area within this salary range. You can review the job titles and duties to determine if the jobs are of interest to you. It is important to search for ALL JOBS, because federal job titles are not as straightforward as we would like, and they are prone to change as new job needs arise in agencies. If you limit your job search to a particular job title with which you are familiar, you may not learn about all of the job openings for which you are qualified—or even those that represent your particular field of interest. For instance, would you automatically think to search for Program Specialist or Management Analyst? Surprisingly, these popular government job titles mean many things. The range of program possibilities is phenomenal - environmental, food and nutrition, transportation, education, health, health insurance, and homeland security. You name it. The government probably has a program specialist or management analyst working on it! Sorting through the long list of jobs will take time, but as you learn the job titles and functions, you will gradually be able to accurately target your job search, and it will likely save you time in the long run.

### Set Up Search Agents in USAJOBS

You can create up to five search agents in USAJOBS to receive emails on a daily, weekly, or monthly basis with specific job titles, geographic region, and grade or salary. But beware: you should not rely only on this system completely. If you do use the ALL SEARCH as described above, there will be some job titles that will not come up with your search agent.

# Application Manager
**www.applicationmanager.gov**

Application Manager is provided by the Office of Personnel Management and powered by USA Staffing™, a tool to submit and track application packages. Application Manager, like a handful of other federal staffing systems, is integrated with USAJOBS to accept USAJOBS Resumes. Application Manager 'takes over' management of the application process once you leave USAJOBS. Application Manager presents any assessments you need to complete, collects any supporting documents that are required or needed, and provides detailed feedback to applicants as the process goes forward. Some agencies will use Application Manager as their only recruitment system.

This website makes applying to multiple announcements easier by keeping on file all of your personal information, the documents you have submitted, and your responses to questionnaires. Application Manager will also help to ensure that your application package is complete.

## Application Manager

**Welcome to USA Staffing™ Application Manager**

**Existing Account? Log In Here:**

User Name: _____
Password: _____

[Go]

Application Manager is an official U.S. Government System. You are authorized to use it subject to Terms and Conditions. Unauthorized use of this system or its information could result in criminal prosecution.

Forgot User Name or Password   Problems Logging In?

**Create an account:**

Create one now -- It's fast, convenient and easy to use all these Application Manager features!

Check out our Quick Start Guide.

[Create an Account]

Instructions on how to apply for a job without using Application Manager

## Avue Central Recruiting System

www.avuecentral.com

Avue Central is a competitor of USAJOBS. This system is developed and maintained by Avue Digital Services, a private industry company providing recruitment services for federal agencies. Avue Central services approximately 25 federal agencies with their resume builder, questionnaire, and essays. Agencies using Avue Central place their job announcements here as well as on the OPM website (www.usajobs.gov). Avue Central is a free, easy-to-use website.

You can input your resume into their database with their resume builder and apply for jobs with any of their client agencies with a simple click. The search screen is simple to scroll through, with as many as twenty job announcements per screen.

*Agencies and Organizations using Avue Central:*

Architect of the Capitol
Carahsoft Technology Corporation
Court Services and Offender Supervision Agency
Department of Justice
Drug Enforcement Administration
Federal Air Marshal Service
Fratelli Coalition Site
International Leadership Foundation
Library Of Congress
Millennium Challenge Corporation

Office of Federal Housing Enterprise Oversight
Peace Corps
Securities and Exchange Commission
Society of American Indian Government Employees
US Agency for International Development
USDA Forest Service
United States Capitol Police
Department Of Agriculture

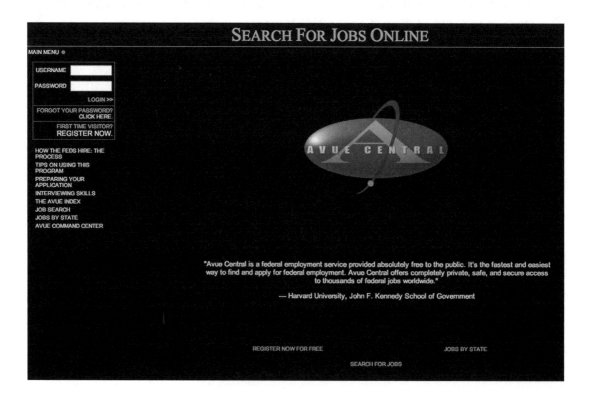

# Resumix™ (U.S. Department of Defense Resume)

Department of Defense agencies (including the military services for their civilian hiring) use Resumix™, a resume-driven system for Civilian Personnel Hiring and Management. NASA also uses Resumix in addition to the USAJOBS Resume Builder for resume collections. Several agencies are working on a new internal recruitment system that will eliminate Resumix, but as of this printing, the Resumix system is still in use.

A key difference between Resumix and the other automated hiring systems we have mentioned is that Resumix does not use your answers to job-specific questions to determine whether, and how well, you are qualified for a job. But like the other systems, it does require a Profile set-up with personnel questions to establish your account and to determine your eligibility for federal employment. After that, the focus is on the content of your resume.

Definition by *Business Wire*, 1996: Resumix uses image processing to store electronic images of candidate and employee resumes. Patented artificial intelligence extracts the specific candidate qualifications (keywords) specified by federal government agencies. An electronic skills and qualifications database is prepared for automatic matching to vacancy requirements. The Resumix system creates lists of the most qualified people for hire, promotion, or reassignment, and are then compiled for review by selecting officials.

In other words, Resumix is a keyword search system. The human resources specialist will search the database with five to seven critical keywords/skills/phrases taken from the vacancy announcements.

Because the Department of Defense agencies use Resumix™, it is tempting to believe that one registration and one resume could be used for all civilian jobs having similar qualifications requirements across all of DOD, Army, Air Force, Navy, and the Marine Corps. Not so! Although the system is commonly used, the requirements are specific to each user. So Army, Navy (including the Marine Corps), and DOD all have unique requirements for their Resumix™ users. This is also true for NASA, which is not part of the DOD.

On the following pages, we provide information about key websites to visit to apply for civilian jobs in the Department of Defense and the military. Remember, you can also find jobs in these departments on the USAJOBS website, but you will be redirected to the specific departmental (e.g., Army, Navy) website to actually apply for a specific job.

## Department of the Navy Civilian Jobs (Resumix)
### https://chart.donhr.navy.mil/

The U.S. Navy and Marine Corps have their own website on which you can post your resume. You may copy and paste your resume into their online resume builder, then search for announcements that match your qualifications. Go to the "Jobs, Jobs, Jobs" page to search for civilian job vacancies by geographic area, salary, or job title.

Internships with the Navy or Marines are also listed on this website. You MUST apply for jobs or internships through this system. The resume builder on this website is very simple and easy to complete.

NOTE: The Department of Navy announcements are not particularly descriptive. They may have "generic" job descriptions instead of specific "duties," like other announcements. These are "Open Inventory" or database announcements.

Jobseekers may not take these employment opportunities seriously because the closing dates for the jobs may be 2012. However, they are real jobs; HR staff will search for the best candidates when a supervisor has a position to fill.

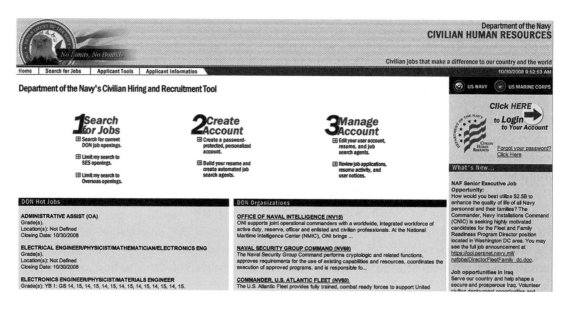

## Strategy Tip
POTENTIAL BUILDER PITFALL! Sometimes a job applicant will forget they are applying to an Army announcement and will update their USAJOBS resume instead of their Army resume. The result is that you may not actually be applying for the Army announcement.

# Department of the Army Civilian Personnel (Resumix)

www.cpol.army.mil

Although the U.S. Army posts its civilian vacancies on the Army site AND the USAJOBS website, you MUST post your resume into the Army's resume builder. If you are interested in civilian positions with the U.S. Army, you might save time by going directly to the Army website to find the announcements and apply for the jobs.

## Agency Job Listing Websites

Most departments and agencies have their own job information websites or pages. They may also provide information to the main government job information site (www.usajobs.gov). If you are focusing your job search on specific agencies, register at these agencies' websites and search for jobs within their listings. Frequently, agencies provide more information on their own websites about jobs and how to apply for them than they include in the announcements placed on USAJOBS. Individual agency websites also include their database registration pages for their on-line application forms.

### Traditional vs. Nontraditional Civil Service

Size breeds complexity! The federal government is comprised of hundreds of separate organizations. Many of these organizations belong to the traditional civil service, and follow a common set of hiring rules. Others, however, lie outside the traditional civil service, and may have their own hiring policies. To complicate things even further, one agency may have different hiring policies within each department. If you are interested in working for any of these agencies, be sure to check the agencies' websites to learn about vacancies.

The fact that not all vacancies are located in one place is both a challenge and an opportunity for you. It is a challenge, because it suggests that you should not rely only on the USAJOBS site when you look for federal jobs, but to also consult homepages of federal agencies for which you might want to work. You can not lose by taking this additional step. And while you are on the agency-specific site, you can learn useful information about the agency, its mission, its culture, and its jobs.

Remember to also keep an eye open for other ways federal agencies recruit and advertise their openings. For example, agencies are increasingly participating in or running their own job fairs. They may recruit through school career centers, and some even use newspaper advertising.

## Strategy Tips
- ✪ Bookmark these sites and check them every week or more frequently.
- ✪ Sign up for automatic emails with job listings.

# Excepted Agencies

Excepted agencies do NOT list on USAJOBS. These agencies utilize some of the "nontraditional" hiring practices. These agencies may post their vacancies on USAJOBS, but you should also check their home pages when you are conducting your federal job search.

Transportation Security Administration, Department of Homeland Security
Federal Reserve System, Board of Governors
Central Intelligence Agency
Defense Intelligence Agency, Department of Defense
Foreign Service, U.S. Department of State
Federal Bureau of Investigation, Department of Justice
Agency for International Development
National Security Agency, Department of Defense
National Imagery and Mapping Agency, Department of Defense
U.S. Nuclear Regulatory Commission
Postal Rate Commission
Health Services and Research Administration, Department of Veterans Affairs (Physicians, nurses, and allied medical personnel)
Judicial Branch
Legislative Branch (including the Government Accountability Office)

*Government Corporations, such as:*
U. S. Postal Service
Tennessee Valley Authority
The Virgin Islands Corporation

*Public International Organizations:*
International Monetary Fund
Pan American Health Organization
United Nations Children's Fund
United Nations Development Program
United Nations Institute
United Nations Population Fund
United Nations Secretariat
World Bank, IFC and MIGA

# Other Websites Worth Checking

Other websites that you may want to frequent are www.washingtonpost.com and www.indeed.com, which will sometimes list federal jobs. If you do find federal announcements on these two sites, the announcements will be short and sweet. It might not contain all of the needed information for you to be competitive against those who have read the announcement on the www.usajobs.gov website, so try to see if you can locate the same announcement on USAJOBS.

## Troutman Method Lesson 2: Interpreting a Vacancy Announcement

The most important point that you need to take away from this step is to read the vacancy announcement very carefully. You not only need to comply with the requirements of the vacancy announcement perfectly, you will also need to use keywords from the announcement to prepare a successful application package.

You will see sections of vacancy announcements in the True Stories. You will see how we analyze the duties, qualifications, and specialized experience for keywords and how we integrate those keywords into the resumes.

## Strategy Tip

Read the vacancy announcement very carefully, paying close attention to these sections: Duties; Qualifications; Knowledge, Skills & Abilities; Questionnaires; and How to Apply.

### Title of Job, Grade, and Salary

Be sure the job is right for you. Some job titles in government are unusual and not typically recognized in the employment world. However, they might be just right for you. For instance:

✪ Budget Analyst, GS-12/13, DE; Salary: $69,764 to $107,854; Executive Office of the President, 1 Vacancy, Washington, DC; Position Information: Career/Career Conditional Position in Competitive Service; Permanent Position

✪ Administrative Assistant, GS-0303-09/09; Promotion Potential to GS-9; Salary: $50,285 to $65,276; Department of Justice, U.S. Attorneys, Executive Office & Office of U.S. Attorneys, Eastern District of New York; Full-time Permanent Career or Career-Conditional Appointment in the Competitive Service

✪ Energy Management Specialist, GS-1102-9/12; Promotion Potential to GS-12; Salary: $36,671 to $84,559; Department of Defense, Defense Logistics Agency, Ft. Belvoir, Fairfax, VA; Full-time Career/Career Conditional

✪ Contract Specialist, GS-1102-9/12; Promotion potential to GS-12; U.S. Secret Service, Department of Homeland Security

## Closing Date

Be aware that applications submitted after the closing date will NOT be considered. Therefore, check the job announcement listings at least weekly so that you will have enough time to submit your applications. If the closing date says "Open Continuously," "Inventory Building," or has a closing date that is far off in the future, then the organization is using this announcement to build an inventory of future job candidates. Names of qualified applicants will be placed in a database for future (and also possibly, current) job openings. Such announcements represent many jobs that the agency expects to open up at any time.

## Who Can Apply

What does "Open to Anyone With or Without Status" mean? If the announcement says "Open to Anyone," then you can apply. "Status" refers to current federal employees and former employees whose length of previous federal employment and type of appointment qualify them for reinstatement. NOTE: Most federal civil service jobs require U.S. citizenship, but jobs in other federal systems (such as the Postal Service, National Institutes of Health, and other agencies) may not. If you are not a U.S. citizen, read this part of the announcement carefully.

You will see this question in the USAJOBS vacancy announcement search. You will click on NO if you are none of these special situations. You will click on YES, if any of these items applies to you.

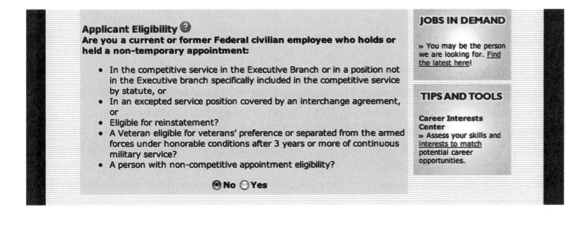

**Applicant Eligibility** ❓
**Are you a current or former Federal civilian employee who holds or held a non-temporary appointment:**

- In the competitive service in the Executive Branch or in a position not in the Executive branch specifically included in the competitive service by statute, or
- In an excepted service position covered by an interchange agreement, or
- Eligible for reinstatement?
- A Veteran eligible for veterans' preference or separated from the armed forces under honorable conditions after 3 years or more of continuous military service?
- A person with non-competitive appointment eligibility?

⦿ No ◯ Yes

**JOBS IN DEMAND**

» You may be the person we are looking for. Find the latest here!

**TIPS AND TOOLS**

**Career Interests Center**
» Assess your skills and interests to match potential career opportunities.

## Strategy Tip

GS-1202-9/12: Vacancy announcements with multiple grade offerings are your best option for career opportunities in government.

## Agency/Office

The office where the job is located is very important. Researching and understanding the office mission could help you write a more targeted resume. The office title could also provide clues about the mission of the job, such as Information Technology, Legal Services, Policy and Planning, or EEO.

## Location/Duty Station

Make sure you are willing to work in the geographic location of the position you are seeking. When hiring new employees, federal agencies must accept applications regardless of where the applicant lives. (For example, an agency must accept an application from a person living in Florida who seeks a job in Alaska). However, the agency may refuse to pay moving and relocation expenses. Read the announcement carefully to find out what your obligations are.

## Knowledge, Skills, and Abilities (KSAs or Competencies)

Read the announcement carefully to see if KSA narratives will be required written on separate sheets of paper, or if the KSAs can be described in the text of your resume. (See Step 7 for more instruction on KSA writing.)

## Duties

Always read the duties carefully because the title of the position may not accurately reflect the duties of the job.

In the True Stories, we mention *one year specialized experience* in almost every example. Pay close attention to this language in the announcement. The HR Specialist will be looking for your One Year Specialized Experience in areas of work similar to the performance level of the announcement.

## Qualifications and One Year Specialized Experience

One year of specialized experience means that you have one year of experience that is specialized in this work and at this level. Read the required qualifications to determine if you have the generalized and specialized experience, or the education that can substitute for it. If the announcement uses the term "one year," it means 52 weeks, 40 hours per week. Relevant experience gained from part-time jobs can be combined to determine how much job-related experience you have. If the hours combine to make one year of specialized experience, then you can be credited with that year.

For many jobs, qualifications are expressed in terms of experience or education, or combinations of the two. Possession of a Bachelor's Degree is often enough to qualify someone for an entry-level (GS-5 or sometimes GS-7) job in many professional or administrative occupations.

For career changers returning to college for another degree, you may qualify for your new career as a GS-5, 7, or 9 based on your education alone. You will probably have to move back in your earnings, but with potential to move ahead in your new career.

## Questionnaires, Core Questions, Vacancy-Specific Questions, and Job-Specific Questions

Many announcements will require you to fill out additional questions as part of your application. This is a Self-Assessment Questionnaire. You will be rating your skill level in the questions. The question format will be multiple choice, yes/no, true/false, check all that apply, and essay questions. You will be graded on your answers – and the grade will determine your score for your application. A human resources specialist gave this instruction to a class at the Environmental Protection Agency: "Give yourself the most credit that you can when answering the questions."

You will learn more about Questionnaires in Step 7.

*Example 1 - Vacancy Specific Questions (from USAJOBS)*

**STEP TWO - (Vacancy Specific Questions - CPSC Career Connection)**

In CPSC Career Connection, you will answer vacancy specific questions necessary to evaluate your qualifications for the specific job to which you are applying. When completed, the information you provided at USAJOBS and the answers to the CPSC Career Connection questions will become your application. You may edit your answers up until midnight EST of the announcement close date. After the vacancy closes the HR office uses the application package to automatically rate, rank and certify candidates.

*Example 2 - Assessment Questionnaire (from USAJOBS)*

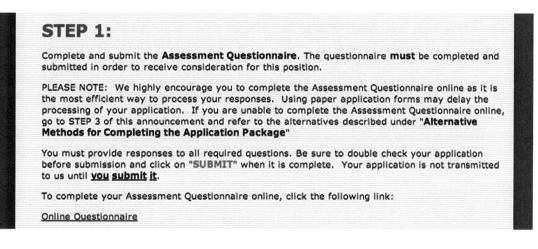

## STEP 1:

Complete and submit the **Assessment Questionnaire**. The questionnaire **must** be completed and submitted in order to receive consideration for this position.

PLEASE NOTE: We highly encourage you to complete the Assessment Questionnaire online as it is the most efficient way to process your responses. Using paper application forms may delay the processing of your application. If you are unable to complete the Assessment Questionnaire online, go to STEP 3 of this announcement and refer to the alternatives described under "**Alternative Methods for Completing the Application Package**"

You must provide responses to all required questions. Be sure to double check your application before submission and click on "SUBMIT" when it is complete. Your application is not transmitted to us until **you submit it**.

To complete your Assessment Questionnaire online, click the following link:

Online Questionnaire

## How to Apply

Follow all of the directions very carefully. Read the instructions to determine what to send with your application and which resume format to use. Sometimes this is not clear. While most agencies now use an online application system that takes you step-by-step through the application process, many still do not. The burden is squarely on the applicant to submit a complete, accurate application in a timely manner. If you are going to take the time to apply for a federal job, be sure you submit a complete application! See Step 8 for more details on applying for jobs.

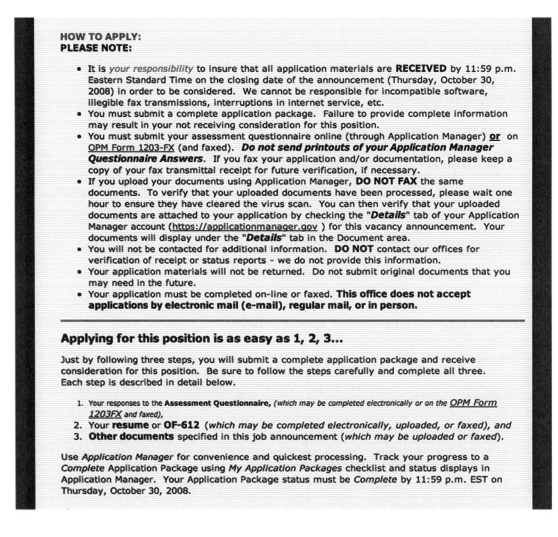

**HOW TO APPLY:**
**PLEASE NOTE:**

- It is *your responsibility* to insure that all application materials are **RECEIVED** by 11:59 p.m. Eastern Standard Time on the closing date of the announcement (Thursday, October 30, 2008) in order to be considered. We cannot be responsible for incompatible software, illegible fax transmissions, interruptions in internet service, etc.
- You must submit a complete application package. Failure to provide complete information may result in your not receiving consideration for this position.
- You must submit your assessment questionnaire online (through Application Manager) **or** on OPM Form 1203-FX (and faxed). ***Do not send printouts of your Application Manager Questionnaire Answers.*** If you fax your application and/or documentation, please keep a copy of your fax transmittal receipt for future verification, if necessary.
- If you upload your documents using Application Manager, **DO NOT FAX** the same documents. To verify that your uploaded documents have been processed, please wait one hour to ensure they have cleared the virus scan. You can then verify that your uploaded documents are attached to your application by checking the **"Details"** tab of your Application Manager account (https://applicationmanager.gov ) for this vacancy announcement. Your documents will display under the **"Details"** tab in the Document area.
- You will not be contacted for additional information. **DO NOT** contact our offices for verification of receipt or status reports - we do not provide this information.
- Your application materials will not be returned. Do not submit original documents that you may need in the future.
- Your application must be completed on-line or faxed. **This office does not accept applications by electronic mail (e-mail), regular mail, or in person.**

### Applying for this position is as easy as 1, 2, 3...

Just by following three steps, you will submit a complete application package and receive consideration for this position. Be sure to follow the steps carefully and complete all three. Each step is described in detail below.

1. Your responses to the **Assessment Questionnaire,** *(which may be completed electronically or on the* OPM Form 1203FX *and faxed),*
2. Your **resume** or **OF-612** *(which may be completed electronically, uploaded, or faxed), and*
3. **Other documents** specified in this job announcement *(which may be uploaded or faxed).*

Use *Application Manager* for convenience and quickest processing. Track your progress to a *Complete* Application Package using *My Application Packages* checklist and status displays in Application Manager. Your Application Package status must be *Complete* by 11:59 p.m. EST on Thursday, October 30, 2008.

## Quote

" I had heard of keywords but didn't take it seriously. I had applied to 400 jobs over the last 2 years trying to get a permanent position in Heidelberg. I was blasting the CPOL Army website, applying to every position, I could find that I thought I could qualify for. When I found out that keywords come from the announcement and I have to customize my resume with specialized experience and keywords, I slowed down with my announcement selection, edited my resumes and finally landed a permanent position with my keyword resumix. Keywords make or break an application for a DOD position. "

*Gary*
*Army Civilian*
*Heidlelberg, Germany*

# STEP FIVE
## Identify Your Keywords

Why keywords are important—three main reasons:

1. If you look around, you will find keywords in just about everything: advertisements, promotions, book covers, websites, and even on your cereal box. In today's "Quick Read," iPod, text messaging, and sound bite world, keywords represent who you are.

2. The vacancy announcement contains a technical description of the position you hope to be hired for. Core competencies contain descriptions of the "value-added" traits the government is looking for in their new hires. Both of these descriptions are filled with keywords. The HR specialists will be looking for these keywords in your resume to help them efficiently and effectively evaluate whether or not you are qualified for the position.

3. Some hiring systems—such as the U.S. Army, Navy, Marine Corps, and some DOD agencies—are using an automated keyword system to search their resume database for candidates whose resumes contain five to eight pre-identified keywords, and these resumes are the ones to get further review. The keywords used to search the database come from the vacancy announcement and the position description. It is critical to get the right keywords into your resume to be considered for positions in these hiring systems.

## Overview

## Troutman Method Lesson 3: Finding Keywords in the Vacancy Announcement

Once you have found a promising vacancy announcement, it is time to analyze the announcement for keywords.

The simple steps outlined here have been successfully used by thousands of federal job applicants to break the vacancy announcement code.

1.  Save the vacancy announcement as an html file.
2.  You will be reviewing these sections from the announcement for keywords:
    -   Duties
    -   Qualifications
    -   Specialized Experience
    -   Knowledge, Skills, and Abilities
    -   Questionnaires
3.  Copy and paste these sections from the announcement into a word processing program such as Word or WordPerfect.
4.  Enlarge the type to 14 to 16 points to make the print more readable.
5.  Separate each sentence by increasing the line spacing for the entire document.
6.  Delete useless words such as "the incumbent will" or "duties will encompass a variety of tasks including."
7.  Underline or highlight keywords and skills that are significant to the position, such as "identifying deficiencies in human performance" and "recommending changes for correction."

## Example: John Wallstone

In this step, we will show you how one of our real life case studies, John Wallstone, identified the keywords from his target announcement. John was a sous chef seeking a federal job as a program analyst at FEMA. Below, John highlighted the key skills in the announcement that a job applicant must have in order to demonstrate that they are qualified for this position. In Step 6 we will show you how John re-wrote his current private industry resume to apply for this position.

**Target Announcement: Program Analyst, GS 9/11/12**

Duties for this position may include all or part of the following:

**Conducts needs assessment surveys** using complex methods for assigned program(s). Collects, analyzes, and maintains data required to manage assigned programs (i.e. historical, statistical, etc). Researches and **investigates best practices** for applications to organization/agency programs or operations. Incumbent conducts studies of efficiency and productivity. Incumbent conducts studies and **analysis of operations, procedures and policies,** and **analyzes staff strengths and weaknesses**, to determine if more efficient or cost effective methods/practices can be achieved or if **customer satisfaction** can be improved.

**Identifies resources required** to support varied levels of program operations. **Compiles budget information** and **performs cost and price comparative analysis** to determine fiscal resources for implementing changes in pricing and practices.

Develops management and/or program evaluation plans, procedures, and methodology. Recommends changes or improvements to **achieve the highest efficiency** in programs and **ensures efficient business processes**. **Manages operations** by **directing staff** to implement recommended changes. **Creates a timeline of implementation** and monitors the development of and evaluates the execution of project(s) and program(s). Incumbent will **develop new pricing and cost accounting procedures** based on analysis of findings. **Oversees vendor contracts** to **ensure efficiency, security, and reduce waste**.

### John's Keyword List

Next, pull out the highlighted words and create a list of keywords. Eliminate duplication and unnecessary words (such as "a" and "the") and use active verbs to create the most succinct, but complete, list that you can. You can also reorder the list alphabetically or group them according to categories depending on which format is easier for you to use.

#### Announcement Keywords (listed alphabetically)

Achieve highest efficiency
Analyze operations, procedures, and policies
Analyze staff strengths/weaknesses
Best practices
Compile budget information
Conduct needs assessment surveys
Create project timeline
Customer satisfaction
Develop pricing and cost accounting procedures
Develop pricing and marketing information
Direct staff
Ensure efficiency, security, and reduce waste
Ensure efficient business processes
Manage operations
Oversee vendor contracts
Perform cost and price comparative analysis
Recommend and implement changes

#### Announcement Keywords (grouped by category)

Achieve highest efficiency
Ensure efficiency, security, and reduce waste
Ensure efficient business processes
Best practices
Customer satisfaction
-----------------------------
Conduct needs assessment surveys
Analyze operations, procedures, and policies
Analyze staff strengths/weaknesses
Perform cost and price comparative analysis
Compile budget information
-----------------------------
Recommend and implement changes
Develop pricing and cost accounting procedures
Develop pricing and marketing information
Direct staff
Create project timeline
Manage operations
Oversee vendor contracts

## More Samples of Keyword Lists

These samples contain actual keyword lists from true federal job seeking stories.
See the Before/After resume samples in this book and on the CD-ROM.

**Sample 1: Constance Jenkins**
**Target Position: Paralegal / Legal Assistant**

*Announcement: Qualifications Section*
Applicants must possess one year of specialized experience equivalent to the next lower
grade level in the Federal service. Specialized Experience is experience which demonstrates
**knowledge of law, rules, regulations, policies, and precedents**, and skill in **interpreting and
applying** them to varying situations. Skill in **analyzing case issues**, summarizing pertinent
data on the issues involved, **developing and/or evaluating evidence, resolving conflicting
data, clarifying factual and legal issues, and recommending appropriate actions**.

GS-7 level: Applicants must have one year of specialized experience equivalent to the GS-5
level. Specialized experience is defined as: performing **legal research** both electronic and
through the use of a law library; applying basic legal principles and concepts, in order to
monitor the performance of panel trustees in the administration of cases; **auditing, reviewing,
and determining the accuracy and completeness** of Trustee Final **Reports**, Accounts and
Final Distribution Reports to ensure proper administration of estates.

GS-9 level: Applicants must have one year of specialized experience equivalent to the GS-7
level. Specialized experience is defined as: reviewing chapter 7 bankruptcy petitions and
schedules for debtor compliance with legal requirements and technical accuracy; **drafting
motions, routine judicial pleadings, various types of memoranda, notices**, etc.; and
**developing draft motions** for default of judgment to reopen a case, defer payment of fees,
and complaints objecting to discharge.

*Announcement Keywords*
Administration of cases
Analyzing cases
Auditing reviewing Trustee Final Reports
Basic legal principles
Clarifying factual and legal issues
Developing evaluating evidence
Interpreting and applying
Laws, rules, regulations, policies, and precedents
Legal principles and concepts
Legal research
Monitor the performance of panel trustees
Recommending actions
Resolving conflicting data

### Sample 2: Benjamin Gaston
### Target Position: Administration / Program Management, GS-0343

*Announcement: Duties Section*

The selectee will serve as a **Management and Program Analyst** and will be responsible for performing a wide range of highly complex duties and for providing **technical guidance and advice**. Duties include but are not limited to the following: developing, administering, coordinating, and **analyzing accountability** and **management programs, identifying problems, recommending solutions, and monitoring progress**; preparing reports and **studies on accountability** and **management activities** for internal and external purposes; responding to **external accountability** and **management evaluations** or studies organized by the Office of Management and Budget (OMB), Office of Inspector General (OIG), Government Accountability Office (GAO), National Archives and Records Administration (NARA), and other oversight agencies

Specialized experience is experience that equipped the applicant with the knowledge, skills, and abilities to perform successfully the duties of the position, and that is typically in or related to **research and analytical studies**.

*Announcement Keywords*

Accountability
Analytical studies
Develop and administer programs
Identify problems
Internal and external purposes
Management activities
Management and Program Analyst
Monitor progress
Prepare reports and studies
Recommend solutions
Research
Technical guidance and advice

## Sample 3: Barbara  Kelly
## Target Position: Accounting And Budget Group, GS-0500

*Announcement: Duties and Specialized Experience sections*

The incumbent will primarily **examine** insured depository institutions. The incumbent will travel within the AOR to visit institutions to **identify** all **factors** and **causes, unsafe and unsound practices**, and **violations of laws and regulations**, which have affected or may affect the **condition and soundness of the institutions**. This position involves **analyzing and classifying loans, liabilities and capital; reviewing lending practices for compliance with regulations** such as **Check 21, Fair and Accurate Credit Transactions Act, and Privacy of Consumer Information**. Meets with **insured depository institution** officials and/or boards of directors to discuss **findings of examination, corrective programs,** and commitments for correction of deficiencies. Develops **recommendations for correction of weaknesses or deficiencies**. Evaluates and **prepares written reports**.

*Announcement Keywords*
Analyzing and classifying loans
Compliance with Check 21
Condition and soundness of institutions
Correction for weaknesses
Corrective programs
Deficiencies
Depository institution
Examine insured depository institutions
Fair and Accurate Credit Transactions Act
Findings of examination
Identify factors and causes
Liabilities and capital
Prepare written reports
Reviewing lending practices
Unsafe and unsound practices
Violations of law and regulations

## What Are Core Competencies?

Consider this scenario: what if you were as qualified as another job applicant from a technical standpoint? How would the hiring officials decide which one of you to select for the job?

Many jobseekers know to list their technical skills in their resume but neglect to list their "soft skills." These soft skills are your core competencies. To stand out above your competition, you must demonstrate your core competencies and show that you can offer something to the organization above and beyond your technical skills. You will, of course, have to be qualified with the right education and generalized or specialized experience, but these core competencies could make the difference in helping you become the best-qualified applicant among your peers.

Therefore, core competencies are another important source for keywords to include in your federal resume.

## How to Use Core Competencies in Your Resume

Core competencies for a particular job opening may be found in the vacancy announcement, agency mission statement, program description, career descriptions on the agency's website, and sometimes in the classification standard for the position (found at www.opm.gov). Review these documents and ask yourself whether the text gives you clues as to the type of person the organization is looking to hire. For example, is customer service or flexibility/adaptability more important for the particular position or organization?

In this step, review the documents listed in the previous paragraph and identify at least five to ten competencies that you can demonstrate in your past accomplishments. Add these competencies to your resume in the Work Experience descriptions for a stronger federal resume!

# Veterans Administration Example

This step features the Veterans Administration set of Core Competencies developed by a group of human resource and organizational development specialists in New York. This list will give you a good starting point for identifying the major core competencies that most agencies are looking for in job applicants.

## Personal Mastery

- ✪ Assumes responsibility for personal development and career goals
- ✪ Takes time to reflect on personal satisfaction and balance between work and personal life
- ✪ Manages self effectively, including time and physical/emotional health
- ✪ Takes initiative for continuous learning
- ✪ Actively seeks information on how one is perceived by others
- ✪ Improves behavior, skills, and knowledge as a result of evaluation and feedback
- ✪ Learns from setbacks or failures as well as from successful efforts

*Resume and KSA Writing Tip*

Personal mastery demonstrates your drive to improve your professional level. These skills are demonstrated by your professional memberships, conferences attended, professional training (college courses and developmental training), skills training, personal interests, non-profit activities, and volunteer participation. If you are a committee leader in your volunteer association, you will be demonstrating personal mastery. You can also demonstrate personal mastery by showing your career progression, accomplishments, committees, and tasks. Resumes that include only duties are not demonstrating personal mastery. You must write about accomplishments and other life components to show a well-developed person who is seeking improvement and personal mastery of skills.

### Interpersonal Effectiveness

✪ Builds and sustains positive relationships
✪ Handles conflicts and negotiations effectively
✪ Earns trust and holds respect
✪ Collaborates and works well with others
✪ Shows sensitivity and compassion for others
✪ Encourages shared decision-making
✪ Recognizes and uses ideas of others
✪ Communicates clearly, both orally and in writing
✪ Listens actively to others
✪ Honors commitments and promises

*Resume and KSA Writing Tip*
Interpersonal skills are a must in today's government and industry jobs. This core competency is one of the most important in government. If you can not get along with others, your career will not progress. These skills and language can be used in a cover letter, KSA statements, or in the descriptions of your work experience. For example, you can include this statement in your Profile Statement (as shown in the examples in the appendix): "Recognized for interpersonal skills with customers and co-workers."

### Customer Service

✪ Understands that customer service is essential to achieving the VA mission
✪ Models commitment to customer service
✪ Understands and meets the needs of internal customers
✪ Manages customer complaints and concerns effectively and promptly
✪ Designs work processes and systems that are responsive to customers
✪ Ensures that daily work and the VA's strategic direction are customer-centered
✪ Uses customer feedback data in planning and providing products and services
✪ Encourages and empowers subordinates to meet or exceed customer needs and expectations
✪ Identifies and rewards behaviors that enhance customer satisfaction

*Resume and KSA Writing Tip*
Most federal agency mission statements include a comment about improving customer service. This is a critical skill in government because of the important focus on services to the American public and the Defense agencies. Always highlight your customer services experiences and knowledge in your federal resume. You can include a customer services statement in your Profile Summary at the top of your resume—for example, "Recognize the importance of customer service. Received more than 25 letters from customers for outstanding service and efficient handling of priority situations."

## Flexibility/Adaptability

- ✪ Responds appropriately to new or changing situations
- ✪ Handles multiple inputs and tasks simultaneously
- ✪ Seeks and welcomes others' ideas
- ✪ Works well with all levels and types of people
- ✪ Accommodates new situations and realities
- ✪ Remains calm in high-pressure situations
- ✪ Makes the most of limited resources
- ✪ Demonstrates resilience in the face of setbacks
- ✪ Understands change management

*Resume and KSA Writing Tip*
Each agency changes its mission, services, customers, and procedures regularly. The government is striving to recruit people who are flexible, willing to change, and demonstrate the ability to manage multiple projects and priorities. You can write a "flexibility" statement in your work experience summary or your Profile statement—for example, "Demonstrated flexibility in handling multiple projects across agencies. Worked successfully under deadlines to achieve program objectives. Willing and able to work extra hours and take over additional tasks to complete project."

## Creative Thinking

- ✪ Appreciates new ideas and approaches
- ✪ Thinks and acts innovatively
- ✪ Looks beyond current reality and the "status quo"
- ✪ Demonstrates willingness to take risks
- ✪ Challenges assumptions
- ✪ Solves problems creatively
- ✪ Demonstrates resourcefulness
- ✪ Fosters creative thinking in others
- ✪ Allows and encourages employees to take risks
- ✪ Identifies opportunities for new projects and acts on them
- ✪ Rewards risk-taking and non-successes and values what was learned

*Resume and KSA Writing Tip*
Creative thinking is becoming more popular in government. We all know that the government is bureaucratic, and it is challenging to change any part of it—even for the better. But the government is recognizing that change is important and inevitable. The government is recruiting creative people who are willing to try new processes, take calculated risks, and even demonstrate entrepreneurial behavior. You can write a "creativity" statement like this: "Created a new process to receive information for website content. Recognized the need for consistent formatting and receiving of information to more efficiently update the intranet site. Designed an online form to assist content editors with organization of thought and information. Resulted in saving 50% of my time."

### Systems Thinking

✪ Understands the complexities of VA healthcare and how it is delivered
✪ Appreciates the consequences of specific actions on other parts of the system
✪ Thinks in context
✪ Knows how one's role relates to others in the organization
✪ Demonstrates awareness of the purpose, process, procedures, and outcomes of one's work
✪ Consistently focuses on the core business of the organization
✪ Asks questions that help others to think in a broader context
✪ Encourages and rewards collaboration

*Resume and KSA Writing Tip*

Systems thinking means being able to work through a complicated system and process. Achieving success in government requires that you work through a system, requiring you to understand how the system works and how to handle your projects appropriately within that framework. A resume or Profile Statement could be the following: "Improved the system of receiving and managing emails from more than 500 customers per week. Categorized the requests, organized the information, and wrote ready responses to consistent inquiries. Streamlined the response time from one day to one hour. "

### Technical Skills

✪ Displays knowledge and skills necessary to perform assigned duties
✪ Understands processes, procedures, standards, methods, and technologies related to assignment
✪ Demonstrates functional and technical literacy
✪ Participates in measuring outcomes of work
✪ Keeps current on new developments in field of expertise
✪ Effectively uses available technology (voice mail, automation, software, etc.)

*Resume and KSA Writing Tip*

You need at least some technical skills for most jobs in government. What technical skills you have, how you use them, and how you are improving on your technical skills are the important elements of this core competency. If you are a subject-matter expert, train co-workers, or serve as a user support professional, make sure to include this information, because it demonstrates that you are continually upgrading your technical skills.

## Organizational Stewardship

✪ Demonstrates commitment to people
✪ Empowers and trusts others
✪ Develops leadership skills and opportunities throughout organization
✪ Develops team-based improvement processes
✪ Promotes future-oriented system change
✪ Supports and encourages lifelong learning throughout the organization
✪ Manages physical, fiscal, and human resources to increase the value of products and services
✪ Builds links between individuals and groups in the organization
✪ Integrates organization into the community
✪ Provides developmental opportunities for employees
✪ Participates in and fully supports 360 degree assessment
✪ Accepts accountability for self, others, and the organization's development
✪ Works to accomplish the organizational business plan

*Resume and KSA Writing Tip*
Organizational stewardship is a core competency for managers, supervisors, and team leaders. It entails knowing, following, and introducing the agency's mission and strategic plan, as well as communicating these goals to all employees. Managers and executives should integrate this element into their application. Here is a good way of saying you have organizational stewardship: "Dedicated, determined, and driven to achieve agency mission objectives."

"***Change Catalyst -- Initiating or Managing Change***
  People with this competence:
  Recognize the need for change and remove barriers
  Challenge the status quo to acknowledge the need for change
  Champion the change and enlist others in its pursuit
  Model the change expected of others"
  --Daniel Goleman, *Working with Emotional Intelligence*, 1998.

## Examples of Core Competencies

Here are real life examples of core competencies from the resumes of our case study examples.

**Administrative Assistant:** Able to manage simultaneous projects and deadlines, and set priorities. Works well in a fast-paced setting. Demonstrate values that require accuracy and quality in work products. (Personal Mastery)

**Attorney:** Skilled in expressing opinions logically and interviewing subjects and witnesses to elicit sensitive information. Able to convey program information effectively. (Interpersonal Effectiveness)

**Warehouse Manager:** Offer exceptional customer service and assist customers, storage depots, and other organizational representatives. (Customer Service)

**Logistics Manager:** Proven track record for meeting targets, developing and implementing effective policies, managing diverse programs, and providing excellent service to internal and external customers. Demonstrated success forging collaborations with all constituencies. Highly developed organizational and supervisory abilities coupled with superb communication skills support an ability to achieve quantifiable program results. Polished, professional presentation. (Organizational Stewardship)

**Public Health Specialist:** Extensive experience developing and coordinating complex, cross-cutting health communication projects which are national in scope and require coordination across broad constituencies. (Flexibility/Adaptability)

**Program Analyst:** Build rapport with internal staff and external departments to improve operations and flow of information. Respond to written and verbal inquiries from the public and the media, adhering to strict communication standards. Represent First Family at charity and press events. (Interpersonal Effectiveness)

**Corps of Engineers Program Manager:** Engage in proactive oral communications with a wide variety of internal and external stakeholders including contractors, colleagues, and federal and state regulatory agencies including the Environmental Protection Agency, to brief them on activities and project progress. Negotiate with stakeholders on matters related to environmental technology. Prepare and present technical training and briefings to corporate executives on effective environmental remediation and restoration. (Interpersonal Effectiveness)

**Vocational Rehabilitation Specialist:** Developed and implemented best organizational and time management practices to improve the delivery of services and staff efficiencies, including utilizing a tickler system (activity due) to address timelines and projects due; and prioritize and implement service importance according to client's needs. Implemented a new organizational/ filing system that improved management of paper documents. (Creative Thinking)

## Example: John Wallstone

Earlier in this chapter, we identified keywords from the announcement that John Wallstone applied to. As you may recall, John applied for a program analyst position at FEMA. Because John is seeking to make an obvious career change, he will need to demonstrate that he has transferable skills to the new position. Often for career change situations, it is the "soft skills" or the core competencies that are the transferable skills.

Studying the announcement for core competency language, we deduce that John should also include some keywords in his federal resume around these core competencies:

✪ **Information Management:** This is actually a technical skill that is implied in the vacancy announcement but not explicitly stated. The announcement contains many information-related duties, such conducting surveys, analysis, budget information, and program applications, and a person who could fulfill these duties must have some background or skill in information management.

✪ **Customer Service:** FEMA's mission is "to reduce the loss of life and property and protect the Nation from all hazards, including natural disasters, acts of terrorism, and other man-made disasters, by leading and supporting the Nation in a risk-based, comprehensive emergency management system of preparedness, protection, response, recovery, and mitigation." According to this mission, FEMA provides a service to our country, so for FEMA and other agencies providing a service to the American public, customer service is often an important core competency to demonstrate.

✪ **Communications:** The new hire will be responsible for directing staff to implement changes, and this level of front line management will always require communication skills or interpersonal effectiveness.

## Senior Executive Service Executive Core Qualifications

These SES ECQs are mandatory for Senior Executive Service positions. Candidates for SES positions will be writing two pages of narratives for each of the five ECQs. Each ECQ will include two or three of your top accomplishments that demonstrates the ECQ and the definitions. These ECQs are very important for positions that are GS-9 and above. They are not mandatory to be written, but could prove to support your qualifications and experience.

### Executive Core Qualifications (ECQs)

If you would like to apply for a Senior Executive Service position in government, you will have to write the five ECQs as part of your application. The best way to begin writing the ECQs is to write your Top Ten List of Accomplishments.

The Top Ten List of Executive Accomplishments can then be mapped into the five ECQs described here. You can find more details and examples on how to write ECQs on OPM's website.

| Leading Change | Leading People | Results Driven | Business Acumen | Building Coalitions |
|---|---|---|---|---|
| Definitions | | | | |
| This core qualification involves the ability to bring about strategic change, both within and outside the organization, to meet organizational goals. Inherent to this ECQ is the ability to establish an organizational vision and to implement it in a continuously changing environment. | This core qualification involves the ability to lead people toward meeting the organization's vision, mission, and goals. Inherent to this ECQ is the ability to provide an inclusive workplace that fosters the development of others, facilitates cooperation and teamwork, and supports constructive resolution of conflicts. | This core qualification involves the ability to meet organizational goals and customer expectations. Inherent to this ECQ is the ability to make decisions that produce high-quality results by applying technical knowledge, analyzing problems, and calculating risks. | This core qualification involves the ability to manage human, financial, and information resources strategically. | This core qualification involves the ability to build coalitions internally and with other federal agencies, state and local governments, nonprofit and private sector organizations, foreign governments, or international organizations to achieve common goals. |
| Leadership Competencies | | | | |
| Creativity and Innovation External Awareness Flexibility Resilience Strategic Thinking Vision | Conflict Management Leveraging Diversity Developing Others Team Building | Accountability Customer Service Decisiveness Entrepreneurship Problem Solving Technical Credibility | Financial Management Human Capital Management Technology Management | Partnering Political Savvy Influencing/ Negotiating |

## Quote

" Kathryn's Outline Format is so easy to follow, understand and write. I rewrote my own block style resume in the small paragraphs and added accomplishments. The Troutman Method works and helped me to structure the duties section of my resume. I had been struggling with advising jobseekers of an easy way to write the all-important experience descriptions to match a federal job announcement. Now I have the format to advise which is easy to update for additional announcements as well. As a Workforce Job Counselor and Center Director, I will advise my clients and staff in this format for all federal positions." "

*Sandy Smith*
*BRAC Center Director*
*Crystal City, VA*

## Merit System Principles

The *Merit System Principles Section 2301* states that "Recruitment should be from qualified individuals from appropriate sources in an endeavor to achieve a work force from all segments of society, and selection and advancement should be determined solely on the basis of relative ability, knowledge, and skills, after fair and open competition which assures that all receive equal opportunity."

This is the reason why the federal application process is so complex.

This is the most important chapter in the book—and in your federal job campaign. When writing a "federal style" resume, the two most important points to remember are these: a federal resume is about two times longer than a private industry resume, and federal resume language is not the same as private industry resume language.

In this step, you will learn about two successful resume formats:
1. USAJOBS federal resume format, which can also be used for other online resume builders such as Resumix and Avue Central.
2. The paper federal resume.

You will also learn the secret to writing a successful federal resume: the outline format with headlines.

## Overview
Federal vs. Private Industry Resume
Checklist: Sources of Information for Your Resume
Helpful Tools for Writing Your Federal or Electronic Resume
Troutman Method Lesson 4: Create Your Federal Resume in the
    Outline Format
Building Your Outline for the Work Experience Section
Important Federal Resume Writing Facts & Resume Writing Tips
Creating Your Basic Resume
Electronic vs. Paper Resume
Sample USAJOBS Federal Resume in Outline Format With Headlines
Sample Paper Federal Resume

## Federal vs. Private Industry Resume

Federal resumes are different from private industry resumes for a number of reasons. Here is a quick list of differences to keep in mind when you are converting your private industry resume into a federal resume.

### Private Industry

Focused on the mission of the business
Profit motivated
Customer service for customers who buy products
Provides a product or service
Markets business to select customer base
One or two pages in length
No social security number, supervisors, or salaries given
Fewer details in work descriptions
Creative, graphic, functional formats are okay
Accomplishments are great
Keywords are desirable
Emphasis on ten years of experience
More succinct writing style
Honors, awards, and recognitions are important

### Federal Resume

Focused on the mission of the agency, programs, and services
Grant and budget motivated
Customer service for millions of people, as well as internal customers
Provides a program or service
Implements Congressional legislation and laws
Markets to and informs the American public (similar to private industry)
Three to five pages is acceptable
Include SSN, supervisors' names, and salaries
More details for work descriptions so that keywords demonstrate your qualifications for a job
Chronological, traditional format
Accomplishments are great
Keywords are needed
Emphasis on ten years of experience
Concise, yet informative content
Honors, awards, and recognitions are more important

## Checklist: Sources of Information for Your Resume

Before you sit down to write your resume, it is very helpful to first collect all of the background information you will need for your writing into one place. Here is a list of items that you will need:

- ❂ Target Vacancy Announcements
- ❂ Other Vacancy Announcements for similar jobs
- ❂ Agency website, including program descriptions and mission language
- ❂ Department of Labor Occupational Listings
- ❂ Classification Standards of desired positions (available at www.opm.gov)
- ❂ Your previous resume
- ❂ Position Descriptions
- ❂ Evaluations
- ❂ Private industry job websites

## Helpful Tools for Writing Your Federal or Electronic Resume

The Resume Place Federal Resume Builder can be found on the CD-ROM of this book or at www.resume-place.com.

Use one of the sample resumes from the CD-ROM as a template to help you build your first federal resume.

## Troutman Method Lesson 4:
## Create Your Federal Resume in the Outline Format

In this step, we will first begin with the hardest part, the heart of your resume: writing your work experience section. Once you have this lesson down, the rest of the step will be much easier. We will teach you how to write the work experience portion of your resume in the outline format.

The outline format for your federal resume was first developed by Kathryn Troutman in her 2000 edition of a cutting-edge resume-writing book—*The Electronic Federal Resume Guidebook*—the first book ever written on Resumix writing for Department of Defense civilians. Since then, outline format has become more popular than ever.

Additionally, Ms. Troutman is a popular federal resume and KSA instructor, teaching the outline format to agency employees across the country. A human resources specialist from the Environmental Protection Agency said, "I wish all resumes looked like this; it is so easy to read and see the skills we need to determine qualifications." A civilian personnel human resources specialist at Walter Reed Army Medical Hospital said of this format, "I love the cause and effect style of writing, it is so easy to read and understand what a person really DOES in their job."

### Features and benefits of the Outline Format:
✪ Headings include **keywords** from the vacancy announcement
✪ Headings are in ALL CAPS for easy reading
✪ Each paragraph in the Work Experience blocks represents a skill set
✪ Paragraphs are easy to read for supervisors and human resources specialists
✪ Paragraph length should be eight to ten lines at most
✪ Separate Duties from Accomplishments
✪ The format is easy to read and looks great in resume builders
✪ Updates are easy—just edit and change the HEADLINES with new keywords
✪ Oversee vendor contracts

# Building Your Outline for the Work Experience Section

We are going to continue with John Wallstone's example, which we began in Step 5. As you may recall, John was a sous chef seeking a federal job as a program analyst.

This case study is a superb example of how it is possible to translate one career to another by analyzing and matching the keywords. Check out the keyword crosswalk from kitchen operations to program analyst. The announcement keywords will become critical language in the next version of his resume, and the description of his responsibilities will focus on these transferable skills rather than the specific menus, recipes, and grocery items mentioned in the previous resume.

## Create your keyword lists

In order to create the outline for your federal resume, you need to start with two key pieces:
Keywords from your previous resume (BEFORE resume keywords)
Keywords from the target vacancy announcement (announcement keywords)

On pages 87-88, we showed you how John created his list of announcement keywords. Also, on page 99 we explained a few core competencies that should be demonstrated in John's resume as well, and these are included in the announcement keyword list. Below on the left is a list of BEFORE resume keywords that we have created from John's private industry resume, which can be found on pages 256-257. Compare these two lists of keywords below.

| Before Resume Keywords | Announcement Keywords |
| --- | --- |
| Catered events | Achieve highest efficiency |
| Cost control measures | Ensure efficiency, security, and reduce waste |
| Customer service agent | Ensure efficient business processes |
| Designed and directed production | Best practices |
| Executive Dining room | Customer satisfaction |
| Food operations | Conduct needs assessment surveys |
| Implement sanitation programs | Analyze operations, procedures, and policies |
| Just in time inventory systems | Analyze staff strengths/weaknesses |
| Lead production teams | Perform cost and price comparative analysis |
| Maintained repeat customer clients | Compile budget information |
| Menu planning | Recommend and implement changes |
| New catering sales | Develop pricing and cost accounting procedures |
| Personal needs of first family | Develop pricing and marketing information |
| Petty cash funds | Direct staff |
| Promote safe food handling | Create project timeline |
| Purchasing, quality, and cost recommendations | Manage operations |
| Quality assurance | Oversee vendor contracts |
| Supervised staff | Information management |
| Updated computer technology | Customer service |
| Vending operations | Communication |

### Keyword Match

Next, we will perform a cross walk, or match, between the two keyword lists in an effort to come up with five – ten major groupings of keyword from both lists. One way to do this is shown below.

*Manage operations*
- Food operations
- Executive Dining Room
- Menu planning
- Achieve highest efficiency
- Best practices
- Analyze operations, procedures, and policies

*Manage projects*
- Catered events
- Conduct needs assessment surveys
- Create project timeline
- Analyze staff strengths/weaknesses

*Manage supply*
- Oversee vendor contracts
- Vending operations
- Just in time inventory systems
- Perform cost and price comparative analysis

*Budget*
- Develop pricing and cost accounting procedures
- Compile budget information
- Petty cash funds
- Perform cost and price comparative analysis
- Develop pricing and marketing information

*Manage staff*
- Direct staff
- Communication
- Lead production teams

## Edit the Categories Into Outline Headers

Looking at John's work experience, it became clear that John spent most of his time managing people, events, budgets, supply, etc. John's experience in managing is exactly what the hiring officials are looking for in this announcement. So in the end, we highlighted his management skills in the outline headings that we came up with. We also included the core competencies in the final list of outline headings, because, as we mentioned in Step 5, these core competencies include many of the transferable skills for career change resumes.

Again, aim to create five – ten headings for the outline of your federal resume.

Here are the final outline headings we identified for John:

| Before Resume Keywords | Announcement Keywords | Outline Headings |
|---|---|---|
| Catered events | Achieve highest efficiency | Operations Management |
| Cost control measures | Ensure efficiency, security, and reduce waste | Project Management |
| Customer service agent | Ensure efficient business processes | Supply Management |
| Designed and directed production | Best practices | Budget / Funds Management |
| Executive Dining room | Customer satisfaction | Logistics Management |
| Food operations | Conduct needs assessment surveys | Personnel Management |
| Implement sanitation programs | Analyze operations, procedures, and policies | Customer Service |
| Just in time inventory systems | Analyze staff strengths/weaknesses | Communications |
| Lead production teams | Perform cost and price comparative analysis | Information Management |
| Maintained repeat customer clients | Compile budget information | |
| Menu planning | Recommend and implement changes | |
| New catering sales | Develop pricing and cost accounting procedures | |
| Personal needs of first family | Develop pricing and marketing information | |
| Petty cash funds | Direct staff | |
| Promote safe food handling | Create project timeline | |
| Purchasing, quality, and cost recommendations | Manage operations | |
| Quality assurance | Oversee vendor contracts | |
| Supervised staff | Information management | |
| Updated computer technology | Customer service | |
| Vending operations | Communication | |

## Fill in the Outline

Now that you have your outline, fill in the outline with descriptions of each skill set under the outline. You can find resume description content in your current resume, the vacancy announcement, other similar vacancy announcements, or the Classification Standards from the Office of Personnel Management web site: www.opm.gov.

Below is a portion of the work experience section based on the outline headings for John Wallstone. You will be able to see many of the keywords in his resume.

Serve as second in command of kitchen staff for First Family of Maryland. Manage kitchen operations and direct staff to ensure efficient business processes and customer satisfaction.

- **Operations Management**: Direct daily operations of full-service kitchen, planning, coordinating, and preparing formal and informal meals and events for up to 3,000 people, both planned in advance and last minute, with range of guests from international dignitaries to constituents. Continually analyze operations, procedures, and policies to achieve highest efficiency and best practices. Recommend and implement range of process improvement initiatives. Implement, apply, and interpret policies, regulations, and directives. Work with senior management to establish goals and objectives.

- **Project Management**: Conduct needs assessment surveys and determine needs based on event specifications and labor demands. Plan event with consideration to protocol, preferences, caliber of event, attendees, and lead time. Create project timeline and assign, monitor, and adjust tasks according to staff strengths/weaknesses to fulfill deadline completion. Review progress and make production and priority adjustments as needed. Manage multiple task lists to complete projects with adjacent deadlines. Resolve problems and issues, including crisis situations. Conduct post-event assessment to identify successes and areas for improvement.

- **Supply Management**: Take inventory and plan orders to regulate flow of product and ensure stock levels meet event and daily needs. Research best products and vendors to comply with state purchasing regulations; establish delivery protocols and resolve delivery problems. Rotate stock, monitor usage and storage to ensure efficiency, sanitation, and security, and reduce waste. Negotiate, administer, and oversee vendor and service contracts. Maintain documentation, verify invoices, and assure prompt payment.

- **Budgeting / Funds Management**: Develop pricing and cost accounting procedures. Analyze and forecast product and labor costs estimates. Apply due diligence to projects to ensure feasibility and cost effectiveness, as well as conduct after-action reviews. Compile budget information and apply generally accepted accounting procedures and state regulations to track expenditures, including petty cash. Perform cost and price and comparative analyses. Develop and implement pricing and marketing information for clients. Identify and resolve budget issues and develop cost-cutting solutions to ensure budget adherence. Brief management and recommend cost control improvements and budget adjustments.

- **Logistics Management**: Integrate logistics of event planning, including manpower and personnel, supply, training, storage, and facilities. Research and plan manpower, equipment, and fiscal resources.

- **Personnel Management**: Direct kitchen and wait staff, promoting teamwork and communication. Provide continual training and coaching to improve employee performance, job knowledge, and career advancement; also, serve as point of contact for benefit information. Write position descriptions and assist in hiring process. Resolve employee issues and provide employee input and feedback to management. Assist in background checks for auxiliary employees and vendors. Train others in security and privacy protection.

- **Customer Service**: Serve as personal and administrative assistant to First Family. Anticipate and respond to needs, maintaining flexible and service-oriented attitude. Purchase personal and business related goods, including supplies, as extension of house staff. Assist in managing schedule and making travel arrangements and appointment reservations, as needed. Protect privacy of First Family and work with Maryland State Police to ensure security precautions are followed at all times.

- **Communications**: Build rapport with internal staff and external departments to improve operations and flow of information. Respond to written and verbal inquiries from the public and the media, adhering to strict communication standards. Represent First Family at charity and press events.

- **Information Management**: Develop and utilize spreadsheets, databases, and professional documents to improve operational readiness, manage projects, and research information. Maintain records on events, including menus, demographics, and after-action reports. Assist in establishing database for mailing list.

## Remember Your Accomplishments

As a final step, John listed his main accomplishments at this position. It is a good idea to separate the duties you performed from the major accomplishments you achieved in order to highlight those accomplishments.

*Key Accomplishments:*
- Plan, coordinate, and execute breakfast, lunch, dinner for First Family and other events, including seated dinners and open houses for up to 4,000, with usually 3-5 events per week, as many as 2 per day.
- Instituted process changes to increase efficiency and change mind-set from reactive to proactive. Created plan to work one meal ahead, allowing time to respond to last minute requests, changes, and events.
- Received letter of appreciation from the White House for organizing luncheon attended by President Bill Clinton with less than 24-hour notice.
- Implemented industrial production system, automated systems, and information management for production, scheduling, and cost control.
- Actively built team mindset and morale, and implemented employee incentive program, stressing interdepartmental cooperation and employees' role in organizational success. Resulted in improved attendance and performance.

## Important Federal Resume Writing Facts

Now that you have written the most difficult portion of your federal resume, it is time to put it all together and add the surrounding sections to make your resume complete. First, let us start with some important resume writing facts and tips.

- ✪ Federal resumes must include compliance details for each job for the last ten years. As noted earlier in this chapter, compliance details include supervisor's name and telephone number; street address, including ZIP code; hours per week; and ending salary.

- ✪ Reverse chronology: Begin with your most recent position and work backward, unless you need to highlight a position that is relevant and not the most recent.

- ✪ Last ten years: Develop an outline of your positions with compliance details to plan the number of job-related positions held within the last ten years.

- ✪ Prior to ten years: If the positions are relevant, include the title of your job, organization, city, state, and dates. A short one-sentence description can be included. Prior to ten years, your supervisor's name, telephone number, specific address, ZIP codes, and salaries may not be relevant, correct, or needed any longer.

- ✪ Students: Include relevant positions only.

- ✪ Retired Military: Combine early positions/assignments.

- ✪ Write your organization's name one time. Do not repeat the name(s) of your organization(s) if you have multiple jobs in the same place.

- ✪ Unpaid volunteer experience is equal to paid work experience for federal job qualifications. You can write about volunteer and community service activities as though it is a job if it will help you qualify for a position. If you are using unpaid work to qualify, always include the number of hours per week in your description. If you have paid employment that qualifies you for the job, then simply summarize your volunteer experience under Community Service.

- ✪ Missing years of experience? Just skip those years and write great descriptions about the positions you have held. You do not need to describe reasons for a gap in your dates. However, be prepared to discuss it in an interview. Many people miss years of employment due to education, travel, and family responsibilities. The new federal resume focuses on experience that is relevant, and not on every job you held or every period in your life.

- ✪ Returning to government after leaving? Feature your GOVERNMENT EXPERIENCE first, then list your BUSINESS EXPERIENCE or OTHER EXPERIENCE second. Even if it is out of the reverse chronology, the personnel specialists will want to see your government positions first.

- ✪ Any military assignments? List the most recent ones first. Include many details on the last ten years. Anything longer than ten years, summarize and edit the text to include only the relevant experience.

## Resume Writing Tips

- ✪ Use plain language. Write professionally and concisely.

- ✪ Eliminate acronyms whenever possible. When you must use them, spell them out the first time used and separate with parentheses, commas, or dashes.

- ✪ Since your space is limited, drop words that do not add value such as "responsible for," "very" and "duties include." Also, see how many times you can delete "the" without changing the meaning.

- ✪ Avoid using the same descriptor twice in the same paragraph, such as "manage," "develop," or "coordinate" and minimize repeating words. Use a thesaurus to maximize descriptors that will bring out skills.

- ✪ Start each sentence with an action verb, and not "I." Use the personal pronoun "I" two times per page, to remind the reader that it is YOUR resume.

- ✪ Active voice is more powerful than passive voice.

- ✪ Use present tense for present work experience, past tense for previous work experience or for projects in the present work experience that have ended. Do not add "s" to your verbs, i.e. plans, manages, and leads, as this is writing in the third person. Write in the first person, without the use of "I."

- ✪ Use ALL CAPS for official position titles. Also, this holds true for titles of roles in jobs, or unofficial, working job titles, such as PROJECT MANAGER, SENIOR STAFF ADVISOR, RECEPTIONIST, when you are describing these in your work experience summary.

- ✪ All caps can be used to identify major functional areas of work. Keep your paragraph length to eight to ten lines.

- ✪ Use more nouns. Nouns are searchable terms in most databases. If you can use "editor" rather than "responsible for compiling documents and preparing a publication," you will be more successful.

- ✪ Include the proper names and generic descriptions of products, software, and equipment. It is difficult to know which words will be in a database. Write both to be sure.

KSAs in the resume? You will read some vacancy announcements that say you should include the Knowledge, Skills, and Abilities in the resume. Use the OUTLINE FORMAT to cover your KSAs, using the keywords from the KSAs in the Outline headlines to bring attention to your KSAs.

## Creating Your Basic Resume

You will need to create both an electronic and paper resume if you are applying for federal jobs. The content in each of these is the same, though the electronic version may be shorter in length than the paper version. To get started, we recommend that you first create a "basic resume" that you will tailor to develop your paper and electronic resumes for different vacancy announcements.

Complete these resume sections in the following order:

1. Format your name and address
2. Write your work experience
   - Create your Outline Format with Headlines
   - Fill in your duties, responsibilities, and projects
   - Highlight skills that support the announcement
   - Include recognition
3. Add your education and training
4. Include Additional Information
5. Write a profile or summary of skills statement in the Additional Information field

More information about each section is provided below.

### Job Information and Personal Data

If you are writing a USAJOBS federal resume, your job information and personal data will be added into your Profile Statement. If you are writing a paper federal resume, put your personal compliance information for federal positions at the top of your resume.

### Federal Job "Compliance" Information

Much of your compliance information is included in the USAJOBS profile set-up. Here are the typical personal compliance details that civil service human resources offices require:

- ✪ Full name, mailing address (with ZIP Code), and day and evening phone numbers (with area code)
- ✪ Social Security Number
- ✪ Country of citizenship
- ✪ Veterans' preference
- ✪ Reinstatement eligibility (If you have been laid off from a federal job, there could be special rules for reinstatement; you will need proof of your status.)
- ✪ Geographic preferences
- ✪ If you will accept positions that are Term, Temp, Part-time, or Full-time
- ✪ Announcement number, title, and grade(s) of the job for which you are applying
- ✪ Highest civilian grade held, job series, and dates

Sample compliance information from paper federal resume:

---

**JOHN WALLSTONE**
123 Dewberry Way • Baltimore, MD 21243
Residence: 410-123-4567 • Office: 202-123-4567
Email: jwallstonecraft@gmail.com

SSN: 123-45-6789                                           Veteran's Preference: N/A
Citizenship: U.S.                           Geographic Preference: Denver, Colorado

---

## Work Experience

We have discussed this section at length earlier in this step. Copy and paste your work into the work experience section.

## Include Recognitions in Job Descriptions

Most federal announcements give instructions that you cannot attach letters of commendation to the application. Therefore, the best way to include a quote from an evaluation or letter is to include a quote from the commendation in the Work Experience section of your resume. Collect any emails or complimentary letters you have received from supervisors, customers, or other important individuals that say you are an outstanding employee or supervisor. The following letters are possible sources to review for good quotes:

- ✪ Outstanding team reviews (as a member or leader of a team)
- ✪ Outstanding performance ratings
- ✪ Customer satisfaction awards or letters
- ✪ Write-ups in company newsletters
- ✪ Employee of the month recognitions
- ✪ Community or volunteer service recognitions
- ✪ Newspaper quotes

Honors from outside organizations, recognition for community service, or achievements from your academic or civic background can also reinforce recognition of your skills.

## Quote Recognitions and Awards

The following are a few examples of how to use the quoted material in your resume:
- ✪ Received Letter of Commendation from the Chief of Naval Material, 20xx.
- ✪ For planning, acquiring, and implementing a CAD/CAM system at 54 Navy sites, received a "Special Act Award" for my accomplishments under this project.

## Include Professional Training Course Lists

For the last five to ten years, list the titles of the relevant courses and year. Include recent computer and technical courses.

*Sample 1*

**Continuing Education and Training**
[date] How to Prepare a Quality IT Offer 0.1 Credits
[date] GSA Vendor Payment Update 0.1 Credits
[date] AM e-Authentication 0.1 Credits
[date] Secure Wireless Technology 0.1 Credits
[date] Proper Use of Non-DoD Contracts 1.0 Credit
[date] GWAC Direct Order Direct Bill Authority 0.1 Credits
[date] Marketing Strategies and Techniques for Small Business 0 Credits
[date] The 1102 Contract Specialist as a Business Manager 0.1 Credits

*Sample 2*

SALES AND MARKETING PROFESSIONAL DEVELOPMENT COURSES

Law of Agency, Real Estate College, Arlington, TX, 30 credit hours, [mo/year]
MS Software Application Training, Work In Texas, Dallas, TX, 10 credit hours, [mo/year]
Acquisition/Procurement Planning I Certification, Management concepts, Washington, DC, 80 credit hours, [mo/year]

## Formatting Your Education

*Sample*

EDUCATION

B.S., Management & Marketing / Finance Minor, 12/19xx, Texas Tech University
GPA: 2.9 out of 4.0; 120 +Semester Hours

RELEVANT COURSEWORK: Economics, Accounting, Cost Accounting, Business Policy & Development, Marketing, Finance, Business Finance, Business Law, International Business.

COMPUTER/TECHNICAL SKILLS: DMSi, Microsoft Office (Word, Excel, PowerPoint, Access). Working knowledge of Access, Lotus, WordPerfect.

## Additional Information / Other Qualifications and Skills

The "Additional Information" field in USAJOBS is a great place to list your summary of skills, areas of expertise, and positions that were part-time or volunteer. You can list travel experiences and special interests.

*Additional Information Ideas*
Associations
Community Service
Computer Skills
Conferences Attended
Consultancies
Honors & Awards
International Travel
Languages
Memberships/Office Activities
Part-time Jobs
Presentations
Publications
Special Interests
Teaching Positions
Volunteer Services

*Sample*

PROFESSIONAL DEGREES, DESIGNATIONS & LICENSES
- Real Estate Broker
- B100 Unlimited General Contractor's license state of Utah
- Certified Insurance Consultant
- Investment Advisor under the 1940 Act
- NASD Principal's License, DPP/BD, Series 6, 22, 39, 63

PERSONAL ACCOMPLISHMENTS
- Private Pilot – Instrument rated
- Commercial Pilot – Hot Air Balloons
- Climbed Kilimanjaro, Huascuran, Rainier
- Only American crewmember on the Soviet team for the Whitbread Round the World race, Ft. Lauderdale to Southampton, England leg, aboard "Fazisi"
- Vice President, Kyrgyz National Biathlon Federation

AVOCATIONS
- Woodworking, Rowing, Skiing, Reading

**Writing a Profile Statement**

Summarize your entire career in one paragraph -- your Profile Statement!

Create a new resume focus for every announcement by changing only about 10–15 lines! Very often in job interviews, an employer will open by saying, "Tell me about yourself." The "Profile" paragraph on page one of your resume provides an opportunity to develop a precise and targeted response with the keywords and skills from the "duties" section of the announcement. For career change resumes, the profile or summary of skills is critical for featuring the skills and most relevant experience for the next career.

The following examples show two formats for writing the introductory paragraph.

*Sample 1*

**PROFESSIONAL PROFILE:**

- BUSINESS DEVELOPMENT: Experienced business developer with outstanding strategic, technical, and organizational leadership skills. Comfortable advising others who are interested in tackling new business start-up challenges. Known for the ability to collaborate with individuals and teams to develop business strategies and manage specific components of strategies to meet measurable performance benchmarks. Recognized as an expert in private sector development, including host-country economic development programs and policies, having served as a Country Director (GS-15) in the Peace Corps, in Kyrgyzstan.

- BUSINESS ACUMEN: Excellent business instincts, including financial and human resource allocation, and leveraging technological resources. Demonstrated ability to provide exceptional customer services by assessing customer needs, meeting quality standards, and evaluating customer satisfaction.

- LEADER OF CHANGE: Accomplished at leading change, starting new companies, and taking them from conceptualization through to completion, also reorganizing existing companies. Skilled at evaluating, negotiating, planning, budgeting, and administering projects and proposals with an emphasis on dollar productive activities. Ability to convince others of the value of a specific course of action

- GOVERNMENT ISSUES: Intensely curious about how things work in politics, the world of investing, community affairs, business, and governmental issues. Always willing to seek the advice of experts in various fields before coming to a conclusion or final decision.

*Sample 2*

**PROFILE**

Information Technology Director with an outstanding record of success delivering enterprise applications and architectures for federal and commercial organizations. Extensive experience developing short and long term Information Technology (IT) strategies, practices, policies, and metrics for highly technical and agile organizations in the public and private sectors. Experienced in all phases of the Software Development Life Cycle (SDLC) from requirements analysis through user acceptance and operational support. Combine results-oriented project management skills with expert technical knowledge of network and IT service offerings to deliver best value solutions for the customer. A decisive and participatory leader with keen business acumen, motivating leadership skills, and extensive knowledge of emerging trends in the information age.

## Highlighting One Year Specialized Experience

Once you have a draft of your Outline resume, go back to your target vacancy announcement and read the Qualifications section again. Look at the One Year Specialized Experience instruction and review their examples. Make sure that your resume hits this specialized experience with examples. We have talked about keywords in this book many times. Make sure that the keywords are in the resume in either the HEADLINES or the text. The goal of the organization and presentation in your resume is to highlight the skills that support your federal job objective. You want to make it easy for the human resources staff to find the information needed to ensure you are qualified for the job. Next, you want your resume to STAND OUT so that the hiring official will want to interview you.

When reviewing applications, the HR specialist will be looking for the relevant experience for their position. So, in your work experience, the position(s) that are most relevant to your target position should be the most in-depth and carefully written. Outstanding resumes keep the reader's attention longer, compelling the reader to move the resume to the "read again later" pile, then with further reading, moved to the "Best Qualified" list. The selecting official will go through the same process as well.

### *Modify the organization for various builders and applications as needed*

Your basic resume can be used for various resume builders. You will have to count characters and follow the directions, but your resume should work for all builders.

### *Review the critical job elements*

Review the duties in the vacancy announcement against your resume AGAIN. Make sure the keywords in the Duties section are visible, that the One Year Specialized Experience is clearly presented, that examples they are seeking are included, and that you have utilized the space in the builder correctly.

### *Read your resume aloud and edit profusely!*

Now that you have drafted your basic federal resume, you will need to edit and decide what is relevant and most important for the position. Most public service resumes are two to five pages in length. However, length is not the most important element of the resume – content is.

### Electronic vs. Paper Resume

If you compare the paper federal resume to the electronic resume, you will see that the content is similar, but the format is different. The electronic resume must be more succinct and ready to copy and paste into an email textbox or resume builder. Since every agency has its own way of recruiting and its own favorite application format, you will have to be prepared to apply for federal jobs with two types of resumes—the USAJOBS (or other online) resume and a paper resume.

At the end of this step, you will see an example of a paper federal resume and the matching electronic federal resume.

Once your electronic and federal resumes are ready, Step 8 will help you understand the various applications requirements for government and learn how to apply for federal jobs.

#### Resume Lengths

If you are writing an electronic resume with a three-page limit, then you should try to fill the three pages. The average length of a USAJOBS federal resume is three to five pages. The format for USAJOBS wastes a lot of white space, which makes it a little bit longer than it really should be. The federal paper resume does not have a page limit, but three to four pages is the recommended length and is better than just two pages.

#### Features of the Paper Federal Resume

The paper federal resume is better-looking than the electronic builder formats and is easier to read: It looks like the paper formatted resumes from the 1990s. And good news: you can write your resume in this format AND copy and paste it successfully into the USAJOBS builder. You can actually get started with this format.

Uses of the paper federal resume:
✪ Paper application – some instructions will state that you can mail, email, or fax your resume. This means you can use a paper resume.
✪ Interview – you can take this formatted resume to the interview for easier reading.
✪ Browse and upload – some builders (Avue Central and applicationmanager.org) will let you browse and upload a paper resume into their system.
✪ This paper resume is great for content for the builder. Just copy and paste into your builder. Formatting features will disappear when you copy and paste into USAJOBS.

Format suggestions for your paper federal resume:
✪ Use the outline format with HEADLINES
✪ Add bulleted lists
✪ Use indentations for more readability
✪ Headings should be in ALL CAPS
✪ Add the Summary to the top (in the electronic resume, the summary is usually included in the Additional Information at the bottom of the resume builder / resume)

In the early years of USAJOBS, you could not copy and paste indented copy, Times Roman font, or bullets into USAJOBS. Now you can take a formatted resume, and copy and paste it into the builder successfully. This resume format is easier to read for human resources specialists, supervisors, and contacts.

The format and bullets can be copied and pasted into USAJOBS correctly. You do not have to write your resume in ASCII format to put it into a builder anymore. The builders are better now!

## Features of the Electronic Federal Resume

A resume builder is an online form where you can either type your resume directly into the builder fields, or you can copy and paste your resume into the fields. We prefer that you write your resume in your favorite word processing software, then copy it into the various builders you will find online at employment websites. Each builder has particular requirements. Make sure you understand the requirements before entering your information.

Formatting suggestions for your electronic federal resume:
- ✪ Write targeted versions of your resume for each application, picking up keywords and skills from the announcement.
- ✪ Research and include key skills.
- ✪ Follow the page length instructions for each resume builder.
- ✪ Use ALL CAPS for highlighting job titles or other important nouns. Do not over-use all caps.
- ✪ Do not use bold, italics, underlining, or other special fonts.
- ✪ Do not use lines, borders, or boxes.
- ✪ Do not use a two-column format.
- ✪ Keep paragraphs to eight to ten lines maximum.
- ✪ Add a hard return between paragraphs to improve readability and add white space.
- ✪ Most resume builders give you space for six jobs.
- ✪ Copy and paste your resume into the resume builders.
- ✪ Keep your passwords.

## Sample USAJOBS Federal Resume In Outline Format With Headlines

| | |
|---|---|
| | GRACE STANFORD<br>20000 Square Road<br>Richmond, VA 20111<br>Day Phone: (222) 222-2222<br>Evening: (333) 333-3333<br>Email: stanfordg@acc.net |
| WORK EXPERIENCE | Credit Card Systems<br>12/20xx - Present<br>Richmond, VA US<br>Salary: $55,000 USD Per Year<br>Hours per week: 40<br><br>FINANCIAL SOLUTIONS CONSULTANT<br><br>MARKET AND CONTRACT ANALYSIS: Provide expertise in market development and analysis, product pricing/positioning, strategic sales; and competitive contract solicitation, development, and quantitative/ qualitative analysis for multi-service, performance-based contracts and service agreements for private sector and government organizations.<br><br>PROJECT TEAM LEAD: Select and lead cross-functional teams comprised of subject matter experts from Operations, Software Engineering, Client Services and Sales. Identify issues, gather and analyze information, and develop action plans for creating customized products and services. Establish project priorities. Monitor timelines. Manage project teams to maximize productivity and meet deadlines.<br><br>CONDUCT ANALYSES for contract solicitations/bid proposals. Analyze solutions options, capacity requirements, materials and services requirements, and capital expenditures. Perform due diligence by conducting financial background investigations.<br><br>MONITOR CONTRACT ADMINISTRATION THROUGH CLOSEOUT: Track and monitor current and expiring contracts to promote renewal. Negotiate termination settlements and change proposals and costs. Represent clients with federal contracts to negotiate contract modifications and terms.<br><br>VENDOR SOURCING AND REVIEW: Evaluate vendor services. Provide market-sensitive pricing for bids, quotes, and RFPs. Advise sales team on strategic pricing negotiation.<br><br>CONDUCT TECHNICAL REVIEW OF CONTRACTS, STATEMENTS OF WORK (SOWS), AND CORRESPONDENCE: Work with management/legal team to develop and review final contracts, SOWs, bids, and proposals to understand liability issues. Recommend improvements or modifications to ensure compliance with standards and policies.<br><br>DEVELOP PROGRAMS AND SERVICES DELIVERY IMPROVEMENTS: Work with software developers to automate information delivery to customers. Verify security controls. |

| WORK EXPERIENCE continued | ACCOMPLISHMENTS:<br><br>• ISO PROJECT TEAM: Currently contributing to the development of a database to track renegotiated contracts and pricing changes to ensure compliance with ISO 9001 standards.<br>• Delivered a $100,000 Service Agreement with a major bank.<br>• Won a contract with one of the largest card issuers in the world through a strategic alliance and successful bid with another company.<br>• Implemented an online email tool that automated an inefficient paper process for contract solicitations and improved internal communications.<br>• Increased revenue from 50% to 100% on assigned and new accounts through personalized customer service.<br>• Promoted within one year to program/product analysis position.<br><br>Charge Cards USA<br>3/20xx - 10/20xx<br>Minto, VA US<br>Salary: $67,000 USD Per Year<br>Hours per week: 40<br><br>ACCOUNT MANAGER<br>CUSTOMER SERVICE/CUSTOMER RESPONSE INQUIRIES: Identified, troubleshot, and resolved electronic system processing problems and errors for operational accounts. Serviced global financial services customer accounts using complex, global transaction telecommunications authorization and settlement systems. Provided proactive problem analysis, management, and resolution of as many as 20 processing problems. Managed service change requests.<br><br>PARTICIPATED IN ANNUAL CAPACITY REVIEWS. Contributed to redefining customer services needs for services upgrades, data conversions, and data center relocations. Worked with Project Management Group to initiate changes. Acting Project Managers in their absence.<br><br>INTERNAL/EXTERNAL LIAISON: Technical, service, and informational liaison to customers. Ensured current, ongoing communication on operating regulations, billing, and compliance issues. Served as Subject Matter Expert and technical advisor for the launch and implementation of special programs and services.<br><br>ACCOMPLISHMENTS:<br><br>• DATACENTER RELOCATION: Exceeded established objectives for a client's datacenter relocation project. Re-prioritized work schedule to expedite service migration. New center opened four weeks ahead of schedule with no disruption of services to client. |

| WORK EXPERIENCE continued | • Eliminated $8M cash loss per day for major customer through innovative problem solving.<br><br>• Saved over $5M annually for Charge Cards, USA and member financial institutions by developing and implementing innovative policy changes.<br><br>• Contributed to profit increases through successful negotiation of systems changes with financial networks outside of Charge Cards, USA.<br><br>• Provided technical recommendations and implementation support for the successful launch of a new charge card product.<br><br>• Qualified for monetary incentives for achieving 100% of performance goals and objectives.<br><br>(Contact Supervisor: Yes, Supervisor's Name: Dan Jones, Supervisor's Phone: (703) 777-7777) |
|---|---|
| EDUCATION | UNIVERSITY OF PHOENIX<br>Reston, VA US<br>Some College Coursework Completed<br>118 Semester Hours<br>Major: Organizational Security<br>GPA: 3.1 out of 4.0<br>Relevant Coursework, Licensures and Certifications:<br>Degree Anticipated: 12/20xx. Completed 118 credit hrs. (98.3% complete)<br><br>• Completed 27 elective credits in B.S. in Organizational Security and Management, a degree program designed to address an increasing national and international need for greater technical competence and professionalism in the security industry.<br><br>• Relevant Courses: Administration Process (focus on program budgets and contract negotiation and preparation); Budget Preparation, Justification, and Management |
| JOB RELATED TRAINING | Intelligent Risk Taking Workshop & Conflict to Consensus Workshop, 20xx<br><br>Effective Communications Skills, Decker Presentation Skills Workshop, 20xx<br><br>Advanced PowerPoint; AMA Critical Thinking<br><br>Large Account Management Process (LAMP), Miller & Heiman, 20xx |

| ADDITIONAL INFORMATION | QUALIFICATIONS SUMMARY |
|---|---|
| | Dynamic, goal-oriented Program Manager / Operations Analyst with over ten years of experience in business development, customer management, operations and budget planning, and performance/ quality management. Outstanding team and project leader with keen presentation, negotiation, and communications skills. Recognized throughout career for productivity excellence, teamwork, accountability, sound decision-making, and strong technical qualifications. Combine cross-functional expertise in the following areas: |
| | **PROGRAM MANAGEMENT & ANALYSIS:** |
| | • Expertise managing, tracking, and monitoring the performance and effectiveness of multi-phase programs and projects, including developing matrices and tracking systems. |
| | • Record of success fostering positive, productive working relationships with customers, project teams, and senior leadership. |
| | • Experience preparing a wide range of written reports, documentation, and analytical summaries of program and operational performance, activities, and profitability. |
| | • Strong computer skills. Proficient using automated systems to track and monitor operations. |
| | **FEDERAL AND PRIVATE SECTOR CONTRACTING & ACQUISITIONS:** |
| | • Career experience developing standard contract methods, procedures, and protocols for non-standard terms and conditions; monitoring contract performance; and negotiating modifications, termination settlements, and other adjustments. |
| | • Academic experience designing, responding to, and qualifying federal Requests for Proposal (RFPs). Career experience with purchase orders, Master Service Agreements, Statements of Work (SOWs), and RFP response coordination. |
| | **COMPUTER SKILLS:** Proficient in: Microsoft Office; Lotus Notes, COGNOS, multiple internal UNIX and Web-based systems (VTRS, VOL, Integrated Billing, Exception Manager, Exception File, Tran History, BASEI, BASEII, Core and Configuration); Multiple financial processing front and back office systems. |

## SAMPLE PAPER FEDERAL RESUME

**GRACE STANFORD**
20000 Square Rd.
Richmond, VA 20111
Evening: (222) 222-2222
Day: (222) 222-2222
Email: stanfordg@acc.net

SSN: xxx-xx-xxxx
U.S. Citizen
Federal Status: N/A
Veteran's Status: N/A

### QUALIFICATIONS SUMMARY

**Dynamic, goal-oriented Program Manager / Operations Analyst** with over ten years of experience in business development, customer management, operations and budget planning, and performance/quality management. Outstanding team and project leader with keen presentation, negotiation, and communications skills. Recognized throughout career for productivity excellence, teamwork, accountability, sound decision-making, and strong technical qualifications. Combine cross-functional expertise in the following areas:

### PROGRAM MANAGEMENT & ANALYSIS

- Expertise managing, tracking, and monitoring the performance and effectiveness of multi-phase programs and projects, including developing matrices and tracking systems.
- Record of success fostering positive, productive working relationships with customers, project teams, and senior leadership.
- Experience preparing a wide range of written reports, documentation, and analytical summaries of program and operational performance, activities, and profitability.
- Strong computer skills. Proficient using automated systems to track and monitor operations.

### FEDERAL AND PRIVATE SECTOR CONTRACTING & ACQUISITIONS

- Pursuing B.S.B.M. degree, University of Phoenix. Degree anticipated 12/20xx. Extensive coursework in Organizational Security with a focus on federal contract administration.
- Comprehensive knowledge of all phases of the federal procurement process, from pre-award to closeout, formal advertising procedures, and performance-based acquisitions.
- Career experience developing standard contract methods, procedures, and protocols for non-standard terms and conditions; monitoring contract performance; and negotiating modifications, termination settlements, and other adjustments.
- Academic experience designing, responding to, and qualifying federal Requests for Proposal (RFPs). Ceer experience with purchase orders, Master Service Agreements, Statements of Work (SOWs), and RFP response coordination.

## PROFESSIONAL EXPERIENCE

**FINANCIAL SOLUTIONS CONSULTANT**                    11/20XX – Present [3 years]
Credit Card Systems
3456 Seger Rd., Richmond, VA 20111
Salary: $55,000; 40+ hours per week
Supervisor:

**MARKET AND CONTRACT ANALYSIS:** Provide expertise in market development and analysis, product pricing/positioning, strategic sales; and competitive contract solicitation, development, and quantitative/qualitative analysis for multi-service, performance-based contracts and service agreements for private sector and government organizations.

**PROJECT TEAM LEAD:** Select and lead cross-functional teams comprised of subject matter experts from Operations, Software Engineering, Client Services, and Sales. Identify issues, gather and analyze information, and develop action plans for creating customized products and services. Establish project priorities. Monitor timelines. Manage project teams to maximize productivity and meet deadlines.

**CONDUCT ANALYSES** for contract solicitations/bid proposals. Analyze solutions options, capacity requirements, materials and services requirements, and capital expenditures. Perform due diligence by conducting financial background investigations. Prepare status reports.

**MONITOR CONTRACT ADMINISTRATION THROUGH CLOSEOUT:** Track and monitor current and expiring contracts to promote renewal. Negotiate termination settlements and change proposals and costs. Represent clients with federal contracts to negotiate contract modifications and terms.

**VENDOR SOURCING AND REVIEW:** Evaluate vendor services. Provide market-sensitive pricing for bids, quotes, and RFPs. Advise sales team on strategic pricing negotiation.

**CONDUCT TECHNICAL REVIEW OF CONTRACTS, STATEMENTS OF WORK (SOWS), AND CORRESPONDENCE:** Work with management/legal team to develop and review final contracts, SOWs, bids, and proposals to understand liability issues. Recommend improvements or modifications to ensure compliance with standards and policies.

**DEVELOP PROGRAMS AND SERVICES DELIVERY IMPROVEMENTS:** Work with software developers to automate information delivery to customers. Verify security controls.

## ACCOMPLISHMENTS

- ISO PROJECT TEAM: Currently contributing to the development of a database to track renegotiated contracts and pricing changes to ensure compliance with ISO 9001 standards.
- Delivered a $100,000 Service Agreement with a major bank.
- Won a contract with one of the largest card issuers in the world through a strategic alliance and successful bid with another company.
- Implemented an online email tool that automated an inefficient paper process for contract solicitations and improved internal communications.
- Increased revenue from 50% to 100% on assigned and new accounts through personalized customer service.
- Promoted within one year to program/product analysis position.

## EDUCATION & CERTIFICATIONS

**B.S., Business/Management / Focus on Organizational Security**

Degree Anticipated: 12/20xx. Completed 118 credit hrs. (98.3% complete)

University of Phoenix, Reston, Virginia, 3.31 GPA

- Completed 27 elective credits in B.S. in Organizational Security and Management, a degree program designed to address an increasing national and international need for greater technical competence and professionalism in the security industry.
- Relevant Courses: Administration Process (focus on program budgets and contract negotiation and preparation); Budget Preparation, Justification and Management

## PROFESSIONAL DEVELOPMENT

Intelligent Risk Taking Workshop & Conflict to Consensus Workshop, 20xx

Effective Communications Skills, Decker Presentation Skills Workshop, 20xx

Advanced Power Point; AMA Critical Thinking

Large Account Management Process (LAMP), Miller & Heiman, 20xx

## HONORS & AWARDS

Cash Award for business enhancement, 20xx; Cash Award for customer satisfaction, 20xx

Certificate of Accomplishment, effective communicating, 20xx

Star Performance Certificates (3), 20xx

## COMPUTER & TECHNICAL SKILLS

Proficient in: Microsoft Office; Lotus Notes, COGNOS, multiple internal UNIX and Web-based systems (VTRS, VOL, Integrated Billing, Exception Manager, Exception File, Tran History, BASEI, BASEII, Core and Configuration); Multiple financial processing front and back office systems.

## 6

The True Stories in the Case Study section of this book will include samples of the Outline Format, the BEFORE private industry resume and the keyword analysis of target announcements.

## Quote

"What I learned from this book *[Ten Steps to a Federal Job, First Edition]* is that the KSA(s) makes or breaks an application. I truly believe that it is more important than any other step in the application process, including the interview. If you don't know how to write a KSA, you will not get a federal job. The book…breaks down the KSA and explains exactly what it should look like. The book even gives sample KSAs so you can model yours around it.

After reading the book, I applied its principles to an application with a federal agency. It was a position I really wanted, and I spent a great deal of time refining my KSAs. And six months later, I was called for an interview. A month after that I was offered the job.

*Jeffrey J. Smith* "

## Top Tips for Writing Winning KSA Narratives

**#1 Give one fantastic example per KSA.** KSAs are no place to talk in generalities. Get very specific about what you did and your results.

**#2 Quantify or qualify your results/accomplishments.** It is better to say that you type 65 wpm than to say you type fast. It is better to say that you came in $12,000 below budget than saying you saved your office money.

**#3 Let the CCAR drive your story.** Context-Challenge-Actions-Results is a winning formula.

**#4 Use a consistent length and format.** Address each KSA statement separately, writing one-half to one full page for each. Your name, social security number, and the job announcement number should be on each page. Page numbers are also useful to the reviewer.

**#5 Write in the first person.** Write in complete sentences and well-crafted paragraphs. Do NOT talk about yourself as though you are someone else. Do NOT use "we." Do NOT omit pronouns altogether (as you would in a resume).

**#6 Proofread your KSAs.** Then proofread it again and again. This is a writing test. Although spell check is a wonderful tool, it is not a substitute for proofreading.

# STEP SEVEN
## Conquer the
## KSAs and Questionnaires

As you are answering the KSA questions, think about your answer as if you were in a live interview. What would you say? What example would you give that would demonstrate you can do this work? In *Step 3: Target Your Top Accomplishments*, you learned to create your top accomplishment record list. Those accomplishments are the beginning of your KSAs. By writing the story surrounding your accomplishment in the KSAs, you will demonstrate that you have the experience necessary to perform the job.

## Overview

What is a KSA or Questionnaire?

Knowledge, Skill, and Ability: The Differences

Troutman Method Lesson 5: Write KSAs Using the Context-Challenge-
    Action-Results Formula

KSA and Questionnaire Formats

KSA Narratives on a Separate Sheet

Questionnaires with Supporting Essays

KSAs in the Resume

Writing the Impossible KSA

Adapting KSAs

Getting Ideas from Google.com

Getting Ideas from the Vacancy Announcement

How Will My KSA Narratives Be Graded?

## What is a KSA or Questionnaire?

Many federal vacancy announcements now require you to write KSAs or questionnaires. You can consider them to be Part 2 of your application. The first part of your application is obviously the resume. You may even be required to submit a third part—required documents such as transcripts, performance evaluations, or military DD-214 forms.

> KSAs are an assessment tool, a test, or procedure used to evaluate an individual's job-related competencies, interests or fitness for employment based on the nature and complexity of the work to be performed in the position to be filled. (MSPB study, Issues of Merit, May 2008)

The purpose of the KSA or questionnaire is to help the hiring officials screen out applicants who do not have the specialized experience needed for the job and help identify the best qualified applicant. Think of KSAs as basically pre-interview questions. Questionnaires serve the same purpose but are most often a set of multiple choice questions addressing the skills that you will use on the job. If you do have the skills and abilities to perform the job, this part of your application will give you the opportunity to express your strengths more thoroughly.

Another important point is this: the KSAs and questionnaires are scored like an examination. So, you need to pay attention to the questions in the KSAs and questionnaires just like you are taking an exam for the position.

Agencies do not always call KSA statements "Knowledge, Skills, and Abilities." Sometimes the written essay portion of the application might be called:
- Quality Ranking Factors
- Narrative Factors
- Technical Qualifications
- Self-Assessment Questionnaire (sometimes with essays)
- Statements of Qualifications
- Selective Placement Factors

You may even find other designation for these statements. Read your vacancy announcement carefully and remember that a KSA by any other name is still a KSA. Follow the advice in this chapter UNLESS the vacancy announcement specifically tells you to do otherwise.

### Commonly Seen KSAs

For many positions, especially in general administrative and management positions, you will likely encounter KSAs that ask you to address seemingly basic knowledge, skills, and abilities. These are some of the commonly seen factors:
- ✪ Communicate orally and/or in writing
- ✪ Plan and organize work (for yourself or for others)
- ✪ Independently plan and carry out multiple assignments
- ✪ Locate and assemble information for various reports, briefings, and conferences
- ✪ Analyze and solve problems
- ✪ Work well with others

## Knowledge, Skill, and Ability: The Differences

Hi Kathryn,

One thing that (I don't think) was discussed on today's telephone training was the clear difference between a Knowledge, a Skill, and an Ability. So if a KSA says "Describe your Knowledge in the area of Network Management," versus "Describe your Skills in the area of Network Management," versus "Describe your ability to manage networks," how do you address these levels in the KSA response? If it says I just need knowledge, would I use training and no hands-on experience, for example?

*Peter Hitchcock*
*U.S. Fish and Wildlife Service*

It can be confusing at times to delineate clearly what is a skill, what is an ability, and what is knowledge. Here is how the government defines each of these terms:

✪ Knowledge: An organized body of information, usually of a factual or procedural nature, which, if applied, makes adequate performance on the job possible.

✪ Skills: The proficient manual, verbal, or mental manipulation of data, people, or things. Observable, quantifiable, and measurable.

✪ Abilities: The power to perform an activity at the present time. Implied is a lack of discernible barriers, either physical or mental, to performing the activity.

To answer Peter Hitchcock's question above, Ligaya Fernandez—a federal human resources expert—writes the following analysis:

**Knowledge** is the basis of our abilities and skills. It pertains to the principles, rules, regulations, or operating systems or procedures. So in [Peter's] example, "Knowledge in the area of network management," he should describe his experience designing architectural structure of network communications. He should describe why he designed a LAN instead of a WAN (or vice versa), for example, and it would help if he describes what it entails to create a LAN versus a WAN. If he had experience setting policy or guidelines in the design and/or use of computer networks, he should describe them under Knowledge. Training and education are also under Knowledge.

**Skill** in the area of network management would include his experience in actually connecting computer network together. Skill is defined as a proficiency, and proficiency is something we can observe or quantify. He should describe his proficiency in working in that operating system (e.g., Novell, Windows, Linux or any others). He can write about how he implemented a network design, operated/maintained computer networks, or performed troubleshooting.

Under **Ability** to manage network, he can describe his experience analyzing network requirements, understanding what the organization needs, resolving network problems, staffing, and mentoring people about the network. If he had experience doing cost-benefit analysis of having a network or the type of network (cable or wireless) to have, he should describe it under Ability.

## Troutman Method Lesson 5:
## Write KSAs Using the Context-Challenge-Action-Results Formula

Your KSAs will be focused around your accomplishments. Ideally, you have already completed Step 3 and have several excellent examples from which to choose.

When writing your KSAs, think of it as telling your story about your accomplishment. To see the whole story, your reader needs to know what you did, why you did it, how you did it, and what you accomplished. This is what is known as the CCAR approach, which stands for CONTEXT, CHALLENGE, ACTION, and RESULTS. The CCAR method is tried and true for developing any type of narrative to highlight your accomplishment, whether for job applications, job interviews, or self-assessments.

Let's define these terms specifically:

✪ **Context:** (Why you did it) Explain the factors contributing to the challenge you faced and the surrounding environment and circumstances. What job title did you hold and what was your level of responsibility? Why did you do what you did in the first place? Budget limits? Staffing changes? Institutional reform? New goals handed down from on high?

✪ **Challenge:** (Problems you faced) State the specific problem you had to address. For example, if the context included widespread institutional reform, what was the specific challenge you faced in your corner of the world that was caused by it and how did you respond to that reform?

✪ **Action:** (What you did and how you did it) Describe the specific steps you took to solve the problem, meet the goal, etc. Generally, it is best NOT to use ordinary examples. Just doing your basic job is not all that remarkable. Instead, look for instances where you took action that went above and beyond the call of duty, applied particularly creative ideas, or put forth Herculean effort. Seek the extraordinary action in what you did.

✪ **Results:** (What you accomplished) Show the outcome of your actions and the difference you made. Quantify your results whenever you can possibly do so. For example, "My quick thinking saved our department $17,000." Again, ignore any examples with mediocre results. Write only about the best you have done.

The CCAR is the crux of your story. It is the core of the KSA that demonstrates your Knowledge, Skills, or Abilities. However, a successful KSA will also feature a strong opening paragraph and an ending with impact. These paragraphs also give you an opportunity to give impressive information beyond your one strong accomplishment. In this way you can show that you understand the agency's mission or tell how many years you have been working in the field.

## Setting the stage – the opening paragraph

The opening lines of your KSA statement are important in establishing an impression of you as a candidate for the job. You want the reader to immediately view you as having the particular Knowledge, Skill, or Ability for the position. It is the perfect place to qualify the scope of your experience, describe the length of your tenure in the field, or just flat-out state you can do the job. The following are some strong lead-ins for opening a KSA statement:

"I have more than seven years' experience working in fast-paced environments processing large volumes of work. I am particularly skilled at stepping out of the day-to-day concerns to see the big picture. Because of this, I have been able to identify and analyze large and complex problems and then develop effective solutions."

"I am very good at reading people, working with them, establishing rapport and trust, and teaching. In addition, I have many years of practical career experience working through problems with others, sometimes difficult ones. As well, I have extensive knowledge of and formal training in counseling, which has served me well."

"My extensive experience creating win-win partnerships between internal and external organizations would be an excellent asset at NASA, where the "Spin-In" model is being used to leverage private sector resources in order to maximize opportunity in the government sector. Garnering stakeholder buy-in, building alliances, and fostering team work has been a strength throughout my career in aerospace engineering. "

## Make a strong summary statement

Just as the opening paragraph of a KSA creates an impression, so too, does the last paragraph. Think of your KSA as a speech where every word counts. The audience stays more interested when each phrase and sentence puts forth new ideas. The closing paragraph can drive home your results, tell about an award or recognition you received for your service, or show a sustained record of success. These are examples of memorable KSA endings:

"The Presidentially-appointed Chair of the Equal Employment Opportunity Commission selected me to draft a key policy memorandum for dissemination to the entire staff on a mission-critical matter. My draft was adopted virtually without change and issued to all employees nationwide. I am highly skilled at written communication in any format, and accurately and convincingly convey ideas, facts, and messages understandable by the intended audience, whatever it may be."

"The Director agreed with my recommendations and we extended the existing contract for two years, resulting in long-term savings of thousands of dollars over the life of the contract."

"Due to my planning, the support program for PTCS was successfully implemented; additionally, I received an Above and Beyond award and monetary bonus for my leadership on this project."

**Example 1: Turning An Accomplishment into a CCAR Narrative**

In this example, you can see how one item from an accomplishment list can become a CCAR story that demonstrates your knowledge, skills, or abilities in a particular area.

**CASE NAME:** JOHN WALLSTONE
**PRIOR POSITION:** Sous Chef, Maryland State Government
**TARGET FEDERAL POSITION:** FEMA Program Specialist, GS 9/11/12
**KSA FACTOR:** Experience Managing Projects

**Accomplishment:** Successfully managed a 425-person party with ten-day lead time. Executed a flawless event.

**CCAR Outline:**
- *Context:* Experience building solid teams to work in tough kitchen environment. In process of hiring a new manager and were short staffed; another chef was on a leave of absence.
- *Challenge:* One of the largest events of my career, 425-person party, while at Government House. Instead of three managers, had only one (myself) to manage the event. Had only ten days lead time.
- *Action:* Planned menu, ordered items, planned work steps, and sequence. Scheduled deliveries carefully to allow for extra post-9/11 security measures. Recruited additional personnel to help.
- *Results:* Event went smoothly; guests and client very pleased. Management gained confidence in me as a project manager.

**Final KSA Story with the Language for a Paper KSA**

CONTEXT: Due to the nature of my career, I have had in-depth experience in leading projects requiring strong interpersonal, group and customer service skills. Kitchens are notorious for their abrasive relationships, which unfortunately can affect the customer; in my kitchens, I actively build solid teams with excellent communications, as well as work with my customers to ensure their satisfaction.

CHALLENGE: One of the largest events I have managed was a 425-person party, while at Government House. In addition to the size of the event, I had two other challenges – we were in the process of hiring a new manager, were presently short-staffed, and another chef had a family emergency requiring a leave of absence. Instead of three managers for the event, I had sole responsibility for it. I knew from the outset that I would need to recruit help from a variety of sources.

ACTIONS: Our lead time for the event was ten days. In that period, I had to plan the menu, determine what items to order, recalculate recipes for mass production, determine what sequence to order and prep food, what items could be ordered pre-cut, what containers and serving items needed to be purchased, and how to store and stage the product while avoiding contamination. (One challenge was receiving, storing, and grilling 420 pounds of chicken, swordfish, and pork.) During this process, I used object-oriented planning, working backward from the final outcome to the initial step. Once the preplanning was completed, I began receiving products and commenced production.

As the event approached, I began to recruit additional personnel. I brought in a retired chef for two days to help with production and a veteran chef for the day of the event. I also resolved problems that occurred, such as last-minute menu changes and retraining inexperienced staff. I worked with my vendors to update my orders, oversaw the delivery and placement of a large rental grill, and directed staff to pick up supplies.

RESULTS: As a result of my planning and problem resolution, the production, staging, and eventual presentation of the food went smoothly. The event was a success; the guests and the client were very pleased. I demonstrated my skills as a planner, organizer, decision maker, and crisis manager, solidifying my management's confidence in me as a project manager. The interruption of our staff by a chef's emergency absence was large enough to jeopardize the event's success. While the potential for widespread chaos existed, I brought a sense of calm, confidence, and leadership to the situation.

## KSA BUILDER AND THE CCAR

The KSA Builder follows the Context-Challenge-Action-Results model for writing examples that will demonstrate your Knowledge, Skills and Abilities. This format gives the staffing specialist and hiring manager readable, interesting and specific examples that they can rate and rank based on the hiring manager's requirements.

Each KSA Builder Form contains fields for writing two examples that support each KSA.

Results: What happened? (quantify with numbers if possible)

Example 2.
Please fill in the following fields to give the human resources staff (another example) of your experience which supports this particular KSA.

Context: Your title and office and dates

Challenge: What was the challenge?

Action: What action did you take?
1.

*Try www.resume-place.com/ksabuilder for writing your CCAR KSAs!*

### Example 2: KSA Critique and Correction

In this critique, a federal human resources professional shows how to strengthen the CCAR elements and effectively demonstrate how the candidate's qualifications match the KSA factor.

**CASE NAME:** ALLISON LEE
**PRIOR POSITION:** Commercial Real Estate Leasing and Sales Broker
**TARGET FEDERAL JOB:** Federal Emergency Management Specialist, Realty Specialist, GS 11/12/13
**KSA Factor:** Knowledge of commonly used contracting rules, regulations, and procedures to obtain routine goods and services.

### BEFORE KSA with Critique Comments

My knowledge of contracting rules, regulations and procedures to obtain routine goods and services is best exemplified by a purchase I facilitated at Global Crossroads Center, in Falls Church, VA. After the purchase was finalized, there was a significant amount of construction work to be completed by the new owner.

I was the listing and selling broker for a six-story, 40,000 SF office building. I used my extensive network created through my innovative marketing and canvassed the community. Within a few weeks, I located a buyer who paid $3.5M. *(Is this the same property at Global? This first bullet is confusing, especially since the last sentence above said the purchase was finalized so why was another buyer located?)*

There were numerous challenges with the property involving asbestos, inadequate fire protection, poor elevators, broken and inoperable windows, heating and air conditioning system problems, etc.

Over a period of nine months, I managed a construction improvement project *(costing how much?)* which involved contracting with various vendors and suppliers and working with various regulatory offices. *(Add this: "I solicited, evaluated, negotiated, and awarded")* I used *(drop "I used")* over seven contracts to bring the building up to code and adhere to regulations to remove the asbestos, increase fire protection, repair and replace several elevators to obtain appropriate licenses, replace windows, and provide short- and long-term solutions to the heating and air conditioning systems.

RESULT: Due to the improvements made under my leadership and the goods and services contracted for use in this construction project, the building owner now enjoys a positive annual cash flow of $720,000. This means the property has doubled in value since it changed ownership in late 20xx.

## AFTER KSA

My knowledge of contracting rules, regulations, and procedures is extensive. I have regularly used this knowledge to obtain routine goods and services.

CONTEXT: One situation that exemplified this knowledge was a purchase I facilitated at Global Crossroads Center in Falls Church, VA. I was the listing and selling broker for a six-story, 40,000 SF office building.

CHALLENGE: There were numerous challenges with the property involving asbestos, inadequate fire protection, poor elevators, broken and inoperable windows, heating and air conditioning system problems, etc. There was a significant amount of construction work that would need to be completed by a new owner after the purchase was finalized.

ACTIONS: Using my extensive networking, innovative marketing, and community canvassing skills, I located a buyer who offered $3.5M within a few weeks. Included in the contract was an agreement that I would manage the construction improvement project. The renovation project was capped at a cost of no more than $750K, and was completed in nine months.

I solicited, evaluated, negotiated, and awarded contracts with numerous vendors, suppliers, and contractors. I contracted services and purchased a fire safety system, elevator repair and replacement, windows, asbestos abatement, and heating and air conditioning equipment, and provided ongoing oversight of each project.

I obtained all appropriate licenses and monitored work for contract compliance, and communicated with all regulatory officials on an ongoing basis. The project required facilitation of more than seven contracts to bring the building up to code and provide all the agreed upon improvements.

RESULT: Due to the improvements made under my leadership and the goods and services contracted for use in this construction project, the building owner enjoys a positive annual cash flow of $720,000. This means the property has doubled in value since it changed ownership in late 20xx.

## KSA and Questionnaire Formats

Agencies consider a number of factors in determining the most appropriate assessment strategy for a particular position. Today's federal applications typically use one of three KSA or Questionnaire formats:

1. KSAs that are written on separate sheets of paper

2. Questionnaires with multiple choice questions and maybe essays (similar to separate sheet KSAs, but shorter)

3. KSAs that are combined into the resume

We will discuss each of these three formats in more detail and include vacancy announcement and response examples. The responses do not apply to the vacancy announcement example provided.

## KSA Narratives on a Separate Sheet

KSA narratives on a separate sheet, sometimes called stand alone or paper KSAs, are specifically written as separate narratives to support each of the areas of knowledge, skills, and abilities listed in the vacancy announcement. There are usually four to six KSAs required for each application.

The KSA narrative should be separate from your resume. Do not merely reference the resume and do not paste your resume into the KSA. A well-crafted narrative is your best tool for standing out from your competition. Sometimes your resume and KSAs will be reviewed by different people. Therefore, each document needs to give an independent account of what you accomplished, but still provide a unified representation of your experience.

Stand-alone KSA narratives are graded with competency-based benchmarks, where various levels of a knowledge, skill or ability earn more or less points depending on your level of experience. For example, you may earn five points for your ability to use Excel to create complex spreadsheets that contain formulas versus two points for the ability to enter data into Excel spreadsheets. Additionally, the HR specialist may have certain points to assign for the use of particular keywords. For best success, explain the most complex level of performance you have ascertained in your experience that demonstrates your competence, and tell that story using keywords and phrases from the vacancy announcement.

## Formatting Tips

Use the CCAR format with a strong opening paragraph and summary statement. Develop your KSA with several descriptive paragraphs, not bullets or an outline. Write in the first person ("I did this or that"). KSAs are typically one-half to one-full page each, single-spaced, and 12-point type is preferred.

## 7

## Vacancy Announcement Example #1

From the Qualifications & Evaluations section of this USAJOBS announcement:

> **HOW YOU WILL BE EVALUATED:**
>
> You will be evaluated to determine if you meet the minimum qualifications required; and on the extent to which your application shows that you possess the knowledges, skills, and abilities associated with this position as defined below. When describing your knowledges, skills, and abilities, please be sure to give examples and explain how often you used these skills, the complexity of the knowledge you possessed, the level of the people you interacted with, the sensitivity of the issues you handled, etc.
>
> 1. Knowledge of office automation systems and information systems and technologies to maintain records, generate reports, and perform a variety of administrative responsibilities and related procedures in support of the Office of the Deputy, Director-Europe.
>
> 2. Knowledge of planning, organizing, and performing work having numerous time pressures and competing priorities.
>
> 3. Knowledge of the policies, procedures, and objectives of DoD programs.
>
> 4. Knowledge of the functional requirements of DoD publications, records, and forms management programs.
>
> 5. Basic knowledge of the procedures related to the Privacy Act and FOIA programs.

Also, from the How To Apply section of this announcement:

> **YOU MUST ALSO SUBMIT:**
> 2. A separate narrative statement that concisely addresses each of the knowledges, skills, and abilities referenced under the section "Knowledge, Skills and Abilities (KSA's)". Make sure that you reference the specific KSA listed on this announcement. If other KSA's are cited, the application will be considered incomplete. Include work experience, education, and training that clearly demonstrates how well you possess each element. FAILURE TO ADDRESS ALL KSA'S ON THIS ANNOUNCEMENT WILL RESULT IN AN INELIGIBLE RATING.

KSAs are clearly required when applying for this position.

**Vacancy Announcement Example #2**

SELECTIVE PLACEMENT FACTORS are knowledge, skills, abilities or special qualifications that are in addition to the minimum requirements but determined to be essential to perform the duties of the position to be filled.

Selective Placement Factor for this position is as follows:

At least 6 months bankruptcy experience which exhibits knowledge of bankruptcy regulations and procedures. Education cannot be substituted for the 6 months bankruptcy experience requirement.

QUALITY RANKING FACTORS are knowledge, skills and abilities which could be expected to enhance significantly the performance of the position.

Quality Ranking Factors for this position are as follows:

1) Knowledge and skill in fact finding, analysis and communication including ability to correspond and
elicit information from debtors, creditors and their counsel.

2) Skill in the use and application of established instructions, procedures, policies, or precedents of the Bankruptcy Code and rules of procedures, local rules of practice, applicable case law, and other reference material.

3) Skill in business arithmetic and familiarity with basic accounting principles.

4) Knowledge of automated office systems.

5) Ability to communicate orally and in writing.

APPLICANTS ARE ENCOURAGED TO SUBMIT A SEPARATE NARRATIVE ADDRESSING THE SELECTIVE PLACEMENT FACTOR AND QUALITY RANKING FACTORS TO ENSURE THAT FULL CREDIT IS RECEIVED FOR THE APPROPRIATE WORK EXPERIENCE AS IT RELATES TO THE POSITION.

This announcement has KSAs by another name. This announcement separates the KSAs into two categories: Selective Placement Factors and Quality Ranking Factors. The announcement clearly states that the Selective Placement Factor is a requirement for the job. A candidate who cannot demonstrate competence with the Selective Placement Factor will not be considered. Although candidates are only "encouraged" to submit separate narratives, these narratives are important in that they will be used to ensure that the applicant receives full credit for their work experience. Not submitting them will adversely affect your rating.

## Response Example

**CASE NAME:** JANE ADDAMS
**PRIOR POSITION:** Acting Manager of Customer Support / Customer Support Specialist
**TARGET FEDERAL JOB:** Information Technology Specialist, GS-2210-12/13

**KSA Factor:** Skill in applying analytical and evaluative techniques and methods to complex technical problems to identify, develop, and propose viable alternatives and long-term solutions.

CONTEXT: During my 25-year career in information technology, I have relied on my skills in analyzing and evaluating technical problems, recommending and developing viable solutions. I have resolved issues in software development, configuration and installation, as well as business process and operations problems.

CHALLENGE: In my first assignment at USPTO, I led a software development effort to improve process monitoring during peak times and load balancing for the group that monitored text search jobs on the Amdahl mainframe computer system. Specifically, I was challenged with delivering a solution that was user-friendly, easy to maintain, and could be delivered in a short timeframe.

ACTIONS: With my team of two developers, I met with the text search (Messenger) support group to determine business requirements. Identifying that simplicity of operations was the key to success, I proposed the system be written in REXX, as opposed to PL/1. This would allow changes to be made quickly and not require that the code be compiled; rather it would just be moved from the Configuration Management (CM) area to the production area. This step would prevent mistakes and possible human error. I also proposed that the data tables for the program be external to the code and not under CM control. Instead, the master tables would be placed in CM and, unless corrupt, the Messenger group could change parameters to adjust load balancing daily.

My team designed and coded an interactive system to their requirements. We received approval from USPTO for the data tables to be external and began the testing phase. During testing, we discovered that starting additional processes this way required that the job be entered into a "super user" group. I assessed the impact and determined alternatives, briefing USPTO on the issue and options, and ultimately receiving a waiver to allow the project to continue.

RESULTS: My team delivered the completed project to the Messenger group on time and within budget. We also provided training and documentation beyond the original statement of work. This program ran successfully, without bug reports for several years.

## Questionnaires with Supporting Essays

As HR specialists seek more efficient ways of assessing applicants, and additional technology becomes readily available, the self-assessment questionnaire is becoming common in federal applications. In this format, you take an online examination to test your level of competence with the knowledge, skills. and abilities required for the position to be filled. Typically, you answer a series of multiple choice or yes/no answers where YOU indicate your level of performance and experience. The number of questions can range from two to over 100 questions! As with any part of the application, read them carefully to ensure you are answering accurately and following the instructions.

Frequently, the multiple choice questions have follow-up essay questions that provide "proof" for your self-examination. The essay answers should read like a stand-alone KSA narrative. Use the CCAR formula to give one strong accomplishment example that shows how your experience meets the qualifications. They can be shorter than paper KSAs but should still provide enough context to allow the reviewer to find the information in your resume.

These questionnaires are popular with federal HR specialists, because the computer automatically grades the assessment, eliminating much of the work of reviewing hundreds of applications. Once the preliminary score is assigned, any corresponding essays, as well as the resume, are reviewed to determine your level of qualifications. To have success with this method of assessment, you must be able to select the highest-scoring answer for almost every question. The best strategy for mastering a self-assessment questionnaire is to consider how you can match an example from your list of accomplishments to the high-scoring answer. Again, only one accomplishment or example of performing that task is needed.

## Strategy Tip
Many applicants do not see themselves as an "expert" on KSAs. However, to be considered an expert, you need only to have performed that KSA independently and have the ability to show someone else how to do it. For a job that truly fits your experience, you will often qualify as an expert.

## Vacancy Announcement Example

---

KNOWLEDGE, SKILLS AND ABILITIES REQUIRED:
Your qualifications will be evaluated on the basis of your level of knowledge, skills, abilities and/or competencies in the following areas:
- Knowledge of the full range of principles and concepts of intelligence collection, analysis, evaluation, interpretation and dissemination of information.
- Knowledge of national intelligence community structure and responsibilities.
- Ability to perform extensive research to interpret intelligence data and present the results in customer usable form; and to analyze data and disseminate finished intelligence.
- Ability to operate laptop and desktop computers and peripherals including external hard drives, scanners, printers, CD/DVD recorders, network hub and switches, digital still and video (single and multiple lens) cameras, global positioning systems and laser range finders.
- Skill in using and controlling classified data and equipment in accordance with established Department of Defense (DOD) security and classification guidelines and procedures.


HOW TO APPLY:

To apply for this position, you must provide a complete Application Package, which includes both of the following:
1. Your responses to the Qualifications Questionnaire, and
2. Your résumé and any other documents specified in the "Required Documents" section of this job announcement.

---

This announcement states clearly that these KSAs will be the basis for your evaluation, but does not give specific instructions for submitting them. In the How to Apply section of the announcement, however, you will see that the required application materials listed are the Qualifications Questionnaire, the resume, and any other required documents. Separate narrative KSA statements are not required to apply for this position.

## Response Example

**CASE NAME:** BARBARA KELLY
**PRIOR POSITION:** Credit Union Area Manager
**TARGET FEDERAL JOBS:** FDIC Compliance Examiner, CG-11

### Announcement Questionnaire Excerpt
My public speaking includes:
Check all that apply
1. Informal presentations to coworkers or supervisors in small group settings.
2. Presentations of technical compliance-related information to peers and/or supervisors in large formal settings.
3. Presentations of audit/internal review findings to senior management or board of directors of financial institutions.
4. Presentations at educational forums for bankers, community groups, or trade associations.
5. Instructor at a school for an employer.
6. Presentations to a civic organization, trade group, religious group, etc.
7. Participant of a public speaking group (e.g., Toastmasters).
8. None of the above.
If you answered other than "None of the above," please describe the circumstances surrounding the positive feedback for your oral presentation that supports your answer choice, and cross reference this to where you gained this experience on your resume.

### Response
Throughout my banking career, I have given numerous public addresses to small and large groups, and have provided substantial internal presentations to senior management and boards of directors. I served for six years ([date] – [date]) as the Secretary to the Acadiana Security Association, a local association that shares information on banking personnel security and physical security issues. In that role, I prepared and reviewed minutes at monthly meetings before the members, which consisted of 45 people. I was re-elected six consecutive years and was consistently praised for my accuracy and reporting skills by law enforcement officials. I coordinated and provided instruction at annual security training with law enforcement, local banks, and credit unions. I always received excellent feedback and return admissions from all who attended.

The Acadiana Security Association held regular seminars covering topics such as bank security, robbery, and fraud. In one example, I spoke to a group of approximately 200 people regarding bank security issues. Attendees were operations personnel from local banks and credit unions who came to gain an understanding of various regulations, risk-management techniques, and other issues. The evaluation slips at the end of the seminar were overwhelmingly positive for my presentation. It was noted that my information was clear and easily understood and that my style was warm and engaging. In another example, I addressed 30-40 people for the Consumer Credit Association's seminar on the Fair Credit Reporting Act. I received positive reviews for that presentation as well.

As the CEO of Educational Association Federal Credit Union ([date] – [date]), I presided over all board meetings, presented updates and briefings, facilitated discussion on business before the board, acted as parliamentarian, and made formal and informal presentations in an official capacity. I addressed groups of up to 50 City of Lafayette employees to convey information on member services. The response was excellent and as a result, membership grew in accordance with growth goals.

## KSAs in the Resume

Some KSAs are not statements, questions, or essays at all. They are merely knowledge, skills, and abilities that should be talked about in your resume using the federal resume outline format. In this case, the KSA factors provide you perfect insight into what the HR specialist will be looking for in the resume. It is your road map to success. You know exactly what your resume needs to say in order to rate well in the application. Because the announcement encourages you to "demonstrate" your experience, featuring accomplishments in the resume that show your competence in these areas are the best way to address them. Your description of your duties and responsibilities can also be used to cover these KSAs.

**Vacancy Announcement Example**

---

HOW YOU WILL BE EVALUATED:

KSA(s) should be reflected within the experience history and not as a separate document. You will be evaluated to determine if you meet the minimum qualifications required; and on the extent to which your application shows that you possess the knowledge, skills and abilities associated with this position as defined below. When describing your knowledge, skills and abilities, please be sure to give examples and explain how often you used these skills, the complexity of the knowledge you possessed, the level of the people you interacted with, the sensitivity of the issues you handled, etc. Applicants are strongly encouraged to address how your experience demonstrates each of these factors to receive full consideration.

1. Knowledge of the military organization and agencies to effectively research and accurately refer customers to appropriate contacts.

2. Skills in using a personal computer and various computer applications; Microsoft Office software; work-processing, database management, desktop publishing, spreadsheets, graphics, and clickbook software, office tracker software.

3. Knowledge of correspondence procedures and skills in writing and editing and proofreading.

4. Ability to organize and prioritize tasks.

---

Sometimes KSAs that should be addressed in the resume are not labeled this clearly. In the absence of specific instructions, you may get in touch with the point of contact listed in the announcement to clarify.

**Response Example**

**CASE NAME:** PATRICIA RICHARDS
**PRIOR POSITION:** Real Estate Office Manager
**TARGET FEDERAL JOBS:** Administrative Assistant Positions, GS-0301-7/9

**KSAs from the Vacancy Announcement**

1)  Oral and written communication.
2)  Control, preparation, and review of incoming and outgoing correspondence.
3)  Setting work priorities and establishing deadlines.
4)  Experience with administrative functions such as budget management, travel planning and reimbursement, and supply requisition or procurement.
5)  Experience with office automation and information systems and equipment.

**Resume Language From One Job Block**

DEVELOPMENT AND MARKETING DIRECTOR / OFFICE MANAGER
March 20xx – Present
Century 21 / Dublin Properties
40+ hours per week
200 Charlotte Blvd., Lafayette, Louisiana 72501
Salary: $35,000 per year
Supervisor:   Dawn Brown (555) 555-5555, permission to contact.

Licensed Commercial Real Estate Agent and FULL-TIME ADMINISTRATIVE PROFESSIONAL in multi-agent office with six licensed agents and four support personnel. Annual revenues exceed $1.6 million, with up to 90 simultaneous listings. Specialties include retail and commercial real estate and development. Serve as Development and Marketing Director, responsible for all internal marketing functions including preparing printed and Web-based materials. Regularly adapt to changing priorities in a fast-paced work environment.

DIRECT OFFICE OPERATIONS AND SUPERVISE FIVE OFFICE STAFF in various clerical and administrative activities. Plan and assign work; set work priorities and establish deadlines; monitor performance of clerical and support functions. Recruit and select office staff, provide on-the-job and other training opportunities, and conduct performance appraisals. Schedule, track, and coordinate payment for office staff training.

COMMUNICATE EFFECTIVELY with contacts at multiple levels of an organization and across various boundaries. Receive and screen visitors and callers, answer the telephone and e-mail, resolve and/or route inquiries, and manage incoming and outgoing correspondence. Excellent interpersonal skills.

MANAGE MULTIPLE PROJECTS in high-paced, ever-changing environment. Fulfill roles of commercial agent, market director, office manager, and project coordinator. WORK AS PART OF A TEAM within and among four distinct entities — rental and office lease, industrial, land, and development. Coordinate and collaborate on various responsibilities and regularly "wear the hat" of other team members. Highly organized; make sound decisions.

Use AUTOMATED INFORMATION AND WORD PROCESSING SYSTEMS to research and determine critical data for property transactions — includes Clerk of Court tax rolls, Clerk of Court and Assessors' computer system for land valuations, and property/ownership details. Use local and national database for marketing purposes; query databases to generate mailing labels or gather pertinent information. Utilize office equipment such as fax machines, copiers, scanners, and multi-line telephone systems.

CONTROL, PREPARE, AND/OR REVIEW INCOMING/OUTGOING CORRESPONDENCE and action documents. Complete memoranda, letters, reports, and other documents in final form or draft, ensuring correct punctuation, spelling, grammar, and conformance with style and industry standards. Proofed marketing brochures, flyers, ads and more on a weekly basis; proofread the work of others. Type 70 words per minute.

MAINTAIN OFFICE RECORDS AND FILING SYSTEMS. Created and maintain the client database. Designed and implemented detailed and efficient filing systems and ensure they are up-to-date and properly maintained. Define procedures for record retention and disposal. Ensure protection and security of files and records.

MANAGE SCHEDULES AND KEEP CALENDARS for owner, other agents, and for major real-estate development projects such as office parks and industrial warehouses. Interface with architects, city officials, subcontractors, zoning officials, and more. Travel and work with contacts in Houston, Dallas, Baton Rouge, and New Orleans. Schedule meetings, negotiate time commitments, and set appointments. Monitor action and suspense dates.

Assist with BUDGET MANAGEMENT and perform SUPPLY PROCUREMENT and office equipment contracts and maintenance. Review and approve supply requisitions, maintain and replenish stock, and forecast needed supplies. Initiate online ordering, verify receipt of supply, coordinate payment, and track inventory.

Prepare LEAVE AND TIME AND ATTENDANCE RECORDS; complete time sheets. Fill out personnel forms as necessary using electronic format.

COORDINATE AND BOOK TRAVEL ARRANGEMENTS. Gather post-trip expense information for bookkeeper.

## Writing the Impossible KSA

Every now and then you may come across a KSA in a vacancy announcement that you feel you just can not write. You are a great fit for the job, but there is one KSA that just stumps you. You have no experience in that area, or perhaps you have never even heard of the program, system, or regulation. Before you give up, consider this.

You can write a truthful, on-target, and effective KSA for the stumper. How? By looking to other areas of your life experience for examples, drawing parallels to what you do know or performing your own research to learn about that KSA. Obviously, you do not want to lie in your answer. You can not manufacture knowledge, skills, and abilities that you do not have. But telling the reviewer what you know and how you know it can fulfill the KSA and keep you on track as an excellent candidate.

### Quote

"After our discussion, I realized that many of the responses [where] I rated myself lower would be at the expert level since people have come to me for assistance on these items. Even when the question refers to very specific reports or unit procedures, there is usually a private industry parallel for it that I have experienced. I do understand that if I respond at an expert level, I need to make sure these are clearly identifiable in my resume to validate my responses."
--*John Naperkoski*

## Knowledge KSA from Life Experience

In this KSA example, the applicant had personal experience from interactions that were not part of her work experience. This is a valid experience for the KSA factor and counts toward the qualifications for the job. While she may not score as high as someone with direct work experience in this area, she will earn points for her explanation, and along with her other strong KSAs, she has a good shot at the job.

**CASE NAME:** HELEN STEIN
**PRIOR POSITION:** IT Specialist
**TARGET FEDERAL JOB:** Centers for Medicare & Medicaid Services, Health Insurance Specialist, GS-0107-12

**KSA Factor:** Knowledge of needs and preferences of people who are elderly or have a chronic illness or disability.

**Response:**
Much of my knowledge of the needs and preferences of people who are elderly or have a chronic illness or disability is the result of personal experiences. As the primary caregiver for my blind, severely disabled elderly sister for the past ten years, I have personal, firsthand knowledge of the needs and preferences of people with chronic illness and disability. And while "book knowledge" is valuable as a facts resource, there is no better teacher than living and caring for a disabled loved-one 24/7, 365 days a year.

Experiencing firsthand the responsibilities of caring for a disabled relative has not only provided me with a knowledge of their needs and preferences, but it has also given me a thorough understanding of what a family experiences when negotiating the maze of health care services. As a result of my experiences, I am very familiar with the insurance and Medicare/Medicaid services that are available to individuals with special needs, as well as those that are not.

I have helped my sister secure coverage under the Medicare and Medicaid programs. I have a thorough knowledge and understanding of the eligibility requirements, coverage for Part A and Part B, and premium payments, as well as the HMO and Private Fee for Service Plans. I coordinate all of her health care and her personal care.

My first-hand knowledge of the needs and preferences of those with chronic illnesses or disability, coupled with previous career experience in the health insurance industry, have provided me with the knowledge base to analyze and understand new information quickly and easily. Whenever I encounter something I do not know, I research materials and resources available or find someone who can share their knowledge so that I can find the best solution to the problem. I am never afraid to ask for guidance, because that is often the best way to gain a better understanding of a subject and learn new information.

### Knowledge KSA from a Parallel Knowledge

Describing how you did what was asked is a great way to show your competence. In this example, an attorney practiced land use and environmental law in Florida, but the issues were different in Colorado, where he was applying. He demonstrated his skills and knowledge with examples from his experience and stated his familiarity with the specific laws in the KSA.

**CASE NAME:** LIONEL TIMMONS
**PRIOR POSITION:** Private Practice Attorney (Solo Practitioner)
**TARGET FEDERAL JOB:** Department of the Interior, Attorney-Advisor and General Attorney, GS-905-14/15

**KSA Factor:** Experience with resource laws administered by the Department, e.g. National Environmental Policy Act, the Mineral Leasing Act Federal Land Policy and Management Act and Endangered Species Act. Provide examples of the issues you have reviewed for legal sufficiency and compliance with applicable case law and/or regulations and the outcome, if applicable.

**Response:**

A specialty throughout my legal career has been in governmental law with an emphasis on land use law and development. In that capacity I have represented numerous governmental entities including St. Johns County, Florida; the Supervisor of Elections, various cities (conflict cases), and numerous fire and water districts. In so doing, I have reviewed and approved a myriad of documents (contracts, leases, memorandums, etc.) for legal form and sufficiency as a prerequisite to a public official's signature.

CONTEXT: I have represented many people before the government who were either opposed or in favor of a land use decision. Invariably this involved working with highly trained professionals such as architects, engineers, planners, environmentalists, and the like. Many of the environmental issues at hand involved surface water management, exotics, wildlife habitats, endangered species, loss of wetlands, and the mining of phosphate minerals. In Florida where I practiced, issues were governed by state resource and land management laws, protected wetlands, and endangered species, among other resources. For example, if a development had an area wherein there lived endangered species such as a gopher tortoise nest, this had to be preserved. Additionally, if a wetland was permitted to be destroyed then at least twice as much wetland or more had to be preserved. These were the environmental issues in my neck of the woods.

CHALLENGE: In one particular case, the government was exacting land to be used for a frontage road from a small church. ACTIONS: My client, the church, merely wanted to build a small school addition to its church and it happened to be in front of an arterial road. The government denied the permit unless they provided a frontage road to alleviate traffic.

We went through the administrative appeals process and simultaneously sued, claiming that the exaction violated the due process and eminent domain clauses of the constitution. RESULTS: In this reported case, the appellate court held that the government could not use the permitting process as a means of "land banking". The outcome caused not only the small church to proceed, but caused the return of numerous lands "banked" by the government.

I am familiar with the resource laws administered by the Department of the Interior such as the National Environmental Policy Act, the Mineral Leasing Act, the Federal Land Policy and Management Act, and the Endangered Species Act. I am knowledgeable of the issues to which these are applied such as endangered species (e.g. osprey and eagle nests, gopher tortoise, and manatee habitats, et al in Florida), environmental habitats (e.g. wetlands, cypress sloughs, et al in Florida), and various solutions, such as conservation easements within the development or purchase of multiple acres per acre of wetlands outside of the development to be deeded to the government. I know how to use my legal acumen to review and analyze issues against these laws and draw conclusions for legal opinion and advice.

### Knowledge KSA from Education

Describing your relevant coursework and featuring accomplishments, awards, and good performance in an academic environment are valid experiences from which to draw for a knowledge KSA. In this case, there is not one CCAR example to describe; therefore a list of her experiences that illustrates what she achieved is given instead.

**CASE NAME:** MONICA CARLTON
**PAST POSITION:** Masters Student and Library Intern
**TARGET POSITION:** Library of Congress, Library Technician, GS 7/8

**KSA Factor:** Knowledge of the history and literature of music.

**Response:**

I have a stellar educational background in the history and literature of music. I graduated magna cum laude from Ministry College in 20xx with a Bachelor of Arts degree, majoring in Music. The music program at Ministry College is history and literature based. To further develop my knowledge of music as well as compliment this degree, I completed the Joint-Degree Program in Music Librarianship at American Christian University in 20xx. As such, I received both a Master of Science in Library Science and a Master of Arts in Musicology.

As a graduate student, I completed 57 credits in the joint-degree graduate program in a period of 23 months, essentially completing a three-year program in two years. Due to my command of the French language, I passed the language requirement before I began my graduate studies. Furthermore, I passed the Library Science and Musicology comprehensive exams the first time I took them. The graduate courses demanded thorough analysis of musical sources and a wide knowledge of music literature. My coursework included Renaissance, Romantic, and 20th-century music, including a seminar on song cycles. All of these courses were based on the history and literature of music. Throughout my program I developed a passion for learning about the role woman composers play in music history and I elected to focus my research on women composers in all of the aforementioned courses.

While studying Music at Ministry College, I took courses in music history ranging from Medieval music to music of the 20th century. I also took a specialized course in Rhythm-and-Blues, as well as a seminar in World music. I gained practical knowledge while singing with the Ministry College Chorale for four years. The repertoire included challenging works by classical composers which reinforced my study of music history and literature.
I also sang with the Collegium Musicum, an ensemble dedicated to the interpretation and performance of early music. Additionally, I studied both solo voice (specializing in classical art songs, particularly those by women composers) and classical piano with private teachers.

I continue to learn about the history and literature of music. I attend the weekly presentations offered by American Christian University's Musicology Colloquium in order to stay connected to current musicological research. I have regularly attended local and national meetings of the American Musicological Society and the Music Library Association. These professional organizations and their meetings offer not only stimulating presentations and debates about current musicological research, but they provide an opportunity to network with researchers.

As a result of the attention I pay to my studies and the growth and development of my career, I have an excellent understanding of music history, as well as an exceptional ability to research and use information resources. I was awarded the Mollie Seltzer Yett Prize for Excellence in Music Academics in recognition of my knowledge and abilities. As a result of my interest in women composers at American Christian University, I developed a research paper on the vocal music of Clara Schumann, the wife of Robert Schumann and a composer in her own right. The research paper was selected from many entries to be presented at the Spring 20xx meeting of the Atlantic Chapter of the Society of Music History, and I received the first place prize of $250.

### Knowledge KSA from Independent Research and Study

When you simply do not have the knowledge being asked for, you can perform independent research, such as Internet research or interviews with experts. A good approach is to explain exactly how and why your knowledge was gained. The following is one example of explaining how knowledge was obtained specifically for the employment application.

> *"I have done extensive research to prepare myself for working for the federal government. I have taken steps to learn more about JCP Printing, Bindery Guideline, and the Code of Federal Regulations. Specifically, I have familiarized myself with the material in the various chapters of the GPO's Title 44 – Public Printing and Documents."*

If you are the best applicant for the position, and you have shown the initiative to learn what you need to know in order to write the impossible KSA, you still have a good chance at landing the job. Just stick close to the question, do your homework, and always, always be truthful.

In the sample below, the applicant's knowledge was gained through personal interaction with a subject matter expert, involvement in a trade association, and through university and other study. Stating what you know and how you know it is a truthful way to show your knowledge and use the keywords of the KSA factor.

**CASE NAME:** TODD GORHAM
**TARGET POSITION:** U.S. Department of Agriculture, Farm Service Agency, County Operations Trainee, GS-5/9

**KSA Factor:** Knowledge of FSA farm programs, practices, and customs.

**Response:**

Over the past five years, I have gained knowledge about the USDA Farm Service Agency by working with Conrad Webb, a second-generation agricultural producer in rural Illinois, and through my work with the Quality Deer Management Association (QDMA).

Working with Conrad, who farms 2,000 acres of corn and beans, I have expanded my knowledge of FSA financial programs, disaster relief, subsidized crop insurance, conservation, commodity loans, and the Conservation Reserve Program. I have spent time with Conrad on his farm soaking up all his knowledge regarding farming and FSA programs.

As a member of QDMA, I have been farming for increased deer habitat in Illinois on two separate parcels of land. I have implemented what I have learned from Conrad into my own plan. I operated large tractors, planters, plows, disks, cultivators, and other field preparation implements. I have planted acres of corn, soybeans, clover, alfalfa, and brassica to increase food sources for deer.

I have developed local co-op's and spoken with fellow sportsmen about effective, economical habitat improvements. I continue to be involved in mentoring local sportsmen on QDMA so they too can increase habitat on their properties.

ADDITIONAL TRAINING: Agricultural Courses; Michigan State University, East Lansing, Michigan; Quality Deer Management Association, Quality Deer Management Association Mid-Michigan Food Plot Days.

## Adapting KSAs

There is no need to reinvent the wheel every time you submit a job application. If you save your KSAs in a word-processing application, you can access and edit them readily each time you prepare a new application. Often, an old KSA can be used again --either verbatim for a similar factor. or adapted to a completely new one. Here is an example of one KSA used three ways. By changing the keywords and the important points of the examples, we can easily put a new slant on an old KSA. The edits between versions are illustrated so you can see how simple this is.

**Case Name:** SAMUEL TARPY
**PRIOR POSITION:** Contract Administrative Assistant, various agencies
**TARGET POSITION:** Correspondence Analyst, Department of the Navy, GS-9

### KSA version 1: Ability to communicate in writing.

My written communication skills are at an expert level as my abilities include presenting complex and technical issues clearly and concisely to diverse audiences of varied levels of understanding.

As a writer for the Correspondent Weekly (20xx – 20xx), a regional political newspaper, I regularly wrote and edited stories on cultural and political topics of local and national interest, and ensured that issues were relevant and meaningful to a wide variety of audiences.

As an Assistant Multimedia Producer in the Corporate Headquarters of Campus Ministries International (date - date), I developed and wrote news stories, audio and video scripts, and talking points in English for a monthly, international satellite broadcast targeting 120 different nations, sometimes incorporating the organization's positions on various topics. I also served as a liaison for fellow staff members in the U.S. and overseas for ongoing audio and video multimedia projects, communicating with them in writing to convey important program information.

In this same role of Assistant Multimedia Producer with a wide international scope, I often utilized my multicultural knowledge to communicate with and understand the nuances of many different audience countries. I corresponded with contacts in many different areas of the world, including developing nations in Africa, Asia, and Latin America, to uncover news stories concerning political, social, and economic issues. I gathered, extracted, verified, and consolidated information through synthesizing stories and issues with various aspects and projects of the ministry.

## 7

## KSA version 2: Ability to proofread and ensure correct grammar, spelling, and punctuation.

My written communication skills are at an expert level. ~~as my abilities.~~ I have had significant experience presenting complex and technical issues clearly and concisely to diverse audiences, each time ensuring correct grammar, spelling, and punctuation in order to maintain correct usage of language. ~~of varied levels of understanding.~~

As a writer for the Correspondent Weekly (date – date), a regional political newspaper, I regularly wrote and edited stories on cultural and political topics of local and national interest. Having responsibility for my work and ~~and ensured that issues were relevant and meaningful to a wide variety of audiences.~~ ensuring that deadlines were met without undue problems, I proofread my stories and ensured adherence to style and correctness, including punctuation and spelling.

As an Assistant Multimedia Producer in the Corporate Headquarters of Campus Ministries International (date - date), I developed and wrote news stories, audio and video scripts, and talking points in English for a monthly, international satellite broadcast targeting 120 different nations. Correct grammar, spelling, and punctuation were imperative to ensure flawless broadcasts and accurate information. I reviewed the work to ensure that all were correct before submitting stories for production. Because I ~~sometimes incorporating the organization's positions on various topics. I also~~ served as a liaison for fellow staff members in the U.S. and overseas for ongoing audio and video multimedia projects, ~~communicating with them in writing to convey important program information~~. I frequently proofread the work of others as well.

In this same role of Assistant Multimedia Producer with a wide international scope, I often utilized my multicultural knowledge to communicate with and to understand the nuances of many different audience countries. I corresponded with contacts in many different areas of the world, including developing nations in Africa, Asia and Latin America, to uncover news stories concerning political, social and economic issues. I gathered, extracted, verified and consolidated information through synthesizing stories and issues with various aspects and projects of the ministry. My excellent command of English grammar and punctuation ensured that the original was accurate for any needed translation.

**KSA version 3: Ability to utilize office automation software.**

In honing my written and communication skills ~~are at an~~ at their current expert level, ~~as my abilities include presenting complex and technical issues clearly and concisely to diverse audiences of varied levels of understanding.~~ I applied my expertise using automated word processing and presentation software such as Microsoft Word and PowerPoint. I have also mastered the use of e-mail and other information transfer systems including Microsoft Outlook, Web mail, and online document sharing programs.

As a writer for the Correspondent Weekly (date – date), a regional political newspaper, I used Microsoft Word to ~~regularly wrote and edited~~ write and edit stories on cultural and political topics of local and national interest and ensured that issues were relevant and meaningful to a wide variety of audiences. I used my organization's web-based email to transmit stories to the editor and used an online document sharing utility to make document edits with other team members in real time.

As an Assistant Multimedia Producer in the Corporate Headquarters of Campus Ministries International (date - date), I developed and wrote news stories, audio and video scripts, and talking points ~~in English for a monthly, international satellite broadcast targeting 120 different nations, sometimes incorporating the organization's positions on various topics.~~ using various software such as Microsoft Word and PowerPoint to arrange copy. I also used Microsoft Outlook to communicate with ~~I also served as a liaison for~~ fellow staff members in the U.S. and overseas ~~for~~ regarding ongoing audio and video multimedia projects. ~~, communicating with them in writing to convey important program information~~.

In this same role of Assistant Multimedia Producer with a wide international scope, I often utilized my multicultural knowledge to communicate with and to understand the nuances of many different audience countries. I corresponded with contacts in many different areas of the world, including developing nations in Africa, Asia and Latin America, to uncover news stories concerning political, social and economic issues. I used online research tools via the Internet to gather~~ed,~~ extract~~ed,~~ verify ~~ied~~ and consolidate~~d~~ information ~~through~~ by synthesizing stories and issues with various aspects and projects of the ministry.

## Getting Ideas from Google.com

For any KSA, but especially when tackling ones where your available content is challenged, use the Internet to research ideas. Most agencies publish documents and manuals that will give you access to information about programs, regulations, and other critical information that can really show intelligent insight in your writing. These are some ideas of things to look at:

1. Agency Mission – Knowing what is important to the agency can help you know which of your experiences will be a good match for the KSA examples. It also shows that you are in the know about the issues and can help solve the problems.
2. Regulations, laws, and orders pertaining to the work – When asked about your Knowledge of the Federal Acquisition Regulations or Title VII of the Civil Rights Act, you can state that you have read it and understand what it means, which is better than stating you do not have experience with it.
3. Relevant current events – Illustrating your knowledge of the events in Iraq could demonstrate how you will be better-equipped than other candidates to work as a Logistics Specialist for agencies serving the war zone.

## Getting Ideas from the Vacancy Announcement

A careful reading of the vacancy announcement, particularly the sections that describe the job responsibilities/duties and qualifications/evaluation methods (including the knowledge, skills, and abilities themselves) may suggest appropriate KSA keywords and examples and trigger relevant memories. As you read the job duties or qualifications from your vacancy announcement, jot down any experiences and training you have had that would specifically qualify you for the job described.

This example is from a vacancy announcement for a GS-9 Paralegal Specialist with the U.S. Trustee Program. As you read the description of job duties, try to identify the many different areas of knowledge, skill, or ability an applicant might have in his/her background that speak directly to the job duties listed:

---

**Major Duties**

The incumbent is responsible for performing a variety of duties that require the application of legal knowledge and financial analysis skills to the examination and processing of cases initiated under the U.S. Bankruptcy Code and are directly in support of the United States Trustee. This includes reviewing chapter 7 or 11 bankruptcy petitions and schedules for legal and procedural compliance with the Bankruptcy Code, related state statutes, etc. In instances of debtor noncompliance with legal requirements, makes recommendations regarding U.S. Trustee action and drafts motions commensurate with recommendations; reviews applications for retention of professionals ensuring qualifications and their necessity; where necessary, drafts motions regarding applications for payment of professionals fees and expenses. Conducts analysis of disclosure statements for legal sufficiency and determines financial condition of debtor and advises attorney or analyst; analyzes facts and technical questions on case administration received by phone or correspondence, answering those that have been settled by interpretations of applicable legal provisions and researching those which present legal issues. As necessary, performs research to assist attorneys and drafts pleadings. Performs thorough audits of trustee final reports to assure all assets have been properly liquidated and accounted for. Participates in monitoring and reviewing the performance of trustees.

---

Six KSAs were required to apply for this position. The following are keyword and top skill ideas right out of the vacancy that can be woven into your descriptions of your accomplishments:

SELECTIVE PLACEMENT FACTOR:
**At least six months bankruptcy experience which exhibits knowledge of bankruptcy regulations and procedures. Education cannot be substituted for the six months bankruptcy experience requirement.** Examination and processing of cases initiated under the U.S. Bankruptcy Code; reviewing chapter 7 or 11 bankruptcy petitions and schedules for legal and procedural compliance with the Bankruptcy Code, related state statutes.

QUALITY RANKING FACTORS
1) **Knowledge and skill in fact finding, analysis, and communication including ability to correspond and elicit information from debtors, creditors, and their counsel.** Performs research to assist attorneys; analyzes facts and technical questions on case administration.

2) **Skill in the use and application of established instructions, procedures, policies or precedents of the Bankruptcy Code and rules of procedures, local rules of practice, applicable case law and other reference material.** Examination and processing of cases initiated under the U.S. Bankruptcy Code; reviewing chapter 7 or 11 bankruptcy petitions and schedules for legal and procedural compliance with the Bankruptcy Code, related state statutes, etc; Participates in monitoring and reviewing the performance of trustees.

3) **Skill in business arithmetic and familiarity with basic accounting principles.** Application of legal knowledge and financial analysis skills; performs thorough audits of trustee final reports to assure all assets have been properly liquidated and accounted for; determines financial condition of debtor; conducts analysis of disclosure statements for legal sufficiency and determines financial condition of debtor and advises attorney or analyst.

4) **Knowledge of automated office systems.** Performs research to assist attorneys.

5) **Ability to communicate orally and in writing.** Makes recommendations regarding U.S. Trustee action and drafts motions commensurate with recommendations; drafts motions regarding applications for payment of professional fees and expenses.

## How Will My KSA Narratives Be Graded?

Your KSAs will be graded by using a "rating and ranking" system called a crediting plan. Your statements can range from Superior to Not Acceptable or may be assigned a numerical score. There is no rule of thumb here, because rating systems vary from one job opening to another and, generally, from one agency to the next. You probably will not know which of the KSAs in the set will be the ones hiring managers consider to be the most important, and you will want to do the best job possible on all of your KSAs.

KSA crediting plans can include points given for different competency-based benchmarks, with more complex experience rating higher than less complex experience. Sometimes the HR specialist may have certain points to assign for the use of particular keywords and certainly the keywords help them to identify how your examples match the benchmark. You will want to explain the most complex level of performance you have ascertained in your experience that demonstrates your competence, and also tell that story using keywords and phrases from the vacancy announcement. The following is a real crediting plan for an Interpersonal Skills KSA.

### Sample: KSA Crediting Plan and Rating Scale, Interpersonal Skills

| Benchmark Level | Level Definition | Level Example |
|---|---|---|
| 5 | Establishes and maintains ongoing working relationships with management, other employees, international or external stakeholders, or customers. Remains courteous when discussing information or eliciting highly sensitive or controversial information from people who are reluctant to give it. Effectively handles situations involving a high degree of tension or discomfort involving people who are demonstrating a high degree of hostility or distress. | Presents controversial findings tactfully to irate organization senior management officials regarding shortcomings of a newly installed computer system, software programs, and associated equipment. |
| 4 | | Mediates disputes concerning system design/architecture, the nature and capacity of data management systems, system resources allocations, or other equally controversial/sensitive matters. |
| 3 | Cooperates and works well with management, other employees, or customers on short-term assignments. Remains courteous when discussing information or eliciting moderately sensitive or controversial information from people who are hesitant to give it. Effectively handles situations involving a moderate degree of tension or discomfort involving people who are demonstrating a moderate degree of hostility or distress. | Courteously and tactfully delivers effective instruction to frustrated customers.<br><br>Provides technical advice to customers and the public on various types of IT such as communication or security systems, data mgmt procedures or analysis, software engineering, or web development. |
| 2 | | Familiarizes new employees with administrative procedures and office systems. |
| 1 | Cooperates and works well with management, other employees, or customers during brief interactions. Remains courteous when discussing information or eliciting non-sensitive or non-controversial information from people who are willing to give it. Effectively handles situations involving little or no tension, discomfort, hostility, or distress. | Response courteously to customers' general inquiries.<br><br>Greets and assists visitors attending a meeting within own organization. |

## Quote

**"** I found a perfect job as a Dining Room Manager at Walter Reed Army Medical Center in Washington, DC on the Army CPOL website. I updated my resume in USAJOBS to add keywords from the announcement. Later, I checked my status on the CPOL site and found that I actually didn't even apply for the job. I should have updated my Army CPOL Resume Builder instead. That was disappointing. Next time, I will concentrate on updating the right resume builder for the right job. **"**

*Sous Chef in Bethesda, MD*

## Strategy Tip

Be sure to update the correct resume builder for the correct announcement. Read the directions carefully in the how to apply section to submit your resume to the right builder.

# STEP EIGHT
## Apply for Jobs

You are ready to start applying for jobs! New federal jobseekers are usually confused when trying to understand the multiple job application systems the government uses. About half of all automated federal applications are processed using question-driven automated systems. Furthermore, despite the federal government's emphasis on automation, some agencies are still using paper applications rather than technology to process job applications. The good news is that with one good resume, and by familiarizing yourself with the different systems, you can adapt your materials to apply for many jobs quickly and relatively easily. This chapter will help you discern what application processes and selection methods the agency is using and how to format your resume and other materials for the application, including online builders.

## Overview

## How Many Applications Will I Need To Submit?

There are about 80,000 to 130,000 open positions posted on USAJOBS every day. An average federal applicant can apply to 20 to 100 positions over a period of four to six months (or years). If your resume is targeted toward a particular federal job title and a correct grade or salary level, you could apply to ten jobs and get referred for all of them. Some federal job applicants could apply to 200 jobs and have no or few referrals to supervisors. The problems can be in any of the following: resume focus, keywords, resume format, your qualifications, your selection of the announcements, your answers in the questionnaire, the profile, how to apply errors, or other application errors.

## Strategy Tip:
When applying for federal jobs, there are two important things to remember:
1) follow the directions on the vacancy announcement, and 2) know the deadline.

## Who Can Apply for Federal Jobs

Every vacancy announcement will be clear about who can apply. Knowing whether you fit the bill and answering the eligibility questions correctly will impact whether you can apply online for the job.

The status question displayed below must be answered on the www.usajobs.gov search screen before you can look at job announcements. This is a good qualifying question. You will have to click YES or NO before the site will search for jobs for you. If you click NO, then the site will automatically return with jobs that are open to anyone. If you do have status, you will have many more jobs to choose from. Approximately 60% of all federal jobs are open to anyone. You could have status if you are a veteran, an outstanding scholar (3.5 GPA overall or in your major), disabled, married to a military person, have worked for the government before, or been laid off by the government.

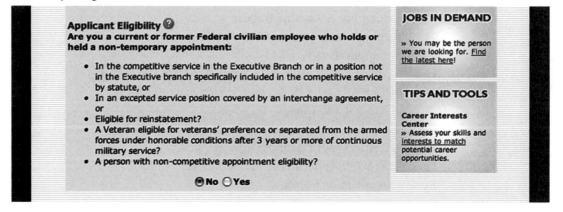

## Read the "How To Apply" Instructions

To apply for a federal position, read the instructions on the "how to apply" tab of the announcement on USAJOBS or other agency website. Since each agency or department of the federal government is a separate entity, each agency may have a slightly different application requirement to apply for positions. The "how to apply" page is critical to the success of your federal job campaign. On that page you will find out what will be required to actually apply for the position.

Beware and be calm: The instructions are slightly unique on most of the announcements. This is a TEST to see if you can FOLLOW DIRECTIONS. Read this page and the QUALI-FICATIONS PAGE CAREFULLY to get all of the instructions. Here are some of the typical combinations of instructions you will find:

✪ Submit your resume to USAJOBS.gov, complete the Questionnaire on applicationmanager. org, and upload PDFs or files of transcripts, DD-214, or other documents online.

✪ Submit your resume to USAJOBS.gov, complete the Questionnaire on applicationmanager.org, and fax your transcripts, DD-214, or other documents.

✪ Submit your resume to USAJOBS.gov, complete the Quickhire Questionnaire, and submit faxes.

✪ Submit your resume to USAJOBS.gov and write narrative KSAs on separate sheets of paper. Fax or copy the KSAs into Additional Information in the USAJOBS builder.

✪ Submit your resume to CPOL.army.mil; either write KSAs separately, or cover the KSAs in the resume. Complete the Self-Nomination form to actually apply for the position.

✪ Answer the questionnaire on applicationmanager.org, submit your resume into USAStaffing online application, and upload or browse to submit your resume and other documents.

✪ DO NOT SUBMIT YOUR RESUME TO USAJOBS. Go to avuecentral.com to create your resume in the builder at that site. Complete the questionnaire at avuecentral.com. Upload other documents into avuecentral.com

✪ Submit your resume into CHART, the U.S. Navy and USMC resume builder and application website. Set up a profile and then complete the Self-Nomination form.

Each resume builder has its own Applicant Profile, so you should complete a Profile for all of the builders: USAJOBS, applicationmanager.org, CPOL, Avue, CHART, WHS, and/or agency-specific websites that are of interest to you.

## Strategy Tip:
Be sure to check off Permanent, Term, and Temp for all builders, so you will be considered for all kinds of positions.

## Package What They Want

Paper Packages: The appearance of your application is important. If you are applying via a paper package, use good quality bond paper. White is customary, but you may use ivory colored paper. Your cover letter, resume, and KSAs should be separate documents. Transcripts can be photocopies and do not need to be official copies. Package your documents in a large envelope so that they do not have to be folded. Do not stable pages together. For paper applications, you may be asked to submit multiple copies. Always comply with the instructions.

Online Applications: For electronic applications, complete all of the pages and questions. Make sure you finish the submission. Sometimes there are at least three steps to applying: Profile/Registration; Resume Builder or Resume Submission; Questions or Essays. Be sure you are not exceeding the maximum number of characters allowed in a field. There is very little formatting that you can do within text fields, but make entries as easy to read as possible.

Combination Online and Fax: If you are asked to apply online, and then fax additional information, make sure you include your Social Security Number (last four digits), name, and announcement number on each page submitted by fax. The agency system will often have a special fax cover sheet that you must print out and submit instead of your own cover sheet. It will contain a bar code that the HR representative will use to match it to the rest of your application.

*SF-171 or OF-612 — Employment Forms*
Very few agencies are still requesting the SF-171 and OF-612 applications, as well as KSAs from candidates. If the list includes a resume, please use the federal resume instead of the form because of the flexibility of the information. Follow their directions on the announcement.

## What to Expect in Various Builders

Understanding what application format the agency is using for their selection process is paramount to successfully submitting your application. Failure to follow the instructions correctly could disqualify your application. The table on the following pages shows you some of the methods used by these agencies. Many agencies use a standard format across the board; however, every agency is different and sometimes you will see variations within an agency, so be sure to read the announcement very carefully. Remember that the number of characters allowed includes spaces and punctuation.

### Strategy Tip:
Keep a log of your passwords and login information for each system. For some agencies, you cannot reset a lost password automatically and may not be able to get the assistance you need before your vacancy deadline.

## Resume Builder Chart

| Name of Agency | Agency Jobs Website | Resume Builder System | Questionnaire System | Job Blocks/ Character Limit | Features |
|---|---|---|---|---|---|
| USAJOBS / OPM | www.usajobs.gov | USAJOBS | USAJOBS | No limit/3000 | Add'l Info, 22,000 char |
| Agriculture | www.usda.gov/da/employ/director.htm | USAJOBS | | No limit/3,000 | Add'l Info, 22,000 char |
| Air Force | www.usajobs.gov | USAJOBS | Application Manager | No limit/3,000 | |
| Army | www.cpol.army.mil | CPOL | N/A | 12,000 total | One field for work exp. |
| AVUE CENTRAL | www.avuecentral.com | AVUE | AVUE | No limit/4,000 | PDs available |
| Bureau of Land Management | www.blm.gov/jobs | USAJOBS | Quickhire | No limit | |
| Central Intelligence Agency | https://www.cia.gov/careers/index.html | CIA Builder | CIA | 1,000 | Short |
| Commerce | www.commerce.gov/JobsCareerOpportunities/index.htm | USAJOBS | Quickhire | No limit/3,000 | |
| Defense Contract Management Agency | www.dcma.mil/careers.htm | CPOL | CPOL Builder | 12,000 total | Paste your work |
| Defense Finance & Accounting Office | www.dfas.mil/careers/post/resumebuilderinfo.html | DFAS Resume Builder | DFAS | No limit/No limit | |
| Defense Logistics Agency | www.hr.dla.mil/prospective | USAJOBS | Application Manager | No limit/No limit | |
| Education | www.ed.gov/about/jobs/open/edhires/index.html | USAJOBS | Quickhire | 3,000 characters | Paste a resume, 16,000 char total |
| Energy | www.energy.gov/careers@energy.htm | USAJOBS or Paper | Quickhire | No limit/3,000 or Paper (N/A) | Different Hiring Processes - Quickhire |
| Environmental Protection Agency | www.epa.gov/ezhire | USAJOBS | EZ Hire | No limit/3,000 | |
| FAA | https://jobs.faa.gov/asap | ASAP | ASAP | 4,000 | 15 minute limit |
| FBI | www.fbijobs.gov | FBIJOBS | Quickhire | No limit/No limit | Paste a resume, 16,000 char total |
| Forest Service | www.fs.fed.us/fsjobs/openings.html | AVUE | AVUE | No limit/4,000 | PDs available |
| Government Accountability Office | www.gao.gov/jobopp.htm | USAJOBS | Quickhire | No limit/3,000 | Paste a resume, 16,000 char total |
| General Services Administration | www.gsa.gov | GSA Jobs | Quickhire | No limit | Paste a resume, 16,000 char total |
| Health & Human Services | www.hhs.gov/careers | HHS Careers/ USAJOBS | Quickhire | No limit | Paste a resume, 16,000 char total |
| HHS National Institutes of Health | www.training.nih.gov/careers/careercenter | NIH/HHS Careers / USAJOBS | Quickhire | No limit | Paste a resume, 16,000 char total |
| Homeland Security | www.dhs.gov/xabout/careers | USAJOBS | Various | No limit/3,000 | Add'l Info, 22,000 char |
| Citizenship & Immigration Services | www.uscis.gov/portal/site/uscis | USAJOBS | Application Manager | No limit/3,000 | Add'l Info, 22,000 char |

| Name of Agency | Agency Jobs Website | Resume Builder System | Questionnaire System | Job Blocks/ Character Limit | Features |
|---|---|---|---|---|---|
| Customs & Border Protection | www.cbp.gov/xp/cgov/careers | USAJOBS | Application Manager | No limit/3,000 | Add'l Info, 22,000 char |
| FEMA | www.fema.gov/career | USAJOBS | Application Manager | No limit/3,000 | |
| Housing & Urban Development | jobsearch.usajobs.opm.gov/a9hudp.asp | USAJOBS/Paper | Application Manager/ paper | No limit/3,000 Paper - no limit | |
| Interior | www.doi.gov/doijobs/jobs.html | USAJOBS | USAJOBS | No limit/3,000 | |
| Justice | www.usdoj.gov | AVUE | AVUE | No limit/4,000 | PDs available |
| Labor | www.dol.gov/dol/jobs.htm | USAJOBS | DOORS | No limit/3,000 | |
| National Aeronautics & Space Administration | www.nasajobs.nasa.gov | USAJOBS | STARS | No limit/3,000 | 6 page resume limit (22,000 characters) |
| National Security Agency | www.nsa.gov/home_html.cfm | NSA Careers | None | | Full text resume |
| Navy | https://chart.donhr.navy.mil | Navy CHART | None | 6/6,000 | |
| Office of Secretary of Defense | https://storm.psd.whs.mil/WHSJobs.html | HRD Resumix | None | no info | Paste a resume |
| Peace Corps | www.avuecentral.com | AVUE | AVUE | No limit/4,000 | PDs available |
| Small Business Administration | www.usajobs.gov | Paper | Paper | No limit | Flexible |
| State Department | careers.state.gov | Various Methods | Paper | No limit | Various application methods, including forms |
| Transportation | careers.dot.gov | USAJOBS/Paper | Quickhire | No limit | Paste a resume, 16,000 char total |
| Transportation Security Agency | www.usajobs.gov | Paper | Paper | No limit | Flexible/paper |
| US Marshals Service | www.avuecentral.com | AVUE | AVUE | No limit/4,000 | PDs available |
| Veterans Affairs | www.va.gov/jobs/Career_Search.asp | USAJOBS/Paper | Paper | No limit/3,000 | Online or paper |
| Washington Headquarters Services | www.whs.mil/HRD | HRD Resumix | N/A | 4 pages + Supp | |

***Disclaimer:*** Research for this spreadsheet was completed on November 15, 2008. Please know that Resume Builders, agency career website addresses, methods of collecting resumes, and other information may change from week to week. We will attempt to stay up-to-date by posting this spreadsheet at www.resume-place.com. Please write builders@resume-place.com for updates that you may have found.

## Tips: Writing For A Resume Builder

1. Read specific instructions for each Resume Builder.

2. If your electronic resume is longer than the Resume Builder character requirements, the extraneous characters could be cut off.

3. Be sure to format your electronic resume to be compatible with the builder. You cannot copy and paste a resume with formatting (bold type, bullets, indentations, etc.) into a builder. The resume will possibly be unreadable and could be rejected.

4. Create your resume in a word processing software in order to check for spelling and grammar mistakes. This is also a helpful way to store your documents from which you can cut and paste, as builders time out. All content should be composed in a word processing software, saved there, and then transferred over. Paste or type your information into each block, as you want it to appear on the resume. Many of the builders allow hard returns to leave blank lines between paragraphs.

5. Be aware that characters like bullets and formatting like bold or italics are usually not allowed. In some cases, this formatting can turn to symbols or gibberish. When you need bullets, use a "+" or a "-". Those characters are typically compatible.

6. Count characters in your job blocks and other categories based on the Resume Builder instructions (Word Count from the Tools menu in Microsoft Word is helpful, or cut and paste it into the actual Resume Builder to get the most accurate count). Make sure you count the spaces.

7. Periodically save your resume as you enter it into the builder to avoid losing your information in the event you get timed out.

## Tips: Keeping Character Count Under Control

1. Take advantage of acronyms wherever possible to save space. Invent your own acronyms for long phrases that pop up frequently. (Example: I drafted 17 successful Motions for Summary Judgment ("MSJ") in one month.)

2. Use one space between sentences instead of two.

3. Cut transitional or introductory words that you do not need, like the word "that" used earlier in this sentence.

4. Use short words like "use," instead of long ones like "utilize." Make this a habit.

5. In a narrative, such as a KSA, cut out the irrelevant. Unless you really need to know a detail to understand the accomplishment, cut it. Make it a habit to consider the usefulness of every word you use. If it can be cut, and the meaning is still clear, cut it.

## Avoiding Application Pitfalls

✪ If the position is an Army position, you MUST apply with your resume in the CPOL builder.

✪ If the position is a Navy position, you MUST apply with your resume in the CHART builder.

✪ If the position is managed and recruited by Avue Central, you must submit and apply directly to Avue Central.

✪ If the position is managed by OPM, and they are using USAJOBS and Application Manager, then you must hit SUBMIT in the system to actually apply for a position.

✪ If the announcement states that you MUST submit additional documents into the system, you MUST do that.

✪ If the announcement states that you must use THEIR FAX Cover, then you MUST do that.

✪ If you submit your user name and password to USAJOBS incorrectly three times, you will be locked out. You can set up another user name and password on the spot – you do NOT have to write to HELP.

✪ You can only have one resume in the Army, Navy, and Washington Headquarter Services (WHS) builders at one time. You will have to change keywords carefully to submit resumes for announcements with close dates.

✪ USAJOBS builder allows you to select Confidential. Do not select Confidential or the supervisor will not be able to see your past employers.

✪ USAJOBS is not viewable by anyone except human resources specialists for the government and agency managers. Most agency managers do not access USAJOBS resumes.

✪ The USAJOBS resumes are searchable by managers, but at the present time, the searchable system is not being used to search for candidates throughout the entire database. Only resumes submitted and positions APPLIED FOR will be accessed.

✪ You MUST hit the SUBMIT, APPLY, or SEND buttons in the various builders. Otherwise, you will not have applied to any job.

✪ The USAJOBS builder gives you the SAVE option at the bottom of the page ONLY. If you GO BACK with content on that page that is not saved, it will be lost.

✪ The USAJOBS builder gives you 3,000 characters (including spaces) for each job. If your current job is longer than 3,000 characters, you can continue that description in the 2nd job block.

## How to Apply: USAJOBS

USAJOBS allows a job seeker to have up to five versions of the resume in the database at once. This makes focusing your resume on a particular job series very easy. You can update your resumes in USAjobs as often as you like. It is a rigid format in that if you wanted to list education before experience, or put your work experience out of chronological order, you would not be able to do that.

Putting a resume in USAJOBS does not mean that you have applied to a job; you are simply storing your resume in the database for later use. You must click "APPLY ONLINE" to start an actual application.

For some announcements, the USAJOBS resume, along with the supplemental data section, is the whole application. For others, the USAJOBS resume is used in tandem with another online system or faxed documents. Follow each step in sequence until you receive a confirmation that your application was sent.

TIP: Put your resume into the USAJOBS online database BEFORE starting an application.

### Step by step: USAJOBS resume and application

1.  Create a USAJOBS account and fill in your profile information.

2.  Use the resume builder in "MY USAJOBS" to create your federal resume. There are many sections to fill in besides work experience and education. Provide as much information as you can that will show your qualifications for the job. You can have up to five different versions in the system at once.

3.  Find your announcement and determine whether you can apply by checking the "who can apply" section.

4.  After your resume is in the system, click "APPLY ONLINE" to start the application process.

5.  USAJOBS will ask you which version of your resume you want to use for that particular application. Select the one targeted for that job.

6.  If the application requires you to complete information on an additional website, your browser will take you there.

7.  Follow all steps through final submission.

## USAJOBS Resume Builder – Five Resumes

*Different set of keywords? Create different resumes in USAJOBS.* You can store up to five different resumes on USAJOBS. If you analyze your keywords for more than one job series, you might want to have different resume versions naming the resume with that job title. The sample below is for the author of this book. She would have different keywords for Writer-Editor, Program and Management Analyst, and Instructional Design Specialist.

---

Welcome back, KATHRYN K TROUTMAN!


Resume Listings and Activity

Resume 1: Writer-Editor, GS-12                     Status: Not Searchable
View | Edit | Delete                               Make Searchable
Format: USAJOBS Resume


Resume 2: Program and Management Analyst, GS-12     Status: Not Searchable
View | Edit | Delete                               Make Searchable
Format: USAJOBS Resume


Resume 3: Instructional Design Specialist, GS-12    Status: Not Searchable
View | Edit | Delete                               Make Searchable
Format: USAJOBS Resume
You have created 3 of 5 possible resumes.

---

## How to Apply: USA Staffing Application Manager

This automated system is frequently used in conjunction with USAJOBS, where https://applicationmanager.gov is the utility for administering the self-assessment and supplemental data questions. You will have the choice of pulling your resume from the USAJOBS online database, or you can upload your resume file. The upload allows greater flexibility in your resume presentation because you can format it however you like.

### Step by step: Application Manager with USAJOBS Resume Retrieval

1. Create a USAJOBS account and fill in your profile information.

2. Use the resume builder in "MY USAJOBS" to create your federal resume.

3. Find your announcement and click "APPLY ONLINE" to start the application process.

4. USAJOBS will ask you which version of your resume you want to use for that particular application. Select the one targeted for that job.

5. Your browser will then direct you to applicationmanager.org to complete the biographical and eligibility information and start the Assessment Questionnaire. You will see that you must create a separate login for Application Manager.

6. Complete all questions and follow all steps including "UPLOAD DOCUMENTS." You will not upload a resume or KSA documents, however, you may need to upload or fax supplemental documents like transcripts or veterans forms.

7. Follow all steps through "SUBMIT MY ANSWERS," or your application will not be submitted.

### Step by step: Application Manager with Resume Upload

1. Go to https://applicationmanager.org and create your login and Profile.

2. Enter the job announcement number or USAJOBS control number (found in the USAJOBS vacancy announcement) to retrieve your target vacancy application.

3. Start the application and complete the biographical and eligibility information as well as the Assessment Questionnaire.

4. Upload and/or fax your resume and other pertinent application documents as well as other information that they might request—last evaluation, DD-214 (veterans), and transcripts, for example.

5. Follow all steps through "SUBMIT MY ANSWERS," or your application will not be submitted.

## How to Apply: AvueCentral.com

This commercial system is used by more than 12 agencies, including the U.S. Forest Service and U.S. Coast Guard. This application is a complex online form with questions and a profile. You submit your resume one time, and then apply for as many positions in the database that Avue Central maintains. However, this can only be done for vacancies in agencies using this system.

Most jobs posted on AvueCentral.com are also posted on USAJOBS. That means that you can search for them in USAJOBS, where there is greater search flexibility and ease of use, and then apply to them through AvueCentral.com as instructed. You can go to AvueCentral.com directly; however, it is often easier to access the application by starting in USAJOBS and clicking "APPLY ONLINE."

### Step by step: Avue Central

1. From the USAJOBS vacancy, click "APPLY ONLINE" and your browser will direct you to that particular vacancy in AvueCentral.com or you can go directly to the Avue Central home page and search for the vacancy.

2. Log on or create your Profile in AvueCentral.com. Click "APPLY NOW" to start the application process.

3. On the left side of the screen, you will see a menu for filling in Mandatory information, such as your work history, education, and KSAs. The application will automatically pull your resume information from your Profile, however you also have the option to revise it for the particular application.

4. Each vacancy announcement in Avue Central has "Job Posting Information" that includes the description that you saw posted in USAJOBS as well as the actual Position Description. Use this Information to write your resume content (keywords).

5. Once you have completed every section in Mandatory information, you will click "SEND APPLICATION" to complete the process.

## Tip:

Some online builders and applications have places to indicate your race, national origin, gender, or medical/disability information. This information is NOT required and it will not adversely affect your application if you decline to answer.

## How to Apply: U.S. Navy's CHART or Army's CPOL

Army CPOL and Navy CHART systems are both keyword systems. The Human Resources specialist will search for the best qualified people based on keywords that are found in either the vacancy announcement or other sources (as described in Step 4, Find the Perfect Job Announcement)

*Open Continuously – Inventory Building – Database Building Announcements.* The Navy announcements have very short "duty" descriptions and list multiple job titles in an occupational series. These are databases where HR professionals will search for qualified candidates when positions become available. These are valuable and real announcements. If you are qualified for these positions you should submit your resume to these databases.

The Army announcements have excellent descriptions of duties and specialized experience. You can find a good keyword description in Army announcements.

### Self-Nomination Process

If your resume is already in the database, you can simply "self-nominate" for a special position that interests you. The Navy uses both Open Continuously announcements and special announcements with closing dates. You will not need to resend or re-submit your resume to the particular database. Make sure your resume is in the right database.

### Step by Step: CHART or CPOL

1.  Create a profile in the pertinent system and fill in your biographical and supplemental data information.

2.  Write the correct length resume paying special attention to whether your content fits within the character limitations.

3.  Paste your resume into the online system ahead of the deadline. Sometimes there are special instructions about how far in advance your resume needs to be submitted.

4.  Self-nominate for the job according to the agency's instructions.

5.  The Supplemental Data Sheet is now part of the Builder and you will complete it online. This is very important in that it shows your eligibility for certain jobs based on whether you have status.

# How to Apply: Paper Applications

Agencies that are still using paper applications may allow several options for your application format. The package usually contains the following: Cover letter, federal resume, KSAs, and supplemental information (such as transcripts).

The package is typically mailed, faxed, or hand delivered. You may use the U.S. Postal Service, or other delivery method to transport your package.

Here is a nice clear set of instructions from a vacancy announcement:

> *Your application will consist of three components. The first component consists of your statement addressing how you meet each of the knowledge, skills, or abilities listed for this vacancy. The second component is your resume. The final component of your application consists of other application materials. Examples of these other materials include your college transcripts (if required) and documentation of veteran status (if applicable). Instructions on completing and submitting these items follow.*

We recommend that you use the preferred paper format, a federal resume. Also in the announcement, usually at the end, is the address to which to send your materials, a number to which to fax it, and perhaps instructions on how to apply with email. If you mail your application, get a delivery confirmation receipt. If you are facing a deadline, fax or email will deliver your application the same day. Whatever the method, if you send your materials ahead of the deadline, you will have time to phone the office to confirm receipt.

Your paper application should include the following:
- A nicely formatted federal resume printed on good quality paper
- KSA narratives (a separate document)
- A cover letter (if allowed)
- Include copies of required supplemental information such as photocopies of transcripts

A Human Resources Specialist will receive your envelope, review the resume for basic qualifications and status, and then rate and rank your KSAs manually by reading for keywords and content. The top candidates will be referred to the hiring supervisor.

## Step by Step: Non-Automated Applications

1. Focus your federal resume (with formatting) on the announcement, picking up the keywords and top skills from the duties, qualifications, and evaluation sections.
2. Add the job title, grade, series, and announcement number to the top of the resume and KSAs. Also, always include your name and the last four digits of your Social Security Number.
3. Write your KSAs for the position.
4. Mail, fax, or email your application to the address (follow their directions). Never use a government postage-paid envelope.
5. Send other information that they may request such as last performance evaluation (if you have one—not mandatory), transcripts, and DD-214. Do not send any attachments if they do not ask for any.

## Cover Letters

Federal job-hunting is a marketing campaign and your application package is your marketing portfolio. You are presenting your unique experiences that not only show how you qualify for the job, but also why you are the best candidate for the job. In business, any good sales pitch does not just tell the features and benefits of a product ONE TIME. It repeats the selling points several times, reviewing features and benefits, giving a demonstration, and then telling the customer how the product will help them achieve their goals. A good federal application package uses sales repetition about your qualifications for the job in this way:

1. Federal Resume – presents detailed work experience, education, specialized experience, and examples

2. KSAs and Questionnaires –highest level of experience demonstrated by your Accomplishment Record

3. Cover Letter – summary of your Best Features and how you will benefit the organization.

### What a Persuasive Cover Letter Can Do

A great cover letter is simply one that creates an impression of you. It directs your reader's attention by showcasing your professionalism. It points out your best traits. Also, the letter can personalize your application package. It is a wonderful chance for you to speak directly to your reader, the hiring supervisor. It is your chance for you to say, "Hey, look at me! I'm the best-qualified, most interesting candidate. Call me!"

Like a goodwill ambassador, a strong cover letter can greet the reader who picks up your application, casting a positive light on you at a critical point in the application process. This letter can impart your passion for the work or the agency's mission and be an enthusiastic voice for your qualifications. Use the cover letter to:

✪ Summarize the best you have to offer
✪ Write about your interests or passions in a particular field or job
✪ Highlight your expertise and qualifications that specifically fit the job
✪ Demonstrate your knowledge of the agency's mission
✪ Showcase your values as an employee
✪ Create a compelling rationale for why you are an outstanding candidate

You cannot use a cover letter with an automated application, but you can write a compelling letter with a "paper" application. The cover letter can sell your best skills and experiences.

## 8

## How to Pitch your Cover Letter and When to Pass

To command attention, your letter cannot be ordinary. It will have interest (passion for the position, agency, or mission), a summary of your skills and qualifications, and a few logistical points that could elicit favorable attention on your application. Some tips for a winning cover letter:

- ✪ Stick to one page. Be clear, well organized, and concise. Senior executive applications could use a one and half page Letter of Interest.
- ✪ Ensure that your letter is free from typos. This is another writing test. Use a proofreader.
- ✪ Focus not on what the government can do for you, but what you can do for the government. Rather than say why you are seeking the job, state what you can provide in performing the job.
- ✪ Put important information that will help qualify you for the job in your resume and KSA statements, as well as the cover letter. The cover letter will not likely be a part of your score and may not be considered part of the official application.
- ✪ Do not name drop or suggest any connections you have with others in the federal government.

Unlike the private sector, federal applications typically do not require a cover letter. Your federal resume and KSAs will prominently display your name, social security number, and the job announcement number, making the cover letter as a reference page obsolete. Once viewed as a requisite, cover letters have nearly disappeared from the landscape of federal applications. In increasingly rare situations, cover letters are required as part of a paper application. In all other instances, they are optional and could possibly be disallowed. When supplemental information is prohibited by the announcement, submitting extra sheets could disqualify you for failing to follow the instructions. Bottom line: read the announcement carefully and then decide the best way to present your materials.

You can use a cover letter typically with these kinds of federal applications:

- ✪ Excepted service positions where there are no KSAs or Questionnaires as part of the application. They will give you instructions to submit only a resume. You can write a letter with these applications to summarize your experience
- ✪ Senior Executive Service applications – the Letter of Interest can summarize why you believe you would be the best candidate for the job.
- ✪ Any "Paper application" where you can fax, mail, or email the resume and KSAs. You can usually also send a short, summary cover letter.
- ✪ If the announcement states, "no cover letters," then do NOT send a cover letter.

What if you want to send a cover letter to make an important statement about relocation, logistics, gaps in dates, etc? You can make a PERSONAL STATEMENT in the Additional Information field in USAJOBS or the Other Information field in Army's CPOL resume builder. You can basically speak to the HR specialist with special information in that summary field.

### Recommended Cover Letter Structure

A solid cover letter is a one-page document with four main elements—each assigned a paragraph in the letter.

#### Paragraph #1: Explain what you are submitting and why

For example: "I am submitting the enclosed resume and KSA set as my application for the position of Public Health Advisor with the National Safety Council." Be sure to reference the job announcement number so that it can be matched to the rest of your application. If you have special or unusual circumstances for seeking the job, explain them here.

#### Paragraph #2: My relevant qualifications include....

In this paragraph, present your qualifications either in narrative (paragraph) form or as bulleted points. Read the vacancy to discern the top skills and use those as a guide for how to organize your summary of experience in the cover letter. This is the best way to show why YOU are the best candidate for the job. It DEMONSTRATES that your qualifications match the needs of the position.

#### Paragraph #3: I would be an asset to your organization because...

Think about the top three to five skills the supervisor is seeking. Think about what you can do to help that supervisor achieve their mission goals. Put yourself inside your reader's head and consider what in your background would make him or her sit up and take notice of your qualifications. You can use core competencies in this section. For example:

> "I have a proven track record of leading enterprise level projects and programs requiring IT investment management, architecture implementation, and policy compliance."

> "I am enthusiastic and flexible, with the ability to travel without limitation on short notice for my job. Because of my excellent physical fitness, I possess great energy and work well in high-pressure environments." OR

> "My work experience in print and online media has keenly developed my ability to work effectively as part of a team. "

#### Paragraph #4: Offer to come in for an interview and offer logistics information

For example: "I am available to meet with you at your convenience to discuss your objectives and my background. You can contact me at either telephone number above. Thank you for your time and consideration. I look forward to your response."

#### Closing/signature

Use a standard business closing and signature. However, list all of the enclosures you are submitting with your application, including your federal resume, KSA narratives, college transcripts, and anything else required in your application. For example:

Sincerely,

Helen R. Waters
Enclosures:

## Explain Special Accommodations Needed for Disabilities

If you are a person with a disability, your letter will be essentially the same as any applicant's. First, you will focus on your skills, interests, objectives, and services you can provide to the organization to which you are applying. Then in a separate paragraph of your cover letter, you might choose to write about the special accommodations you will need to perform at the highest level of your capability.

For instance:

"I am a person with a 90% visual disability. In order to perform effectively in my position, I would simply need special software on the computer so that I could listen to my email and other data. I have excellent health and hearing capabilities, so I am a high-performing employee with the exception of sight capability. I travel easily with a cane and learn new physical environments very quickly. I have a positive attitude and am willing to work hard and learn new policies, procedures, and programs."

It is your decision whether you will write about your disability and special accommodations in your initial application. Keep in mind, though, that agencies do have resources to help such individuals with special software, hardware, and physical accommodations so that they can have a meaningful, well-paid position. The federal government is hiring people with disabilities!

Discuss with your State Rehabilitation Specialist, job search counselor, and your family how you might communicate your particular strengths and your special needs. This is a personal decision, whether to tell the potential hiring manager about your disability or not. Nevertheless, the federal government is mandated to hire thousands of employees with disabilities in the next few years.

Special Emphasis Officers—Human Resource Staff—are tasked with finding qualified, skilled people with disabilities to hire into positions that can accommodate special needs employees. If you are working through a State Rehab Counselor, have a Schedule A letter stating that you have a disability. Then you can seek a position in government without going through the "competitive process" of writing KSAs and applying for announced positions. It could be important to tell the Special Emphasis Officer and Hiring Supervisor of your disability and your strengths, skills, and interest in working for the federal government.

Public service agencies have excellent job opportunities for all people—those with and without disabilities. However, hiring managers and personnel staff need to know the special accommodations that you will require to determine if the job will work for your skills and abilities. I believe that if you are forthright, positive, informative, and honest about your capabilities, the HR Specialists and panels will work with you to achieve a win-win job situation for you and the agency.

## Other Special Circumstances And Handling Objectives

The cover letter provides an opportunity to describe other special circumstances and resume date situations that you may not have another way to mention. In addition, you can turn an idiosyncrasy into a positive. Information to include would be details about your ability to commute or relocate or an explanation for unusual or inconsistent information in your resume. Decide carefully which information you will mention. If it could play a negative part in the selection process, leave it out. Examples that can work in your favor or preempt problems are:

✪ DO NOT LIVE IN COMMUTING AREA

"As I am relocating from Louisiana to Maryland, I have already secured a residence in Baltimore and can begin work immediately."

✪ SEEKING TO RELOCATE FOR FAMILY REASONS

"I am seeking a position in Portland, Oregon to be near my mother who is aging and requires my attention."

✪ GAP IN DATES DUE TO EDUCATION

"I was a full-time student from 20xx to 20xx and finished my Bachelor's degree in Human Resources at University of Maryland, College Park."

✪ RETURNING TO GOVERNMENT

"I accepted a position with SAIC for two years as a government contractor in order to develop specialized skills in networking, so that I could return to government with new specialized skills and experience."

✪ SEVERAL JOBS WERE LOST DUE TO COMPANY CLOSINGS

"My career in retail (mortgage, real estate, contracting, finance, and other failing industry) has been affected by the economy. I have survived fairly well, but now, desire to work for a more stable organization – the U.S. Government – where I can contribute determination and specialized skills to help manage programs for the American Public."

✪ UNEXPLAINED TERMINATION IN EMPLOYMENT

"I left my medical residency due to a personal medical condition that has been resolved. There is no further inability to perform my work as a medical professional."

✪ OVER QUALIFIED

"As my application materials demonstrate, my qualifications exceed those required for the position for which I am applying. I am prepared to accept and enthusiastically perform in this position as I am making a career transition."

✪ GAP IN EMPLOYMENT

"During the five year period from 20xx – 20xx, I took time away from my career to assist my very ill parents who have since passed. I remained current on happenings in my field and returned to work as a more effective employee."

In the absence of a need to explain special circumstances, keep the cover letter simple. Avoid unforced errors by staying brief, to the point, and focusing on your strengths. Rather than imparting your philosophy or viewpoints, stick to the facts of your demonstrated experience, accomplishments, and qualifications.

## Cover Letter Sample

**Deborah Thomas**
8042 Harwell Court
Bethesda, MD 21228
Phone: 301-555-5555
Email: dthomas@hmail.com

July 21, 20xx

Internal Revenue Service
Attention: Sharla Houston
5333 Garden Road
Memphis, TN 38118

Dear Ms. Houston:

Enclosed is my application responding to **Vacancy Announcement # 08ME1-SBE0091-343-14-CH, Management and Program Analyst.** I have included my Federal Resume, KSA narratives, and other requested documentation, which highlights my professional experience and relevant accomplishments over the last ten years. I currently live in an area commutable to D.C.

I can offer the **Small Business/Self Employed Business Unit** of the IRS proven Project Management experience. I have a successful track record in specialized, technical human resources management in these five areas:

- More than 11 years experience in executive positions in human resources with a focus on **leadership coaching and development**.
- Proven expertise in developing and managing **human resources policies** and procedures for dynamically changing organizations.
- As VP, Human Resources, U.S. Food Service, **strategic recruitment** and the design of a Management Development Program; produced six top leaders for challenging markets.
- Proven experience in devising, implementing, and leading **succession plans** for training, development, and refreshing the pipeline of management candidates and technical personnel.
- Experienced **training director** with vision; expert in consulting with managers on required training, mission changes, and work demands.

My experience in these areas in private industry would provide a unique viewpoint from which to support those working in Small Business and Self Employed programs at the IRS.

I would like to have the opportunity to offer my extensive experience to the Small Business/Self-Employed Business Unit. I look forward to a possible opportunity to meet in person for an interview. Thank you for your consideration of my application materials.

Sincerely,


Deborah Thomas


*Enclosures: Federal Resume and KSA Narratives*

Draft your Cover Letter with our Online Template, used successfully by thousands of job seekers at http://www.resume-place.com/fedres_builder/cover_letter.

## Facts to Know About Deadlines

✪ Applications for federal job vacancies will be accepted only while the vacancy is "open." Exception: Veterans with 30% disability can apply for positions after a closing date, as long as there is no selection made on a position. The veteran would need to email or write the HR specialist for this consideration.

✪ Application Manager and Quickhire Questionnaires deadline: 11:59 PM Eastern Standard Time on the due date.

✪ It is recommended that you submit your applications at least 8 hours before any deadline. Beware: If you put your user name and password in the system incorrectly three times, you could get rejected from the system. For USAJOBS you can create another user name and password within minutes.

✪ Avuecentral.com Questionnaires and resumes: 11:59 PM Eastern Standard Time.

✪ USAJOBS announcements: check the "how to apply" page for directions on deadline and how to apply.

✪ Most paper applications: 5 pm of the time zone of the address of the agency. Beware: If you submit by fax, the fax could be busy. Do not wait until the last hour.

✪ Postmark by 5 pm - this means your package must be postmarked by 5 pm of the time zone of job.

✪ Received by 5 pm - this means they must receive it by 5 pm of time zone of job.

✪ Mailing: best to send by Return Receipt Requested, so you have notice that the package was received in the mailroom.

✪ "Open" periods can range from a few days to approximately four weeks. "One month open" means that they are looking at lots of applicants. "Extended deadline" means they have not received enough applicants.

✪ Re-announced announcement with new deadline: they re-announced the same position again with some change. You would have to apply again.

✪ Open Inventory: announcements that are basically database collections of resumes for future searches. These are real databases (submit your resume). The U.S. Navy and CHART system are mostly Open Inventory, so are the Air Force announcements through USAJOBS. The HR specialists use this system for searching for applicants. These are "real" jobs, but the deadlines and timeline for a contact is unknown.

✪ Open Until Filled: this is also a database announcement collecting resumes until they have hired a number of applicants for many locations.

✪ First Cut-off, Second Cut-off, etc. dates. If you can make an early cut-off, go ahead, but they will usually still view resumes until the last cut-off. The HR specialist will view the resumes collected on the cut-off dates.

✪ If you apply on-line, do NOT send the same package by mail.

# How Federal Job Applications Are Processed

The number of resumes referred to the selecting official can range from 3 to 30, depending on the system. Key steps in federal hiring that involve job applicants interaction:

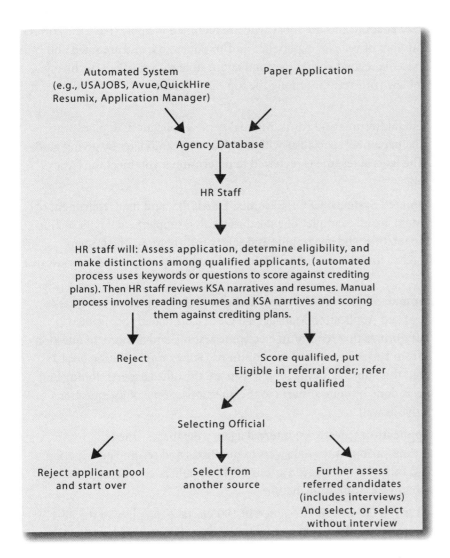

## Review: Application Formats

There are at least six ways to apply for a federal job. The vacancy announcements are different in their instructions for "how to apply."

Here is a review of the various "how to apply" instructions, application formats, and rating and ranking processes. The first cut applicants are those who are qualified to apply (have the correct status), have the correct number of years of experience and/or education, and are rated and ranked high enough to go to the second cut. The second cut or final step is where the hiring supervisor or panel will review your resume among the top candidates.

- ✪ **Paper Application:** Federal Resume and KSAs. Manual paper application. Replaces the SF-171 and OF-612. The personnel specialists will rate and rank candidates by giving grades to KSA applications. The federal resume is reviewed to determine if you meet the basic qualifications of the job.

- ✪ **Resume-Driven Automated Systems:** CPOL Resumix, USAJOBS, and the Department of the Navy's CHART system are all examples of a database with a supplemental data section which provides specific job title, and geographic and salary information. The human resources recruiter searches for best candidates (rates and ranks) by searching for keywords/skills in your resume.

- ✪ **Question-Driven Automated Systems:** Electronic Resume and Occupational and Task Questions. Avue Central and Application Manager, an OPM-automated recruitment system, are examples of formats that require an electronic resume and answers to questions. You will rate yourself from 1 to 5 on many of the questions (For example: Rating level 1: you know nothing about this subject; Rating level 5: you are the office expert). Rating and ranking of applications is done by your answers to the questions. Some of the questions could be a short narrative as well.

- ✪ **Resume Only with Application Questions:** Internal agency databases. The HR professionals rate and rank various ways—answers to questions and resume information. The FAA, CIA, FBI, and other agencies have various on-line applications, questionnaires, tests, and systems to obtain applicant information.

- ✪ **Optional Form OF-612:** The OF-612 was designed in 1995 to take the place of the SF-171, however it is not the preferred method of applying. It contains all of the information that you will write in your federal resume, but it is rigid for the applicant. You will almost always have a choice to use a resume rather than the OF-612. When there is a choice, it is better to use the federal outline format resume shown in this book.

- ✪ **SF-171:** The SF-171 was eliminated in 1995 by the Office of Personnel Management and has not been renewed by the Office of Management and Budget. BUT some agencies still list the SF-171 as an acceptable form of application for a federal job. This author recommends that you not use the SF-171 now for a job application. You should try first to submit the federal-style resume. A second-best choice would be the OF-612. Many agencies still state in their instructions that you can submit an OF-612, SF-171f or resume. The best format is the resume.

## Quote

"When one has applied for a federal position, it is important to follow-up every 2-4 weeks with the human resource contact on status of the vacancy announcement, through email and by phone call. "

*Jeff Clopein*
*State Government to VR Program Specialist*
*U.S. Department of Education/RSA*

# STEP NINE
## Make Sure to Follow Through

In order to be successful, you need to track and follow-up with your applications. This chapter will give you the tools and tips you need to find out the status of your application and what to do next.

## Overview

How Long Does It Take To Get a Response To My Application?

What Happened To My Application Package?

Follow-Up Techniques Summary

Paper Applications: You Mean I Can Contact HR?

How To Contact the HR Person

Sample Scripts

Submitting a Freedom of Information Act Request

Electronic Applications

Tracking Your Application on USAJOBS

Not Selected? What's Next?

## How Long Does It Take To Get a Response To My Application?

Right now, the Office of Personnel Management is working with agencies to reduce the length of the hiring process to a total of 45 days, from the closing date of the announcement to the interview date. In many cases, you might hear back from the agency within a month after the closing date on the announcement. If the announcement is "open continuous," then it could take much longer before a position becomes available to be filled. (See page 66 for more information about this type of announcement.)

### Strategy Tip
Be aware that the electronic job application process is typically faster than the paper application process.

## What Happened To My Application Package?

Here are the various things that can happen to the position openings:
- The position could be FILLED. If you are one of the finalists, you will be contacted for a telephone or personal interview. The supervisor will SELECT one of the applicants. If you were not selected for either the interview or the job, then you may not be contacted at all regarding your application.
- The announcement closing date could be EXTENDED, because they did not receive enough applications.
- The recruitment could go through certain steps (review of applications, qualified persons "certified," and interviews), and then the position can be CANCELLED.
- The announcement could be CANCELLED due to budget cuts or the announcement was written incorrectly. The announcement might be posted again. You will have to re-apply, because previous applicant materials are discarded.

Be prepared for the fact that you may spend hours on your package, and the announcement could end up getting cancelled.

### Strategy Tip: Play the Application Game
The best philosophy here is to apply for as many of these positions as you can. With the government's response time to applications, it is better if you keep applying. The sheer volume of your effort and energy will pay off.

## Follow-Up Techniques Summary

### Paper Applications
If you submit a paper application package and have not heard anything in 30 to 45 days, you could contact the person listed on the announcement by letter, email, phone, or fax. Follow the sample scripts provided in this chapter. Be informative, pleasant, persevering, and genuinely interested in the status of your application.

### Electronic Applications
USAJOBS and some agencies have automated systems where you can check the status of your application, though not all automated systems provide information about applications received.

## Paper Applications: You Mean I Can Contact HR?

Most federal job applicants are not aware that they can contact the HR personnel handling their application. Asking questions, gaining information, developing a relationship, and becoming known are helpful parts of the application process. You can track and follow-up on most of the steps your application follows through in the system. Some of the online application systems are even set up to ensure that you will be contacted.

Vacancy announcements typically include the name of a human resources contact responsible for many aspects of the application process. This HR person may have created the vacancy announcement, posted it on USAJOBS and other websites, and may communicate with the hiring supervisor. They may coordinate the review of the packages and be part of the rating and ranking process to determine who will get an interview. This HR person is a great resource for you.

*Just a reminder, they are busy!*
Human resources staff are occupied with multiple announcements, various aspects of announcement development, reviewing packages, and responding to supervisor needs. Use diplomacy and consideration when contacting them about your package. Your goal is to be remembered favorably!

If you are told by the HR office that you were not rated "qualified" and you feel you really were, you can ask for reconsideration. Agencies have different procedures for this, but it's probably best to ask in writing to the attention of the Human Resources officer. Your rating (or non-selection) is unfortunate, but mistakes do happen. The office will not be able to consider any new information, only what you submitted with your application.

## How To Contact the HR Person

✪ **Telephone:** You probably will not reach the HR person with your first call, so be ready with a good voicemail message. Practice your message before calling.

✪ **What if you try calling and there is continually no answer?** If the phone is always busy, or you leave a voicemail and never receive a call back, here is what you can do: research another vacancy announcement with the same agency (preferably at the same grade level), look for a contact name and phone on that announcement, and call him or her. They are probably co-workers and this person may be able to tell you what happened to the recruiter you are seeking. It is possible that they changed jobs, are on vacation, or are on detail to another agency. HR staff people are usually very helpful and informative. And, they may be able to answer your question themselves.

✪ **Email:** By all means, use this method if it is recommended.

✪ **Fax:** Sometimes only a fax number is provided. In this case, write inquiries simply and clearly, making sure to include your contact information.

✪ **No personal contact information:** If there is no name or personal contact information, but there is an address, you may write a letter. If there is no address, but a database, you cannot contact anyone. Just submit your application and cross your fingers.

---

**Human Resources Specialist's Insight**

"Customer service is not what it should be in many HR offices—we just don't have enough people. If you have not sent your application by some method that gets you a receipt, I would call the agency and make sure they have your application. I have seen applications get misfiled, put in wrong folders, and otherwise mishandled. If you are calling four weeks later and the agency did not get your application, it is too late to do anything about it. Also (and most readers of this book will not make this mistake), if you are calling before the final due date, you can make sure that the HR office has everything it needs (DD214, SF-50, performance appraisal, and so forth) to consider you. In our office, if you don't submit necessary paperwork (say DD214 for VEOA jobs), you're out—we're not going to call you and ask for it."

# Sample Scripts

## Telephone

*1st Message –*
*30 days after the closing date*

> "Hi, Ms. Rogers, this is Kathryn Troutman from San Diego, CA. I'm inquiring about my application for Writer-Editor, GS-7, announcement 20205, which I submitted on April 5, 20xx. I'd like to know the status of my package, or when the packages are being reviewed. Can you please return my call, or leave a voicemail at (410) 777-7777? The best time to reach me is 8 to 10 am. Thank you."

*2nd Message –*
*2 to 4 weeks after the HR person responds to your message by voicemail*

> "Hi, Ms. Rogers, this is Kathryn Troutman again. Thanks for your voicemail on Monday, April 25th regarding announcement 20205, Writer-Editor. I'm checking again on the status of my application. I am still very interested in the job, but other opportunities are appearing. I hope that a decision will be made soon, and I can be interviewed. I want this job and I believe I can make a positive contribution to your agency. I need a job and I've been looking 6 months. My voicemail again is (410) 777-7777."

*3rd Contact –*
*2 to 4 weeks after the 2nd contact (this time, make it by fax or email)*

> To: Susan Rogers, HR Staff for Announcement 20205, Writer-Editor
> From: Kathryn Troutman, SSN 220-00-0000
> Re: Position of Writer-Editor, Closing Date April 5, 20xx

> Hello, Ms. Rogers, I'm still hopeful that I'm in the list of Best Qualified Candidates for this position. I've been reading about your agency in the newspaper and see that there are new programs for housing and construction. I would be able to start immediately. Can you please let me know if this position still exists? I am determined to get a federal job, and I really like the mission of your agency. I could contribute a lot and be very effective there. If another person has been selected, I'd really like to know so that I can pursue other positions. Thanks so much for your help. I look forward to your call. My number is (410) 777-7777. The best time to reach me is 8 to 10 am.

### You Have Been Told You Are Not Getting The Job (Telephone)

"Hello, Ms. Rogers, This is Kathryn Troutman. I got the notice that I was not hired for the job (Announcement 20205, Writer-Editor). When you have a few minutes, I would really appreciate your help with knowing why I was not selected. I'd really like to work for the government in your agency and I felt I was perfectly qualified. If you could take a few minutes and call me back or leave a voicemail, I would appreciate knowing what I could do improve in my resume or my qualifications for future applications. Thanks so much for your help. My number is (410) 777-7777. The best time to reach me is 8 to 10 am."

### You Are Getting An Interview – Congratulations! (Telephone)

"Hello, Ms. Rogers, this is Kathryn Troutman, Thanks so much for the opportunity to interview for the Writer-Editor job, announcement 20205. I am very pleased! I would like to know if you can give me some insight into the interview system. Will there be one person or a panel interviewing me? Also, will the interview follow specific questions? And if so, would I be able to receive these questions ahead of time? I am beginning my research and preparation for the interview now. I look forward to this opportunity. Thanks for any information you can provide! My number is (410) 777-7777. The best time to reach me is 8 to 10 am."

### After The Interview – Thank You Note!

Dear Ms. Rogers:
Thank you so much for your time last Wednesday. I enjoyed meeting you and hearing about your agency. I believe that I would be an asset to your organization and feel certain that I would be able to learn quickly about your mission and programs.
I look forward to your decision and hope that I can begin my career at the Office of _____ at the Department of _____.

Thank you again.

Sincerely,
Kathryn Troutman

## Sample Questions for Applicants to Ask Human Resources

*1. Can you clarify something from the announcement for me?*

If you do not understand exactly a certain request of the vacancy announcement, ask for clarification. If the person you are talking to is not the named contact person, be sure to get his or her name.

*2. Have you received all my materials?*

Many vacancy announcements require you to submit materials by different methods. For example, you may have to use a Quickhire online application system which follows two steps: 1) submit information on-line, and 2) fax or mail your transcripts. It is a good idea to check to see if all your materials have been received before the closing date. Some electronic application systems, like CPOL, list the status of your application materials. If you mail any materials, remember to save your receipts.

*3. What is the status of my application?*

The federal job application process can take a while. You can call to check on the status of your application, but we suggest that you wait about a month after the closing date. You may learn that you did or did not get on the list submitted to the selecting official, or that interviews are being conducted.

*4. How can I improve future applications?*

This is REALLY IMPORTANT. If you learn that you did not get referred for a position, ask the contact person to tell you what you should do to improve future applications. You may learn that you missed a selective factor. You may learn that you were not qualified for a particular grade. You may learn that you did not score highly on your KSAs. You may also learn that you scored very well, but were in competition with a highly qualified group of applicants.

The HR representative usually will not go into great detail, but may tell you what your overall score was, where your KSA's were weak, and where you ranked among the pool of applicants. If you did not get the job you were seeking, then talking on the phone with the people who read and scored your materials can be the most valuable five or ten minutes you can spend in this whole process.

## Submitting a Freedom of Information Act (FOIA) Request

If all else fails, you can send a request to the Freedom of Information Act contact person in the agency. Write and request for the records you want. Each office has a designated staff that answers them on a timely basis, usually within 20 business days of receipt of the request. Under FOIA, you may request records, not information. So do not ask questions, but rather state which specific documents you are seeking.

Research the agency's contact information and FOIA regulations. Internet search terms including the agency's name and FOIA will lead you to the specific instructions for submitting your request. Follow any instructions given by the specific agency you are petitioning. Be prepared to pay a reasonable processing fee (up to $25) when your request exceeds two hours of search time or 100 pages of documents.

If your FOIA request goes unanswered, which is rare, you can also write to your Congressperson or Senator to get this information. This should be an absolute last resort, as these requests take more time and circumvent the processes that the agency has already in place to help you.

Suggested letter for FOIA request:

Kathryn Troutman
89 Mellor Ave.
Baltimore, MD 21228
(410) 744-4324

Sept. 20, 20xx

Re: Employment application records request, July 20, 20xx
Department of Homeland Security, Transportation Security Administration
    Announcement No. 20202, Writer-Editor, GS-301-12

Freedom of Information Act Office
11th Floor, East Tower
Arlington, VA 22202
Attention: FOIA Officer

Dear Mr. _____,

This letter is to request all records in control of the agency related to my application for the position of Writer-Editor, GS-301-12 under vacancy announcement number 20202. I am making this request under the Freedom of Information Act in accordance with the instructions and regulations found on your agency's website.

These documents can be sent to me at kathryn@aol.com or to the above address.

Thank you for your help. I can be reached at the above address or at 410-744-4324, M-F, 9 to 5 EST. I appreciate your assistance.

Sincerely,

Kathryn Troutman

## Electronic Applications

Tracking electronic applications could be easier in some situations but could also present a different set of challenges. For example, when a computer rates and ranks your application, it is difficult to get human feedback on shortcomings with your resume when you are not found qualified for a position.

Furthermore, agencies differ in their application management. For example, in the military sectors, the U.S. Army has an excellent system for tracking the activity that has occurred with your online resume in the database. You can view your resume online and also see how many times, and when, your resume has been "pulled" for an announcement. The U.S. Navy and Air Force also each have their own individual tracking systems as well. Therefore, if you are applying to an agency with an independent tracking system, check their websites to learn more about how they operate.

## Tracking Your Application on USAJOBS

For the most part, we will focus our discussion on how you can track your electronic application on USAJOBS, because this will account for the majority of the electronic applications submitted.

You can check the status of your federal applications online anytime. If you have an account in USAJOBS "My Resume," you can go to the "my applications" page where you can track and follow-up with your federal applications. You can also check in the Office of Personnel Management's Questionnaire site, www.applicationmanager.org.

When a federal agency uses USAJOBS to manage their resumes and applications, the human resources specialist will periodically update your resume account online. That way you can follow the activity in your applications.

Here are the typical responses that you may find, and ideas about how to handle each response:

- ✪ **Application started:** You began the application, but you did not complete it.

- ✪ **Application complete:** You applied correctly, but no one looked at the resume yet. You will have to wait longer to see any activity on your application.

- ✪ **Announcement cancelled:** The job announcement has been cancelled for various reasons. It could be reposted, so check back periodically and apply again if you see a new announcement for the same position. They will not keep your resume on file.

- ✪ **Application pending:** The HR Specialist pulled the resumes, and they are reviewing them now. You will have to wait for further action and the next note by the HR Specialist to see if you have been referred to a selecting official.

✪ **You are not minimally qualified or you do not meet minimum qualifications:**
The HR specialist reviewed your resume, questionnaire, and profile, and you are not even minimally qualified.

Here are possible reasons:
- You do not meet minimum qualification requirements listed in the vacancy announcement, such as work experience, education, or selective factors.
- You applied for a job that was only open to current federal employees or other applicants with special eligibility, such as veterans or former federal employees.
- Your original profile in USAJOBS has something checked off that takes you out of consideration. For instance, you may have checked off that you will not accept any term position. You will not be considered if the job is a non-permanent position.

Now what do you do?
- Find the vacancy announcement if you still have it.
- Review your resume against the announcement.
- Review the Work Experience section of your resume (especially the last eight years).
- See if the Work Experience section demonstrates that you have the specialized experience for the position. If not, continue to work on the resume and re-submit.

✪ If you **are qualified**, this is very good news. Your resume and questionnaire met the minimum qualifications. What do you do now? Wait to see what happens next. You could be in the running to get referred to the supervisor.

## Application Manager

**Welcome to USA Staffing™ Application Manager**

**Existing Account? Log In Here:**

User Name: _____

Password: _____

[ Go ]

Application Manager is an official U.S. Government System. You are authorized to use it subject to Terms and Conditions. Unauthorized use of this system or its information could result in criminal prosecution.

Forgot User Name or Password   Problems Logging In?

**Create an account:**

Create one now -- It's fast, convenient and easy to use all these Application Manager features!

Check out our Quick Start Guide.

[ Create an Account ]

Instructions on how to apply for a job without using Application Manager

✪ **Your application was not referred:** Based on your responses to the questions, you did not receive a score high enough to be referred to the selecting official. The minimum score for minimum qualifications is 70. You may have scored more than 70, thus meeting the minimum qualifications, but did not rank high enough to be considered "best qualified" and referred to a selecting official. The highest score for most applicants is 100. Veterans can add a five- or ten-point preference and achieve the highest score of 110.

✪ If you are **referred to a supervisor or referred for selection consideration**, this means that your resume is on the supervisor's desk, and you are a finalist for an interview (if they interview for the job) or for an offer. What do you do now? Wait to see if you get called for an interview.

✪ You may also **receive a job offer online**. Congratulations! Though most job offers will come by phone or e-mail by the human resources specialist recruiting this position, the USAJOBS Application Manager or the Army's CPOL answer tracking page can actually offer you a job online, even without an interview. Occasionally supervisors do not interview people for federal positions, especially at the GS-9 level. Also, you may see the job offer here after the HR specialist calls and offers you the job. What do you do now? Do not accept the offer on the phone the minute they call you. Thank them and sound very pleased and upbeat. Ask if you can think about the offer for a day and call back the next day with your response. You need to review the position, salary, location, and benefits and determine whether you will negotiate your job offer.

✪ If you are **called in for an interview**
Read *Step 10: Interviewing 101*.

## Strategy Tip
Save the vacancy announcements as HTML or Word files, so that you can monitor the results of your applications. Once the deadline passes, they are no longer viewable online.

## Not Selected? What's Next?

If you get a letter saying you are "Qualified," it means you were minimally qualified, not "Best Qualified."

If you received a letter saying you were found "qualified," that is all that you will get from the agency. More than likely, your consideration for the job stops here. To move into the next phase of the hiring process, that is, to get an interview, you must have been rated "best qualified" for the job. Meaning that, based on the review of your knowledge, skills, and abilities, you were rated one of the best from among the group of applicants who were found qualified for the job. Other language that you may see is that you were "referred" to the selecting official, or that you were placed on the "certificate."

Again, you need to talk to the personnel staffing specialist who reviewed your resume and KSAs. You need to know why you were not qualified (or not "best qualified"). If you do not find out, how will you know what to change for the next announcement? It can be difficult to get the HR specialist assigned to your announcement on the phone, but if you can persevere to make contact with someone, it would help you tremendously. They have the information you need and there could be a simple explanation. Here are a few of the basic reasons your application could be found "not qualified" when in fact you are qualified:

- They could not see your qualifications quickly in your resume.
- They could not see specific qualifications, such as the one year of specialized experience.
- They could not see keywords from the announcement in your work experience descriptions.

Here is a telephone script you can use to call the personnel staff who handled the recruitment:

"Hello, I'm Kathryn Troutman. I received my letter that I was found not qualified for the position Writer-Editor, GS 301-12, Announcement No. 10101. I would like to request a few moments of your time so that I can know what I did not have in my application to be considered qualified for the position. I am intent on obtaining a federal position as a Writer-Editor. I have the education and experience needed for the position. Please help me to understand why I was not selected. I appreciate your time very much. Thanks. I am available at (410) 744-4324 during the days, Monday through Friday, 9-5, EST."

## Quote

" You completed my application package (federal paper resume and KSAs) in June 20xx and I began applying for positions with the VA. I just wanted to let you know I was hired today (12/26/xx). I sent out a total of 14 applications and was interviewed six times. Thank you so much for your help. "

*KeRita Anakoro*

# STEP TEN
## Interviewing 101

The federal government uses many different approaches to interviewing. Managers vary their interviewing techniques and processes to develop an understanding of you as a candidate for their position. The interview will depend on the type of position, as well as the information the manager needs to obtain to determine if you are the best "fit" for the position. This section will help you understand these approaches and provide some practical tips on preparing for interviews.

## Overview

Key Points

Types of Interviews: 3 Basic Formats

Types of Interview Questions

Types of Interviews: 3 Basic Methods

Parts of the Interview

Questions to Ask the Interviewer

After the Interview

Non-Verbal Communication

Steps to Prepare for an Interview

EEO and Rating Systems

Final Tips

## Key Points

This chapter contains a large amount of information to digest. Here are the key points to remember:

### Know the paperwork

Know the vacancy announcement, agency mission, and office function. Read your resume and KSAs out loud with enthusiasm. Become convinced that you are very well qualified for the job and that the agency NEEDS you to help achieve their mission.

### Do the necessary research

Go online to research the agency, department, and position. Read press releases about the organization. Go to www.washingtonpost.com and search for the organization to see if there are any recent news events.

### Practice

In front of a mirror, tape recorder, video camera, family member, friend, or anyone who volunteers to listen to you.

### Confidence, knowledge, and skills

In order to "sell" yourself for a new position, you have to believe in your abilities. Read books and listen to tapes that will help boost your confidence and give you the support you need to "brag" about your work skills.

# Types of Interviews: 3 Basic Formats

Interviews may be conducted in person or over the phone, and may include an interview panel. Interview elements may include several categories, including:

- ✪ Behavioral
- ✪ Technical
- ✪ Competency

All of the interview methods listed above call for some preparation on your part. However, you need to understand which type of interview you will be participating in. When you are contacted for the interview, it is appropriate for you to request information regarding the type and method of interviewing that will be conducted.

Let's discuss the different interviewing methods listed above.

## Behavioral Interviewing

Be prepared for a new interview format, the Behavior-Based Interview. Be prepared to give examples in your answer to seven to ten questions that will be situation- or experience-based. If you have an example of how you led a team, provided training, or managed a project, be prepared to talk about the project and teamwork. The best answers are examples that demonstrate your past performance.

You will see typical questions that could be asked in most interviews. Most panel members or individual supervisor / interviewers will prepare seven to ten questions. The same questions are asked of all the interviewees. The answers are graded. So, be prepared to give examples that demonstrate your knowledge, skills, and abilities.

If you have written your KSAs from Step 7, the KSA narrative / examples could be the basis of your accomplishments for the Behavior-Based Interview. However, you will have to practice speaking about your accomplishments. Even the most seasoned speakers, briefers, and media experts take training in speaking, presentation, and content development. Jobseekers should spend more time writing examples (their "message") that support their best strengths, and practice speaking these elements.

*Behavioral Interview: Sample Questions*

- "Your supervisor has left an assignment for you, and has left on a week long vacation. The assignment is due when she returns. You do not completely understand the assignment – what would you do?"

- "You have been responsible for dealing with a particularly challenging client, who has indicated in their latest phone call, that they are thinking of taking their business someplace else. How would you handle the situation?"

- "The successful candidate for this position will be working with some highly-trained individuals who have been with the organization for a long time. How will you approach them?"

- "Tell me about a time when you took it upon yourself to accomplish a task on the job without being asked."

*Tips for Preparing for a Behavioral Interview*

Prior to the interview, spend some time identifying behaviors that would be critical to success in the position – and do an honest assessment!

Do a "Google" search and look for behavioral interview questions – and practice!

Spend some time thinking through mistakes you have made in the workplace – what would you do differently – in other words, how would you change your behavior the next time?

*Open-Ended and Behavioral Questions*

From a report by the Merit Systems Protection Board:

FOR THE SUPERVISORS: Ask effective questions. As we've indicated, effective interview questions are based on job analysis to ensure that they are job-related. Effective interview questions are also usually open-ended and behavioral, so that they will elicit useful responses.

APPLICANT INSIGHT: Open-ended questions are questions that require the candidate to provide details, and cannot be answered in one word (such as "yes" or "excellent"). Such questions are much more effective than closed-ended questions at developing insight into a candidate's experience and abilities.

For example, the closed-ended question, "Can you write effectively?" can be answered with an uninformative "Yes" — a response that sheds little light on the candidate's level of performance in this area.

An open-ended question such as, "Describe the types of documents you have written, reviewed, or edited," requires the candidate to provide specifics, and provides much more insight into the candidate's writing accomplishments.

There is a place for the closed-ended question. For example, to learn whether a candidate is willing to travel frequently or can start work on a given date, it is perfectly appropriate to ask a closed-ended question.

Behavioral questions are just that: questions that ask the candidate to describe behaviors — responses, actions, and accomplishments in actual situations. The case for the behavioral question is more subtle than the case for open-ended questions. Although research indicates that both behavioral questions ("What did you do?") and hypothetical questions ("What would you do?") can be effective, many researchers and practitioners generally recommend the behavioral question for two reasons. First, behavioral questions can provide greater insight into how the candidate will perform on the job, because the best predictor of future behavior is past behavior. Second, behavioral questions may be more reliable than hypothetical questions. Because the response can be verified through reference checks or other means, it is more difficult to fabricate an inaccurate or untruthful answer to a behavioral question than to a hypothetical one.

*Read the entire report here: http://www.mspb.gov/studies/interview.htm*

## Technical Interviewing

Technical interviews are focused on providing the selecting official with additional information regarding the technical or functional skills of the applicant.

*Sample Questions*

- "Describe your experience with accounting principles, practices, and techniques."

- "Describe your experience in applying program management theories and processes."

- "This position requires experience in scientific research – provide us with information on your role and/or participation in performing basic and/or applied research."

- "How do you keep abreast of new developments in your profession or industry? On a scale of 1-10, how up to date are you?"

- "How does your degree in (major) prepare you for a career in (occupation/industry), or to excel as a (position title)."

- "In your current job/school situation, what types of decisions do you make without consulting your immediate supervisor?"

"On a scale of 1-5, how would you assess your technical skills and why?"

*Tips for Preparing for a Technical Interview*

Closely review the technical requirements listed in the vacancy announcement, and develop a mental inventory of your skills for each requirement.

Identify questions you may have regarding the technical requirements of the work – this will demonstrate your ability to prepare as well as your technical skill level.

Check with college professors, peers, and counselors regarding information on the technical challenges and issues facing the organization; develop scenarios for problem-solving!

## Competency Interviewing

An employment interview in which the competencies have been defined by the organization, and in which applicants are asked questions to determine their possession of the competencies required for the position. These interviews may seem like the behavioral interview described above.

*Sample Questions*

- Problem Solving: "Give me an example of a time when you had to develop a new solution to an old problem."

- Team Work: "Describe a time when you used your teambuilding skills to gain buy-in for a project or idea."

- Communication: "Describe a time when you had to communicate under difficult circumstances, either verbally or in writing."

*Tips for Preparing for a Competency Interview*

Spend some time thinking about mistakes you have made on the job or in school – how would you explain them to an interviewer – and what have you learned from those mistakes.

Research the organization's website to identify organizational competencies and values, and assess how you would fit in to the organization.

Research practice questions and work with peers or counselors to practice responding to questions.

## Types of Interview Questions

In addition to the different types of interview questions already described, you will likely get additional questions from some of the categories listed below:

*Traditional Questions*

The standard interview questions that ask what you may do in a given situation. These questions are more hypothetical and allow you to give best-case answers; they concentrate little on your actual experience.

- "Tell me about yourself." (An all-inclusive question. Also "Why should I hire you?" or "What about this job interests you?" Keep this response job-related and refer to your KSAs and competencies. Give a two-minute commercial selling yourself for the position.)
- "Describe a major obstacle you have overcome."
- "Are you a hard worker?"
- "What are your strengths?"
- "Where do you see yourself in five years?"

*Situational Questions*

Similar to the behavior-based questions, these questions are not so much questions as they are scenarios or situations you could encounter in the new job. The interviewer is looking for how you would react and respond to these situations.

- "We are always looking for new ideas to increase productivity, improve morale, and reduce costs. Tell me about an idea you have that could yield positive results."
- "If you were to go in and find a center not running as efficiently as you expect it could, what would you do?"
- "You find you double scheduled your manager for two appointments at the same time. How do you handle the error an hour before the appointments?"

*Difficult/Negative Questions*

These questions put you on the spot. They can be designed to increase your level of stress to see how you will respond. The questions themselves should be answered by giving the most positive responses you can and by showing ways you are trying to improve.

- "Describe a time when your work performance was poor."
- "What are your weaknesses?" (List only one. Let the interviewer ask for more.)
- "Tell me about a time when your work was criticized."
- "Describe a difficult problem you've had to deal with." (Best to keep your answer work-related, not personal)

*Illegal Questions*

Not mentioned as a possible format, these are questions that should not be asked and do not need to be answered. Interviewers should not ask any questions regarding race, gender, religion, marital status, sexual orientation, or national origin.

*Unanswerable*

If you are asked an unanswerable question, the best thing to do is to be honest. Refocus on something you can do and demonstrate how you can meet the position's specific needs.

# Types of Interviews: 3 Basic Methods

## Telephone Interview

The telephone interview can be either a pre-screening interview, or it can be the full interview, as though you are sitting in the office with the supervisor or the panel. During a telephone interview, you can have notes in front of you to help you with your responses. Just do not rely too heavily on the notes—you do not want to sound as though you are reading from a script. Remember, the Selecting Official is mainly interested in determining whether you should be invited to further participate in the process.

Tips:
✪ Get dressed comfortably
✪ Be prepared, relaxed, and confident
✪ Have your resume and the announcement in front of you
✪ Create your skills and accomplishments list and have them with you
✪ Be seated in a quiet room at a big table
✪ If you are on a cell phone, make sure it is clear and has plenty of battery

## Individual/One-on-One Interview

You may be invited in for a face-to-face interview with the Selecting Official and/or other members of the staff or Selection Panel. In a few cases, especially when a candidate or an interviewer is unable to attend the face-to-face interview, a more formal interview can be conducted by telephone. If there has been no pre-screening interview, the face-to-face interview will be the first step in your interview process. The face-to-face interview can either be individual/one-on-one or group/panel. You may be called in for a preliminary interview (either individual or group), then be invited back for another (or multiple) interviews with the Selecting Official, staff members, and/or members of the Selection Committee who will then meet and make a decision regarding your qualifications.

This type of interview is often conducted across a desk in a question and answer format. However, in recent years more interviewers have opted to make the experience more comfortable and may have each of you sit in chairs on the same side of the desk and make the dialogue more conversational. This all will depend on who is conducting the interview.

## Group/Panel Interview

The third type of interview is the group/panel interview, during which you are interviewed by two or more interviewers who are either directly related to the position (supervisor, co-workers, subordinates), members of the department, and/or members of the Selection Committee. Usually each member of the panel has questions to ask, but there have been interviews where only one person has done the asking, and the others involved are there simply to observe.

Tip: If given a choice, try to get a seat at the end of the table so you can make eye contact with more of the panel members.

## Parts of the Interview

During the actual interview, you can anticipate spending between 30 minutes and one hour with the interviewer or panel. Some interviews are shorter; others can be as long as several hours to a full day. Often, you will be told in advance how long the interview should be. The interview typically begins with introductions and an explanation of the position. It then moves into a question-and-answer session where you are asked a majority of the questions, and ends with an opportunity for you to ask some questions about the position.

### Opening

This is your opportunity to make a good first impression—first impressions do count, and the first two minutes of the interview are critical. They will make the interviewer decide if he/she wants to keep paying attention to what you have to say. A good deal of small talk typically occurs during this time as you and the interviewer(s) get to know each other. Again, you will be given some background about the position, and this is often when you will be asked the first question, something usually along the lines of "Tell me about yourself."

### Body

As you move into the body of the interview, you will be asked a number of questions (traditional, behavior-based, competency-based, situational, difficult, etc.) that will help the interviewer(s) determine your KSAs, competencies, and experience in relation to what the agency is seeking for the position at hand.

In general, when responding to questions, you always want to provide examples demonstrating your KSAs and competencies. Your specific experiences and examples will set you apart from the competition, and your ability to effectively articulate how you are the best candidate for the position can make all the difference in whether you receive an offer for the position. In other words, you want to be able to show them, not just tell them, why you are qualified.

Confidence in describing increasingly more responsible and complex assignments and experiences translates into good marks on the interviewer's "scorecard," used to compare the candidates. If the interviewer has to pull information from the candidate, the resulting impression is weak.

### Closing

At the end of the interview, you will be given an opportunity to ask questions or bring up any selling points that were not discussed during the interview. Take advantage of this opportunity.

If at the end of the interview you feel you have not had the opportunity to elaborate on a particular experience, explain a relevant skill, or demonstrate a specific expertise, now is the time to do it. If you have a portfolio with examples of work you have done, you may bring it to the interviewer's attention at this point if you have not already. Do not take up too much time; it is, after all, the end of the interview. Nevertheless, do not miss an opportunity to sell yourself for the position.

Once you have asked your questions, and made any extra points, do not forget to thank the interviewer for his/her time and reiterate once again your qualifications for the position. This will enable you to leave on a high note—summarizing your qualifications one last time so the interviewer(s) will remember at the end of the interview why you should be the candidate hired for the position. You may also ask when you should hear back from them and let them know you will be looking forward to that.

## Questions to Ask the Interviewer

By all means, ask questions of the interviewer. The questions you want to ask the interviewer should be ones you are truly interested in getting answers to. You will want to limit the number of questions you ask at the end of the interview to no more than four. If you are interested in something the interviewer talks about during the interview, ask about it. Questions encourage dialogue, and dialogue can make the interview more conversational and more comfortable. Again, do not overdo it. The questions you ask should help you determine whether or not this is the right job for you.

In order to prepare questions in advance, take a look at the Position Description (PD) and KSAs—is there anything you would like the interviewer to explain or elaborate upon? See if you have generated any questions from the research you have done. Be careful that you do not ask questions that you should already know the answer to (something listed in the PD, for example).

Have ten questions prepared for the interviewer. Only ask the ones which were not addressed during your discussion.

Here are a few general examples:
- "What is the most significant challenge of this position?"
- "What is the most important contribution you would like to see made in this position in the next two months?"
- "Are there opportunities for creativity and problem-solving skills to be put to use?"
- "Beyond the job description, what are the expectations of this position?"

## After the Interview

Thank you letters should be written graciously, promptly, and carefully. Think about the best form for your thank you. If the interviewer tells you he/she plans to make a decision that night, then you should e-mail promptly. At the same time, if you are applying to an agency that prides itself on doing personalized work for clients, you may want to send a handwritten message on a nice card. Either way, thank the interviewer for his/her time, gently reminding them of your interest in the position, and the valuable contributions you would bring to the organization. Do not miss that last chance to market yourself!

## Non-Verbal Communication

It is also important to think about your non-verbal communication when you are preparing for the interview. First impressions are made immediately based upon how you entered the room, whether or not you made eye contact, and how you presented yourself through your dress, habits, and mannerisms. Needless to say, non-verbals can significantly influence the interview.

Here are some non-verbal pointers to keep in mind:

✪ Entrance. Exude confidence.

✪ Handshake. Should be firm, but not too aggressive.

✪ Personal grooming. Clean, neat, professional dress, and do not overdo make-up, cologne/ perfume, or jewelry.

✪ Tone of voice and volume. You want to sound interested (with inflection), no monotone; but do not be too boisterous, overbearing, or funny.

✪ Eye contact. Maintain eye contact with the person you are speaking to. During a panel interview, look at the person who is asking the question. It is acceptable to look up while you are thinking, or to look around at each of the interviewers, but you want to avoid staring off into space, keeping someone in a deadlock stare, or constantly moving your eyes from person to person like you are at a tennis match.

✪ Enthusiasm. Act like this is the job for you. No one wants to hire someone who is not excited about the opportunity. Just do not come across as over-zealous.

✪ Posture/body language. Do not slump back in the chair. Do not get too comfortable because this can suggest boredom or lack of interest. However, do not seem too eager, whether by sitting on the edge of your chair or invading someone's personal space.

✪ Nervous habits (fidgeting, repeating the phrases umm and ahhh while you speak, shaking your leg, playing with a pen or paper, taking your glasses on and off, etc.). We all have nervous habits. During an interview your goal should be to minimize yours. That is why practice is so important—to help you identify what your nervous habits are. Identification is the first step to eliminating the habit. For example, if you find that you play with items in front of you, do not have them there during the interview.

✪ Smile. Again, you want to be as positive as you can throughout the entire interview.

## Steps to Prepare for an Interview

*Step 1:* Find and print the target announcement

*Step 2:* Analyze the job description

The interviewer will base questions on job analysis. Job analysis is the process of looking at a position (or, more broadly, the work of an organization) to identify essential functions and duties, and the competencies, knowledge, skills, and abilities needed to perform the work.

*Step 3:* Prepare your answers

Prepare a one-minute response to the "Tell me about yourself" question. Write five success stories to answer behavioral interview questions, ("Tell me about a time when…" or "Give me an example of a time…"). Prepare answers to the most common interview questions that will best present your skills, talents, and accomplishments:

- Why did you leave your last position?
- What do you know about our organization?
- What are your goals/Where do you see yourself in 5 years?
- What are your strengths and weaknesses?
- Why would you like to work for this organization?
- What is your most significant achievement?
- How would your last boss and colleagues describe you?
- Why should we hire you?
- What are your salary expectations?

*Step 4:* Research background on the agency and office – learn the latest news and challenges

Here are a few ideas to jump start your research:

- Find the mission of the organization from the vacancy announcement
- Find the agency's website, look up the history of the agency, and other news
- Research any recent events with the agency or office at: http://www.govexec.com/ and www.washingtonpost.com
- Check out President Bush's Management Agenda: http://www.whitehouse.gov/results/agenda/report8-04/PMA_report.pdf
- Is your target agency mentioned in the Management Agenda?
- What are the major issues or concerns of the agency?

*Step 5:* Study the structured interview system utilized by interviewers

Review the structured interview sample chart provided for you on the CD-ROM to get an idea of how the interviewer will view or rate your responses.

*Step 6:* Read about interviewing for federal jobs

Study this chapter, but you can also look online for even more information.

*Step 7:* Practice, practice, and practice your interview techniques

Practice in front of the mirror or with a friend for feedback.

*Step 8:* Be confident with your research and your ability to do the job

## EEO and Rating Systems

Be prepared to also expect the following during your interview:

### EEO (Equal Employment Opportunity) Involvement

In order to decrease the possibility of any grievances, an EEO representative is usually, but not always, present during an interview. The EEO representative ensures there is consistency with the questions asked and the length of the interview. The EEO representative also ensures that no illegal questions are asked. The presence of a third-party observer is to try to make sure each candidate is treated equally throughout the interview process.

### Rating Systems

Many agencies use rating systems during the interview process. A rating system is a means for the Selection Committee to measure one candidate against another based upon pre-formulated measures or scales. When rating systems are used, interviewers typically have a sheet, or scorecard, to use during the interview to rate the candidates' responses to the questions asked. At the end, the candidates can be compared, based upon their scores.

## Final Tips

*Before the Interview*

✪ Be prepared!

✪ Be memorable! Media training expert TJ Walker from www.worldwidemedia.com recommends that you have a story or message prepared so that you will be remembered at the "water cooler."

✪ Try to find out what kind of interview to expect, i.e. behavioral, technical, etc. Feel free to ask when scheduling the interview.

✪ Remember nothing will make you look worse than not knowing what you put on your own resume.

✪ Have your references' permission. These might be former managers, professors, friends of your family (but not family members), or people who know you through community service. You want them to be prepared to praise you. It would be beneficial to provide your references with the following information: the job for which you are applying, the name of the organization, and a copy of your resume.

*During the Interview*

✪ Arrive 10 to 15 minutes early for your interview.

✪ Dress appropriately! Ironed clothes, including skirts (at knee length or longer), nice slacks, or a suit. Keep your interview outfit simple and professional. Be conservative (until you get hired).

✪ Carry these items to the interview
    A copy of your references (for which you already have permission)
    Paper on which to take notes
    Directions to the interview site
    A copy of your resume
    Pen

✪ Be aware of your body language and eye contact. Stand and greet your interviewer with a firm handshake and a smile. Crossed-arms appear to be defensive, fidgeting may make everyone nervous, and a lack of eye contact may be interpreted as an untrustworthy person. Instead, nod while listening to show you are attentive and alert, and most importantly, sit and stand upright.

✪ Think before you answer; if you do not have a clear understanding of a question, ask for clarification. It is okay to take a moment to pause. If you need more time, ask to have the question repeated. But only do this once.

✪ Express yourself clearly and with confidence, not conceit. Keep your answers concise and to the point.

✪ Show a sincere interest in the office and position.

✪ Highlight yourself in your examples and stories, not your co-workers, team members, or supervisors.

✪ Focus on what you can contribute to the organization rather than what the employer can do for you. Do not ask about salary or benefits until the employer brings it up.

✪ Do not start a political discussion.

✪ Do not place blame or be negative about past employers.

✪ If some volunteer work you have done demonstrates a specific skill, use that experience as an example. To demonstrate your qualifications, you may go beyond your professional experiences to draw on other relevant examples.

✪ Be honest. Too much embellishing of one's experience/education, or falsifying, is a serious mistake.

✪ End the interview on a positive note indicating how you feel you are a good fit for the position at hand, and how you can make a contribution to the organization. Ask about the next step, as most offers are not extended on the spot.

✪ Thank the interviewer and ask for a business card. This will provide you with the necessary contact information for following up.

## Negotiating for a Federal Job

*Final Words from the author and Federal Career Coach, Kathryn Troutman*

Congratulations on being offered a position with the federal government! Here are a few final tips to help you negotiate your job offer.

### JOBSEEKER QUESTION:

I received a call from a Human Resource Specialist with a job offer, but I did not accept the job on the spot. I asked if I could call back the next day to think about the salary and benefits. The salary range for this GS-9 position is $39,795 to $51,738. I currently make $44,000. How do you go about negotiating for the higher salary range? What factors go into the agency's decision?

### KATHRYN'S ANSWER:

You can negotiate certain financial benefits with the Supervisor who is recruiting this position. Keep in mind that you will need to prove Superior Skills to receive a higher step than Step 1.

Each government job has a range of salary and grade or pay band. There is a range that the HR Specialist and Supervisor may have in mind to offer you -- depending on your years of experience, specialized experience, and critical skills, and the budget of the agency. You should have NO PROBLEM getting $44,000. I personally think that a person should strive for a minimum of 10% increase for a new position, so I would say that you could ask for $48,000 for this job.

Also, keep these following points in mind:

### Government Pay Scale Information

Check out the General Schedule Pay Scale page at
http://www.opm.gov/oca/08tables/html/gs.asp.

### Ask For A Higher Step Within Grade If You Can Prove Superior Skills

You do have the ability to negotiate your Step within your grade level. You can request a GS-9 Step 7 ($47,757), or any step you choose, based on any of the following reasons:

✪ Wanting a 10% raise from your previous salary for career development and advancement objectives.

✪ Proving your salary was $44K or higher with a W-2. This can help the supervisor see your objective in negotiating for a higher step.

✪ Stating you have extensive expenses involved in travel and relocation to the new position (because they might NOT specifically pay for the relocation expenses).

✪ Demonstrating that you have specialized experience that the agency will benefit by greatly, upon your hire into the position.

✪ Having critical, superior skills, education, and abilities that will greatly enhance the agency's mission and office services.

❂ Needing a minimum of Step 7 ($47,757) since you will be relocating to a geographic area with a higher economy, requiring additional income to support your family and needs.

❂ Providing any additional reason you can think of to justify why you should be paid more.

## Request for Tuition Reimbursement for Student Loans

Some agencies contribute payment toward student loans: up to $500 per month or $10K per year (up to $60K total). You can read about the government policy for hiring incentives at the website. You may be able to get the tuition reimbursement if the agency has the funds or accepts the program for new hires. See the U.S. Code at: http://www4.law.cornell.edu/uscode/5/5379.html

## Critical Hiring Need or Severe Shortage - Recruitment Bonus Incentive

Some agencies may pay a Recruitment Bonus Incentive for Critical Skills or Severe Shortage positions. Each agency is different and some may have critical job shortages. The agency could pay up to 25% of the annual salary. You can read the definitions of Critical Hiring Need or Severe Shortage at www.opm.gov.

## Request for Relocation Allowance

If the vacancy announcement does not state that they will NOT pay for relocation, you can ask if they will pay for relocation costs. If the announcement says that they WILL NOT pay for relocation, then you will not be able to negotiate this point.

## Be Confident

Be confident that you are highly skilled, ready to commit, and dedicated to public service. When you ask for your higher step, tuition reimbursement, or other request, you should be confident that the government WANTS TO HIRE YOU. They have selected you and they do not want to start the hiring process over!

## Negotiating Is Negotiating

When you negotiate, do not worry that they will take away your offer, because they will not. But remember that there is also no guarantee for any agreement on your requests. This is pure negotiation. If you have justifiable reasons and expertise for the job, you might be able to settle on agreeable terms. Keep in mind that you do not know about the budget the office has for hiring this position, so there could be unknown financial considerations for the agency.

Good luck with your negotiating! Please write to me if you have any recommendations or success stories for negotiating with Federal Human Resources Specialists or Supervisors.

# TOP TEN PROJECTED HIRES BY PROFESSIONAL FIELD

Fiscal Year 2007-2009
Bureau of Labor, *Career Guide to Industries, Federal Government, Excluding the Postal Service,*
2006-07 Edition

| Field | Projected Hires | Agencies Hiring |
|---|---|---|
| 1. Security & Protection | 35,620 | 8 |
| 2. Medical & Public Health | 35,350 | 6 |
| 3. Compliance & Enforcement | 27,243 | 12 |
| 4. Administrative/Program Management | 14,305 | 24 |
| 5. IT | 11,562 | 23 |
| 6. Business & Industry | 11,407 | 13 |
| 7. Engineering | 10,712 | 13 |
| 8. Budget/Accounting | 9,841 | 12 |
| 9. Legal | 9,691 | 20 |
| 10. Social Sciences | 4,151 | 10 |

# CASE STUDIES
## Federal Resume and KSA Real Stories

On the following pages you will find our case studies of real life experiences people have had in landing their federal jobs. These case studies are selected to match the top ten jobs that the federal government will be hiring in 2009, plus an additional case study about a job in Iraq.

Many of these case studies are shortened for printing in this book. Please find the complete case studies on the CD-ROM. An additional 13 case studies are also included on the CD-ROM. See the full listing of these case studies in the table of contents on pages iii and iv.

Use these case studies to help you understand how to write a successful federal resume. Read them to learn how to translate your private industry resume into a federal resume, and get important tips from the professional resume writers who prepared these cases.

# HAROLD DENTON

## Security & Protection

#1 in professional fields for projected government hiring in FY 2007 - 2009
35,620 projected to be hired in 2009

Includes intelligence analysis, international relations, foreign affairs, security administration, transportation security officer, park ranger, correctional officer, and police officer.

| Top Hiring Agencies | No. of Employees | Projected Hires |
|---|---|---|
| Department of Homeland Security | 41,701 | 23,746 |
| Department of Justice | 20,418 | 5,609 |
| Department of Defense | 10,149 | 4,886 |
| Department of Veteran Affairs | 2,552 | 929 |
| Department of Interior | 3,731 | 261 |
| Department of Treasury | 153 | 95 |
| Nuclear Regulatory Commission | 105 | 55 |
| Office of Personnel Management | 38 | 39 |
| Total (all agencies) | | 35,620 |

Partnership for Public Service, *Where the Jobs Are: Mission Critical Opportunities for America*, July 2007, http://ourpublicservice.org/OPS/publications/viewcontentdetails.php?id=118

# Facts

**Past Position:** Security Interviewer
**Past Salary:** $30,000
**Target Federal Job:** Personnel Security Specialist, GS-0080-09/11

# Qualifications

Harold worked as a personnel security specialist for a government contractor for four years. His salary was considerably less than the pay for GS-9 in the federal government even though he performed complex duties, and had an excellent record with both the contractor and with the Army. He targeted GS-9 because he possessed more than one year of specialized experience equivalent to the GS-7 level in federal employment and his Master's Degree showed that he qualified based on both experience and education.

VETERAN'S PREFERENCE: 5 points

# Starting Salary

$45,751 - $58,698 USD per year. Harold would like to move to a new location and is very flexible. Any location and position at this grade would be a substantial increase in salary and an opportunity to use his skills.

# Promotion/Promotional Potential

This job has a promotion potential up to GS-11. Harold feels that by getting his "foot in the door" at GS-9 would be a big salary increase and put him in a position for future moves in his career path.

# Results

Harold had been seeking a federal job for two years with little success. Although he has an MBA and almost 20 years combined military and civilian experience he was only able to find entry level employment at the contract level and was unsuccessful in finding a job he thought he deserved. After totally revamping his resume content and format to include keywords and experience found in announcements for his target series, Security and Protection, he applied for several positions with OPM, Department of State, and Homeland Security for personnel security specialist positions and was rated best qualified every time. He was interviewed for five positions and had offers from all over the country from several government agencies as well as other large government contractors. He accepted a GS-9 position in San Diego, CA. His resume is still searchable within USA Jobs and he continues to receive e-mails and phone messages about new opportunities.

# Target Job Announcement

A listing of the knowledge, skills, and abilities were not required to be provided in a separate narrative format and there was no assessment questionnaire requested. This meant that all the pertinent information needed to be included within the resume. All the skills for Security Specialists were fundamentally the same for many agencies. Since one resume could be used for the personnel security specialist positions we expected a good opportunity for referrals or selection.

Department of Army / Army Intelligence Command

| | |
|---|---|
| SALARY RANGE:<br>45,751.00 - 58,698.00 USD per year | OPEN PERIOD:<br>Tuesday, September 09, 20xx to Wed, December 31, 20xx |
| Salary Series & Grade: GG-0080-09/12 | POSITION INFORMATION: This is a full-time position. |
| PROMOTION POTENTIAL: 11 | DUTY LOCATIONS: 1 vacancy - Anne Arundel County, MD |

**Major Duties:**

Serves as security specialist performing the full range of moderately difficult to complex personnel security duties and assignments in **adjudicating personnel security investigations involving Active Army, Army Reserve, National Guard, DA civilians, and contractor personnel.**

You will **adjudicate investigative reports** and case files involving derogatory, conflicting data from personnel security, counterintelligence, or criminal investigations.

-Through **knowledge of principles, policy and procedures used in administering the personnel security program and adjudication of security clearance** and SCI access eligibility; for adjudication of SCI access and clearance conversions for the contractor support program and of **investigative activities.**

**Analyzes complex rebuttals** to Letters of Intent **and prepares final decision letter to subject providing the nexus for action taken**.

**Provides face to face interviews and follow-up determinations** in making relevant eligibility decisions on personnel for specific MOS Enlistment Option Programs under the U.S. Army Personnel Security Screening Program (PSSP).

**Adjudicates investigative reports and case files involving derogatory, conflicting or questionable data from personnel security, counterintelligence, or criminal investigations or received from other sources and renders decisions on the eligibility of personnel for collateral security clearances and access to Sensitive Compartmented Information.**

-**Based on thorough review of case files, grants clearances or prepares Letters of Intent to deny/revoke access/security clearance.**

**Knowledge, Skills and Abilities:**

1. **Knowledge of personnel security investigation process** to include the relationship of the requestors, the investigators and the adjudicators involved.

2.**Ability to provide assistance on technical matters** to lower level personnel and demonstrate expert knowledge of all aspect so the adjudicative process.

3. **Ability to effectively communicate both orally and in writing and possess excellent interpersonal skills.**

# Resume Writing Tips

Use these tips to help you transform your private industry resume into a targeted federal resume. The BEFORE and AFTER resumes are featured on the following pages.

## BEFORE – Private Industry Resume

### Resume Problem
Harold's resume was long on information and short on definition and clarity. The paragraphs were too long for someone to read and pick out the important data and lacked focus on the targeted position.

## AFTER – Federal Resume Focused Toward Target Position

### Resume Solution
Harold's resume was revised and reorganized using the OUTLINE FORMAT. His experience, skills, knowledge, and abilities were grouped into clearly defined paragraphs using KEY WORDS and PHRASES from the announcement. By providing a clear and organized resume, the Human Resource screeners or an electronic screening program could easily detect the key words and information in the resume and pass it on for further review.

Harold Denton
5490 Old Springs Place
St. Louis, MO 65003
Email: XXXXX@XXX.com
Home: (XXX) - XXX-XXXX
Work: (XXX) - XXX-XXXX, Cell: (XXX) - XXX-XXXX


PROFESSIONAL EXPERIENCE

LMNO COMMUNICATIONS, US Army Recruiting Command/5BDE, St Louis, Ops Div, St. Louis, MO
Security Interviewer, United States Recruiting Command, 20XX – Present (4 years)

Serves as a Personnel Security Assistant responsible to perform clerical/administrative duties. Receives and processes requests for SCI access. Conduct interviews, prepare security packets, conduct personnel reliability program interviews. Uses a wide variety of Department of Defense, Department of the Army, and Training and Doctrine Command regulations and directives governing enlistment eligibility. Initiates request for personnel security investigations; conducts local file checks; evaluates and notifies other organizations of unfavorable actions. Performs various information security related issues including: directing security violation/compromise investigation; review and analyze associated reports of findings; determines and directs necessary remedial action. Knowledge of national level, DoD, and Army personnel security policies and procedures, theories and principles of personnel security, a wide range of security administration programs, countermeasures, and background investigative techniques. Manages administrative duties, processing requests for Top Secret Security Clearances SCI access through the Joint Personnel Adjudication System (JPAS), and the Guidance Counselors Redesign (GCR); maintains a 98% accuracy rate.


Detachment Supervisor/Security Manager, United States Recruiting Command 20XX – 20XX (3 Years)

Served as Interim Detachment Commander/Security Manager, overseeing daily operations for 15 Security Interviewers and 5 civilian contractors throughout a 10-state area; supervised 3 military personnel. Reviewed and screened personnel security for soldiers requiring Secret and Top Secret clearances, serving as the principle advisor to a detachment commander. Interviewed military intelligence personnel as an impartial entity to ensure best-qualified individuals were selected for enlistment. Generated reports detailing pending and current clearances. Performs duties as an adjudicator for Military Police Applicants. Completed the Defense Security Service Personnel Security Manager and the Personnel Security Adjudications Training. Oversees the process of submission and acceptance of over 5,000 requests for Top Secret security clearances and 40,000 requests for Secret security clearances annually. Works with TRADOC Installation Security Managers to ensure Soldiers have been processed for the proper interim clearances. Prepares after action reports identifying deficiencies and provides recommendations for corrective action.

Harold Denton
5490 Old Springs Place
St. Louis, MO 65003
Home: (XXX) - XXX-XXXX
Work: (XXX) - XXX-XXXX, Cell: (XXX) - XXX-XXXX
Email: XXXXX@XXX.com
Social Security Number: XXX-XX-XXXX
Citizenship: United States
Veterans Preference: +5 points
Security Clearance: Interim Top Security Clearance

Objective                    Job Title, Pay scale-series-grade, Agency, Location
                             Job Announcement Number: _____

PROFESSIONAL EXPERIENCE:

XX/20XX to Present, (4 years) SECURITY INTERVIEWER,
LMNO COMMUNICATIONS, Contractor for United States Recruiting Command,
5BDE, St. Louis, Operations Division, St. Louis, MO
40 hours per week, Salary: $30,000 per year,
Supervisor: Tim Peterson, 555-555-5555, may contact

**CONDUCT FACE-TO-FACE INTERVIEWS, RESEARCH, AND EVALUATE SOURCE DOCUMENTS** IN ORDER TO PREPARE SECURITY PACKETS. Carry out interviews to determine applicants' eligibility for top-secret clearance and conduct personnel reliability program interviews. Complete record searches to gather information about applicants seeking federal security clearances. Evaluate requests to **ensure compliance with security regulations and policies**. Consult with Central Clearance Facility (CCF) for adjudication or guidance when needed. Obtain waivers and make administrative corrections to applications when required. Maintain Sensitive Compartmented Information (SCI) access-related files, records, reports, rosters, and messages for all supported personnel. Forward completed clearance to Office of Personnel Management, (OPM) and the Central Clearance Facility for processing.

REQUEST **AND PERFORM INVESTIGATIONS** for personnel security investigations; conduct local file checks; evaluate and notify other organizations of unfavorable actions. **Direct security violation/compromise investigations, review and analyze associated reports of findings; determine and direct necessary remedial action.** On occasion, acted as an Intermittent SPIN Investigator to provide follow up investigation on special cases and forwarded results to United States Investigative Services (USIS).

**ADJUDICATE INVESTIGATIVE REPORTS, following background investigations, review results to determine if candidate should be awarded security clearance**. Review and consider all available information to ensure individual's loyalty, reliability, and trustworthiness. Review and adjudicate reports and case files involving derogatory or conflicting data from personnel security investigations. Written results are included with final packet.

POSSESS **THOROUGH KNOWLEDGE OF SECURITY PERSONNEL PRINCIPLES, POLICY, AND PROCEDURES**. Utilize knowledge of national level Department of Defense (DOD) and Army personnel security policies, procedures, theories and principles, security administration programs, counter-measures, and background investigative techniques. Provide advice and guidance to colleagues on proper interpretation of laws and their application in specific situations.

PROVIDE A WIDE RANGE OF ADMINISTRATIVE SUPPORT AND ASSISTANCE to the United States Recruiting Command (USAREC) / (SCI) mission. Manage administrative and clerical support; process requests for SCI access and Top Secret Security Clearances. Monitor work in progress, project deadlines, and office organization. Review documents to ensure proper grammar, spelling, punctuation, format, and adherence to procedures. Utilize proprietary software including Joint Personnel Adjudication System (JPAS) and Guidance Counselors Redesign (GCR). Administer the personnel security program and adjudication of security clearance and SCI access eligibility and clearance conversions.

**PREPARE WRITTEN CORRESPONDENCE, ANALYSES, AND REPORTS. Analyze complex correspondence and prepare responses including recommendation for next action.** Reports include both narrative and numerical formats encompassing quantitative or qualitative analyses, identify anomalies, and make recommendations for improvement. Use a variety of office equipment and software including Word Perfect, Word, Excel, and PowerPoint.

20XX – 20XX (3 years), SUPERVISOR/SECURITY MANAGER,
LMNO COMMUNICATIONS, Contractor for United States Recruiting Command,
5BDE, St. Louis, Operations Division, St. Louis, MO
40 hours per week, Salary: $28, 500 per year,
Supervisor: Tim Peterson, 555-555-5555, may contact

**UTILIZED WIDE RANGING KNOWLEDGE OF SECURITY PERSONNEL POLICIES, REGULATIONS, AND PROCEDURES to support investigative activities, jurisdiction, and requirements of the Office of Personnel Management and US Army.** Interpreted federal laws, regulations, operating policies, and procedures in security personnel management including Equal Employment Opportunity and Privacy Act, among others.

**ENGAGED IN PROACTIVE ORAL COMMUNICATIONS WITH A WIDE VARIETY OF STAKEHOLDERS** including officers, service members, and colleagues in order to provide information, advocated for new approaches, and responded to a wide range of questions. Provided advice and counsel on sensitive matters. **Demonstrated superior interpersonal skills, using professionalism, tact, and courtesy on all occasions, even when under pressure or delivering negative information.**

**MANAGED THE TECHNICAL AND FUNCTIONAL WORK OF CONTRACT SECURITY INTERVIEWERS** located at the Personnel Security Screening Program (PSSP) detachment and 65 Military Entrance Processing Stations (MEPS) located throughout the United States. Reviewed and evaluated personnel security for soldiers requiring Secret and Top Secret clearances, interviewed military intelligence personnel as an impartial entity to ensure best-qualified individuals were selected for enlistment. **Appropriately applied a wide variety of Department of Defense, Department of the Army, and Training and Doctrine Command regulations and directives governing enlistment eligibility.**

**CONDUCTED INVESTIGATIVE ANALYSIS AND EVALUATED ADJUDICATIONS; provided guidance and information to subordinates regarding adjudications and technical advice.** Studied, reviewed, and recommended new procedures, policies, and programs. Performed difficult and complex personnel security duties and assignments in adjudicating personnel security investigations involving Active Army, Army Reserve, National Guard, DA civilians, and contractor personnel. **Based on thorough review of case files, granted clearances or prepared Letters of Intent to deny/revoke access/security clearance.** Analyzed rebuttals to Letters of Intent and prepared final decision letters to subject providing recommendation for action to be taken.

# STEPHANIE MONROE

**REGISTERED NURSE WORKING AS A FEDERAL CONTRACTOR TO PUBLIC HEALTH ADVISOR**

**MEDICAL, HOSPITAL, DENTAL, AND PUBLIC HEALTH GROUP, GS-0600**

## Medical and Public Health

#2 in professional fields for projected government hiring in FY 2007 - 2009
35,350 projected to be hired in 2009

Includes physician (all disciplines), nursing, dietician/nutrition, occupational. and rehabilitation therapy, radiology, pharmacy, industrial hygiene, and consumer safety.

| Top Hiring Agencies | No. of Employees | Projected Hires |
|---|---|---|
| Department of Veterans Affairs | 78,950 | 28,041 |
| Department of Defense | 6,161 | 3,767 |
| Department of Health and Human Services | 13,055 | 3,447 |
| Department of Labor | 442 | 63 |
| Department of Agriculture | 393 | 27 |
| Department of Energy | 26 | 5 |
| Total (all agencies) | | 35,350 |

Partnership for Public Service, *Where the Jobs Are: Mission Critical Opportunities for America*, July 2007, http://ourpublicservice.org/OPS/publications/viewcontentdetails.php?id=118

## Facts

**Past Position:** Program Coordinator / Government Contractor
**Past Salary:** $69,000
**Target Federal Job:** Public Health Advisor, CMS, Department of Health and Human Services, GS-685-9/11/12

## Qualifications

Stephanie wanted to be rated as "best qualified" so that she would be referred to the selecting official. In addition to submitting a resume, she also had to complete a questionnaire and write KSAs. The questionnaire was complex and she read through the questions several times to be sure she selected the best answer for her experience.

**TIP:** If a separate certificate is issued for each grade, it can be advantageous for candidates to apply for multiple grades and hopefully appear on multiple certificates. The more certificates you are on, the better your chances to be selected.

## Starting Salary

$48,108 - $90,698 USD per year

## Promotion/Promotional Potential

This position offers non-competitive promotion potential to a grade 14. This candidate was pleased that her new federal position offered a much better benefits package than she had received with her contract position. This included transit subsidies, flextime, telecommuting, and a job training program that added even more value to her new position.

## Results

This candidate had worked as a federal contract employee in a program coordination and technical support role, but her contract was about to expire. With no guarantee of continued employment, she decided to apply for this federal position. She wanted to continue contributing her program management, healthcare administration, and analytical skills on a permanent, long-term basis. Plus, she was confident that with her nursing background and Master's degree in Healthcare administration, she would be in a great position to advance within the federal government. With a totally revamped resume and KSAs, she qualified for THREE federal positions and was offered her top choice federal position.

**TIP:** Answering the "highest" answer on the questionnaire is important, but your resume and KSAs must support the multiple choice answers you selected. You may even lose points for not supporting your answers in your resume and KSAs.

# Target Job Announcement

## Public Health Advisor, GS-685-11/12/13/14
- The Public Health Advisor serves as principal representative and provides comprehensive technical and administrative advice and assistance to an assigned department in operating a large program.
- These positions are in various geographical locations throughout the DHHS.

### Major Duties:
The Public Health Advisor carries out **large scale public health projects and/or programs. Designs, develops, implements, manages and evaluates all aspects of large, complex, politically sensitive, or developmental special projects or programs.** Provides **leadership to agencies and organizations** in developing, extending and/or improving their health care systems, strategies and services. **Manages awards, grants, cooperative agreements** and comparable funding sources for contracts. Performs advisory and assistance functions. Serves as principal representative and provides **technical and administrative advice** and assistance to an assigned department in operating a large program.

### How You Will Be Evaluated:
Your application will be evaluated and rated under Category Rating and Selection procedures. Category rating combines the applicant's total qualifying experience and education/training into a single quality category.
If you meet the basic qualification requirements, we will further evaluate your entire application package to determine the quality and extent of your experience, education, training, etc., for placement in one of the following categories:
1. Best Qualified - Meets the Minimum Qualification Requirements and excels in most requirements of the position;
2. Well Qualified - Meets the Minimum Qualification Requirements and meets most requirements of the position;
3. Qualified - Meets the Minimum Qualification Requirements, but do not possess the relevant competencies to a substantive degree.

### SPECIAL NOTES:
- This position is being announced for multiple locations and multiple grades. You must specifically identify all locations and all grades for which you desire consideration. You will receive consideration only for locations and/or grades indicated in your online application.
- Be sure to apply only for locations for which you will accept an offer of employment. If you are offered employment, it will be for only one of the locations you indicated in your online application. That is, you will not be offered a choice of locations.

### Essay questions from Questionnaire:
1) Describe your experience in providing direction and leadership in the development of major initiatives, programs and contracts to carry out your organization's mission.
2) Please provide 1-2 examples of your working knowledge of public health and health-related programs, concepts, practices, and procedures.
3) In the space provided, cite examples of your education and/or experience that have provided you with an understanding of the importance of unique cultural issues which impact on treatment effectiveness.

# Resume Writing Tips

Use these tips to help you transform your private industry resume into a targeted federal resume. The BEFORE and AFTER resumes are featured on the following pages.

## BEFORE – Private Industry Resume

### Resume Problem

Stephanie's resume was more suitable for the private sector and did not really highlight her extensive experience and skills. Her resume was not developed for the announcement and did not include the keywords from the announcement.

**TIP:** It is important to spell out your experience, skills, knowledge, and abilities; Human Resources evaluates what you write and does not make assumptions about what you did.

## AFTER – Federal Resume Focused Toward Target Position

### Resume Solution

Put resume into an outline format, greatly expanding knowledge, skills and abilities. Eliminated bullets, lines, and other formatting found in the original version so that the resume could be used for federal online builders and could be printed for interview presentation. Used target language and keywords from the announcement. Added accomplishments and content to ensure the resume matched the KSAs and questionnaire. Deleted jobs that were not relevant to the position she was seeking. Prepared KSAs using the CCAR format (context, challenge, action, result) to convey the candidate's story in a more powerful way. To accommodate the character limitations of the USA Job resume builder, Job Block 1 was divided into two and the experience continued in Job Block 2.

Keyword List:
- Large scale public health projects and/or programs experience
- Manage special projects or programs
- Provide leadership to agencies and organizations
- Program analysis
- Data analysis
- Public Health research
- Develop and improve health care systems, strategies, and services
- Policy development
- Regulatory compliance
- Manage awards, grants, cooperative agreements, funding, contracts
- Technical and administrative advisor

**STEPHANIE MONROE, RN**
555 West Rd.
Annapolis, MD 22222
smonroe@aol.com

## Summary

Healthcare Professional with excellent academic credentials, a strong clinical and administrative background, and solid experience in nursing field program development and implementation. Track record of increasing awareness, treatment, and prevention of public health issues. Youth program development and health risk assessment experience. Project management and team leadership experience. Former School Health nurse with public speaking experience. Applied health research and social and behavioral program research.

EDUCATION Master of Science, Healthcare Administration, May 20xx
Bloomberg School of Public Health, The Johns Hopkins University
Bachelor of Science in Nursing, University of Delaware, May 19xx
Public Health Program Administration, Analysis and Management

## EXPERIENCE

**Program Coordinator,** August 20xx – Present
Contractor to CMS, Baltimore, MD

Contract employee responsible for providing technical assistance, program analysis, and content expertise on multiple child and adolescent mental health initiatives for CMS, Substance Abuse and Mental Health Services division.
- Collaborate across federal agencies, national associations, and other key partners on child mental health program development at the federal, state, and local levels.
- Analyze, evaluate, and develop program guidelines, goals, components, and strategies for the grant program.
- Interact with federal, state, and local resources for developing media and outreach material to reach across multiple agencies and communities.
- Interfaced with community partners to effectively target and reach at-risk populations.
- Bring together multidisciplinary teams to develop prevention and outreach strategies and to discuss changes/updates in provider protocols.

**Medical Case Manager,** *HIV Client Services,* *August 20xx – October 20xx*
Contractor to Baltimore County Govt., Baltimore, MD
- Coordinated delivery of care for HIV persons in homecare settings. Collaborated with multidisciplinary teams to manage cases and maximize quality of patient care.
- Performed physical and psychosocial assessments of clients to determine homecare/DME requirements.

- Served as specialty educational resource for newly diagnosed clients/families, providing information and counseling on HIV treatments and support.
- Served as a grant proposal reviewer for STD/HIV programs.
- Monitored various grants/contracts to ensure compliance of award conditions.

**Grant Manager,** September 20xx – September 20xx
University of Maryland, Health and Mental Hygiene, College Park, MD

Managed this federal grant program. Serve as primary liaison to the Maryland's Department of Health and Mental Hygiene. Monitored the contractual and fiscal obligations of a grant for rape prevention and education.

- Oversaw implementation of the Rape and Sexual Assault Prevention Program in the public school system and rape crisis centers throughout Maryland.
- Conducted grantee site visits; provide training and technical assistance, including curriculum specialist services and program evaluation procedures and resources.
- Conducted a statewide evaluation of the school-based program.
- Developed a statewide media campaign to raise awareness of rape and sexual assault in Maryland.

*STEPHANIE MONROE, RN*

555 West Rd.
Annapolis, MD 22222
smonroe@aol.com
Contact Phone: 222-222-2222
Contact Email: smonroe@aol.com

US Citizen
Social Security Number: xxx-xx-xxxx
Veteran's Preference: N/A
Highest Previous Grade: N/A

PROFESSIONAL PROFILE

Public Health Professional and Registered Nurse with more than **five years experience in managing large scale public health care projects and programs.** Skilled in program evaluation, implementation, and management. Demonstrated ability to develop, implement, and evaluate effective health programs and strategies to further the national mental health, youth violence prevention, and HIV prevention agendas for at risk populations. Solid research experience with the Bloomberg School of Public Health. **Leadership** expertise in **policy development, regulatory review, coalition building, and clinical practice**. Extensive experience evaluating public health care needs, managing staff, and managing grants, contracts, funding, and operating budgets. Outstanding project management competencies. Track record of increasing awareness, treatment, and prevention of public health issues. Skilled clinician and effective leader with a reputation for contributing to morale and productivity.

PROFESSIONAL EXPERIENCE

09/20xx to present, PROGRAM COORDINATOR, CMS, Contract Employee, Baltimore, MD, 40+ hours per week, $69,000 per year, Supervisor Name, (202) 222-2222, do not contact.

**TECHNICAL CONSULTANT** AND ANALYST ON SUBSTANCE ABUSE AND MENTAL HEALTH SERVICES: Contract employee providing expert, on-site **technical assistance, administrative advice, program analysis, content expertise, and program evaluation** on a wide variety of complex, national HIV and mental health programs for mental health initiatives.

APPLY QUANTITATIVE AND QUALITATIVE METHODS TO **EVALUATE AND IMPROVE NATIONAL PROGRAMS** such as the Mary Barnes HIV Prevention Grant program. Strategize and make recommendations on data collection as well as data analysis. Monitor program evaluation, review results, and provide comprehensive written recommendations for use in the final report.

RESEARCH AND **ANALYZE COMPLEX, POLITICALLY-SENSITIVE SPECIAL PROJECTS** AND PUBLIC HEALTH PROGRAMS; develop detailed program plans, complete with actions required, responsibility, and due dates for school- and community-based mental health initiatives, including youth violence prevention and HIV prevention. Monitor, track, and document program implementation and progress; make mid-course corrections to adjust for changing priorities or interim results. Evaluate effectiveness of programs and make recommendations for program enhancement.

ENGAGE IN PROACTIVE ORAL COMMUNICATIONS AND COLLABORATIONS WITH A WIDE VARIETY OF INTERNAL AND EXTERNAL STAKEHOLDERS including government executives, contractors, providers, mental health and national association professionals, researchers, experts, and other federal, state, and local government public health and educational professionals, family members, and consumers, to communicate strategic vision for youth violence prevention and HIV prevention programs. Prepare briefings, technical papers, and reports.

FORM MUTUALLY BENEFICIAL ALLIANCES: Develop resources and collaborations among academics, government officials, and national organizations to form alliances for mutual benefit. Promote best practices. Participate on high visibility projects to build a collaborative vision on youth violence prevention and HIV prevention and other child and youth mental health issues.

REGULATORY ANALYST: ANALYZE AND INTERPRET COMPLEX, FEDERAL LEGISLATION AND REQUIREMENTS, including the Mary Barnes Memorial Act (MBMA), Health Insurance Portability and Accountability Act (HIPAA), Government Performance and Results Act (GPRA), SAMHSA National Outcome Measures (NOMs), Office of Management and Budget (OMB), and other relevant federal regulations, policies, and procedures. Ensure regulatory compliance of all programs and initiatives.

09/20xx to present, PROGRAM COORDINATOR, CMS, Contract Employee, Baltimore, MD, 40+ hours per week, $69,000 per year, Supervisor Name, (202) 222-2222, do not contact.

JOB BLOCK 1 CONTINUED:
ADVANCE KNOWLEDGE AND SKILLS IN CHILD AND YOUTH MENTAL HEALTH FIELD THROUGH PROFESSIONAL DEVELOPMENT including youth violence prevention and HIV through attendance at professional conferences, symposia, and workshops, research and review of professional and peer reviewed journals, and best practices. Interpret and integrate significant developments in the mental health promotion, youth violence prevention, and HIV prevention fields into analyses, technical guidance, and other work.

PREPARE AND PRESENT WRITTEN STRATEGIES, REPORTS, ISSUE PAPERS, MEMORANDA, AND ANALYSES related to child mental health, youth violence prevention, implementation of evidence-based programs, HIV prevention, project management, and best practices. Prepare technical analyses and talking points used to brief executive personnel and/or to prepare Congressional briefings. Develop, implement, monitor, and track complex, technical action plans for child mental health update as required. Disseminate written materials supporting and promoting the agency's strategic vision to government and research audiences. Prepare recommendations and analyses for program and agency leadership on public health programming in children's mental health, youth violence prevention, and HIV prevention.

ANALYZE, EVALUATE, AND DEVELOP PROGRAM guidelines, goals, and components for safe schools healthy students. Review Requests for Application and provide in-depth analyses on program elements, integrating best practices compatible with long and short-term public mental health policies and goals.

ACCOMPLISHMENTS:
+ Consistently recognized by supervisors and colleagues for quality of written work as well as effectiveness in building collaborative relationships with various constituencies.
+ Selected for consultation on multiple high visibility strategic planning initiatives as content expert in child mental health, youth violence prevention, and HIV prevention programming.

EDUCATION

20xx, Master of Science, Healthcare Administration, Bloomberg School of Public Health, The Johns Hopkins University, Baltimore, MD GPA - 3.5

19xx, Bachelor of Science in Nursing, University of Delaware, 121 semester hours, GPA 3.7

# LIONEL RICHMOND

**INSURANCE INVESTIGATOR SEEKS POSITION IN GOVERNMENT AS INVESTIGATOR**

**INVESTIGATION GROUP, GS-1800**

## Compliance and Enforcement

#3 in professional fields for projected government hiring in FY 2007 - 2009
27,243 projected to be hired in 2009

Includes inspectors, investigators (including criminal), customs and border patrol, and protection, import specialist and customs inspection.

| Top Ten Hiring Agencies | No. of Employees | Projected Hires |
|---|---|---|
| Department of Homeland Security | 49,316 | 20,026 |
| Department of Justice | 26,436 | 4,534 |
| Department of Agriculture | 7,673 | 831 |
| Department of Labor | 4,512 | 750 |
| Office of Personnel Management | 1,632 | 636 |
| Environmental Protection Agency | 2,279 | 240 |
| Department of Commerce | 232 | 78 |
| Equal Opportuntiy Commission | 825 | 65 |
| Department of Education | 95 | 34 |
| Securities and Exchange Commission | 173 | 24 |
| Total (all agencies) | | 27,243 |

Partnership for Public Service, *Where the Jobs Are: Mission Critical Opportunities for America*, July 2007, http://ourpublicservice.org/OPS/publications/viewcontentdetails.php?id=118

## Facts

**Past Position:** Material Damage Appraiser
**Past Salary**: $58,000
**Target Federal Job:** Investigator, GS-1801-5/7/9

## Qualifications

Applicant has a background in auto insurance claims and investigations, but no government experience. Lionel also has outstanding oral communication and interpersonal skills, resulting from several years as an "on air" talent for radio.

## Starting Salary

$26,264 - $51,738 USD per year (more depending upon location)

## Promotion/Promotional Potential

This was a GS-5/7/9 position; there was no promotion potential mentioned in the announcement with this position. However, Lionel was anxious to get a position with more security and benefits.

## Results

Lionel wanted to get into the government as an investigator. He wanted to use his criminal justice degree, as well as several years of experience conducting investigations for the insurance industry. His application was referred to selecting officials.

## Target Job Announcement

Criminal Investigator (Special Agent)
Department Of Justice / Bureau of Alcohol, Tobacco, Firearms, & Explosives
Additional Duty Location Info: many vacancies - throughout the Nation, US

Major Job Duties:

Investigates criminal violations of Federal laws within the enforcement jurisdiction of the Department of Justice. Conducts investigations of violations relating to explosives, firearms, arson, and alcohol and tobacco diversion. Gathers and analyzes evidence through investigative leads, seizures and arrests, execution of search warrants and a variety of other means. Prepares concise criminal investigative case reports. Testifies for the government in court or before grand juries. Travel may be considerable, depending upon assignments.

PROMOTION POTENTIAL: The full performance level for this position is Grade 13. NOTE: Promotions are based upon performance and must receive supervisory approval.

## Resume Writing Tips

Use these tips to help you transform your private industry resume into a targeted federal resume. The BEFORE and AFTER resumes are featured on the following pages.

### BEFORE – Private Industry Resume

#### Resume Problem
This was Lionel's first application for a federal job; he really did not know how to approach applying for this position in terms of his resume or KSAs. His existing resume was more like a private sector resume and was not focused on his skills or abilities and did not include any accomplishments to demonstrate that he could achieve results. In addition, Lionel is not a veteran. Entry into the investigative field can be very challenging when much of the competition is coming out of the military and using veteran's preference. Therefore, it is even more important in these situations to demonstrate all of your skills and experience and back it up with powerful accomplishments.

**TIP:** Lionel recognized that getting a federal position would be a process and did not expect immediate results. In addition, he was willing to take an entry-level position, with a possible pay cut so that he could get into the government. He was also willing to apply across multiple grades and agencies, including those outside the DOD and DHS where most veterans apply, to maximize his chances of getting rated best qualified. If you do not indicate that you are willing to be considered for lower grades, you will only be considered for the highest grade for which you are eligible.

### AFTER – Federal Resume Focused Toward Target Position

#### Resume Solution
Lionel's new resume utilized the Outline Format with headlines in all caps. The headlines were written using the keywords from the announcement, making his specialized experience very clear for the human resources specialist and supervisor.

# LIONEL RICHMOND

*Seeking a position in the field of*
**Law Enforcement**

CITY • STATE • FEDERAL • PRIVATE

•Highly motivated, analytical professional with strong work ethic and professional goals.
•Meet challenges head on; work well in stressful situations and in fast-past setting.
•Maintain excellent research, organization, time-management, problem solving, assessment and resolution skills.

---
### EDUCATION
---

**Bachelor of Arts, Criminal Justice – 20xx**
Temple University, Philadelphia, PA

---
## PROFESSIONAL EXPERIENCE
---

**ABC Insurance**                                      2/xx-Present [3 years]
*Damage Appraiser*
Contacts policy holders and claimants to schedule appointments for vehicle inspection. Explain claims resolution process. Monitor supplemental damage. Provide exceptional customer service. Investigate fraudulent insurance claims. Process stolen and recovered vehicles. Settle total losses. Mitigate rental expenses and storage charges.

**WXXX 110.3 FM/WZZZ 112.9 FM**                        9/xx-Present [2 years]
*Weekend On-Air Talent*
Handle daily disc jockey responsibilities. Deliver public service announcements. Produce and provide voice-overs for local commercials. Assist in determining program format. Knowledgeable of Scott system. Execute on-site promotions and contests at client locations, station appearances and clubs.

**WCBA 95.5FM**                                        12/xx-9/xx [3 years]
*On-Air Talent / Promotions*
Weekend on-air talent. Promotions Street Squad- responsible for set up of promotions at client locations and station promotions. Execute on-site promotions and contests at client locations, station appearances and clubs. Produce commercials for the programming department.

**John's Insurance** 9/xx-9/xx [1 year]
*Total Loss Specialist*
Contacted and negotiated settlement of total loss vehicles. Prepared arrangements for the removal of salvaged vehicles. Coordinated rental and storage end dates and mitigated charges. Monitored titles, lien status and supplemental damage. Reviewed estimates from body shops to ensure proper parts usage. Prepared estimates for damaged vehicles. Provided exceptional customer service.

**Auto Insurance** 9/xx-9/xx [2 years]
*Claims Representative*
Conducted client interviews regarding bodily injury and property damage claims. Settled bodily injury claims prior to litigation. Investigated fraudulent insurance claims through extensive witness interviews, detailed analysis of police reports and scene investigations. Handled stolen and recovered vehicles; settled total losses. Assisted in the resolution of a Texas hailstorm claim -the largest catastrophe in company history.

**Enterprise Rent-A-Car** 8/xx-2/xx
*Manager Trainee*
Established communication between insurance companies and auto body repair facilities. Managed business-to-business accounts. Handled contracts and account receivables. Provided exceptional customer service. Exceeded designated sales goals. Completed vehicle inspections.

---
**TECHNOLOGY SKILLS**
---

Microsoft Word, PowerPoint, Microsoft Outlook, Excel, Internet Research, Media Touch, Scott Systems, CJIS and Data Entry.

Lionel Richmond
1234 Mercury Court
Temple Hills, MD 20708

Contact Phone: xxx-xxx-xxxx
Contact Email: lmrichmond@abcmail.com

US Citizen
Social Security Number: xxx-xx-xxxx
Veteran's Preference: N/A
Highest Previous Grade: N/A

Announcement: Entry Level Criminal Investigator, GS-1801-5/7/9

PROFESSIONAL PROFILE

Skilled fact finder with a Criminal Justice degree and experience conducting investigations involving multiple parties and allegations. Outstanding organizational, oral communication, and interpersonal skills to work with diverse employees and customers in stressful and crisis management situations. Goal oriented, high energy individual with excellent attention to detail. Proven analytical skills; ability to investigate and evaluate facts and draw appropriate conclusions. Polished, professional presentation.

PROFESSIONAL EXPERIENCE

02/20xx to present [3 years], MATERIAL DAMAGE APPRAISER, ABC Insurance, 678 Jefferson Boulevard, Baltimore, MD, 40 hours per week, $58,517 per year, Jay Smith, 443-123-4567, may contact.

PLAN AND CONDUCT INVESTIGATIONS of complex motor vehicle accidents, theft and forced entry. Investigations include on-scene investigation, examination of the vehicle, interviews of witnesses and participants, collection of evidence, review of medical records, analysis of soft tissue injuries, and related issues. Prepare mock diagrams to illustrate circumstances. Use established analytical and investigative techniques to conduct investigations. Investigations are thorough and timely. Determine liability and loss; evaluate claims for on-going medical treatment. Coordinate with state and local law enforcement as appropriate.

ANALYZE, EVALUATE, AND INTERPRET INFORMATION FROM INVESTIGATIONS and formulate conclusions about the investigation. Use experience and objective judgment to make decisions about liability and loss. Evaluate opportunities for early settlement based on analysis; negotiate settlements when appropriate. Determine whether claims are fraudulent; refer to proper enforcement personnel if fraud is indicated.

ENGAGE IN EFFECTIVE, PROACTIVE ORAL COMMUNICATIONS, often under difficult or highly emotional circumstances, with widely diverse individuals. Develop questions, interview claimants, and other parties. Conduct follow-up when appropriate. Coordinate with other departments, including legal, to prepare cases for trial or subrogation. Demonstrate tact, professionalism, and courtesy on all occasions.

MANAGE UP TO 25 CLAIMS CONCURRENTLY; plan and organize work in order to meet work objectives and goals. Determine approaches to claims, based on an understanding of company's overall priorities. Coordinate with others to solve unique or highly complex problems. Set deadlines and milestones; ensure all timeframes and administrative requirements are met. Authorize claims payments.

PREPARE A WIDE RANGE OF WRITTEN CORRESPONDENCE AND REPORTS; reports are detailed, factual, and well developed. Conclusions are based on analysis and evaluation of evidence, witness statements, and interviews. Prepare affidavits in cases of theft. Utilize Word, Excel, Outlook, Claims Workbench, and proprietary software to prepare numerical and narrative reports for management. Reports include all supporting documentation and are used in prosecutions of fraudulent and other claims.

RESEARCH, INTERPRET AND APPLY traffic regulations and policy coverage when adjudicating and investigating claims. Determine coverage and apply best practices to conclude claims.

PROMOTE TEAM APPROACH to work. Share information and seek input from internal and external sources; build consensus to ensure optimal efficiency and effectiveness, as well as technical compliance. Develop collaborative relationships with colleagues to identify potential issues and enhance effectiveness. Mentor less experienced personnel; train and assist others with complex, controversial, and difficult cases.

DEMONSTRATE OUTSTANDING CUSTOMER SERVICE to a broad range of internal and external customers, often under difficult circumstances. All interactions are professional, courteous, and tactful, despite occasional provocation by insured and their representatives. Provide timely service.

KEY ACCOMPLISHMENTS: Through careful analysis and follow-through, identified case of insurance fraud. Worked closely with local and federal law enforcement on several investigations of vehicular manslaughter. Analyzed and researched claim of policyholder; determined negligence on part of owner.

12/20xx to 09/20xx [2 years], ON-AIR TALENT/PROMOTIONS, WCBA, 95.5 FM, 4900 Radio Drive, Anywhere, MD, 30 hours per week, $12,668 per year, Ryan Seagram, 301-999-9999, may contact.

DEMONSTRATED OUTSTANDING ORAL COMMUNICATION SKILLS on live radio. Read or ad-libbed scripts to identify station, introduce and close shows, and announce station breaks, commercials, and public service information. Prepared and created shows by gathering information from wire copy, periodicals, computer, and television. Read news flashes to keep audience informed of important events. Recorded interviews of guest, musical, or other famous or public personalities; edit interviews. Interviewed guests to entertain audience. Answered phone lines and interviewed members of listening audience who telephone musical requests. Aired station contests according to the specifications of the program director. Hosted and assisted at charity functions and attend live, in-person appearances. Provided live reports from site of event. Maintained and built strong personal community involvement. Demonstrated professionalism, courtesy, and tact on all occasions.

09/20xx to 09/20xx [3 years] TOTAL LOSS SPECIALIST, John's Insurance, 1234 Insurance Road, Silver Spring, MD, 40 hours per week, $40,199 per year, Chris Smith, 301-123-4567, may contact.

MANAGED AND COORDINATED TOTAL LOSS VEHICLE CLAIMS, consistent with customer coverage. Evaluated damage and negotiated settlements with claimants. Prepared arrangements with local vendors for the removal of salvaged vehicles; coordinated rental and storage arrangements for customers. Handled an average of 100 claims per month.

PREPARED, ANALYZED, AND EVALUATED ESTIMATES from body shops to ensure estimates were accurate and reflected options available for repairing vehicles consistent with customer contracts and corporate standards. Identified anomalies and resolved them. Monitored and tracked repairs to ensure timely completion of work and restoration of vehicles. Checked titles, lien status, and supplemental damage to ensure claim accuracy and policy coverage.

DEMONSTRATED OUTSTANDING CUSTOMER SERVICE to a broad range of internal and external customers, often under difficult circumstances. All interactions were professional, courteous, and tactful, despite occasional provocation by insured and their representatives. Provided timely service.

09/20xx to 09/20xx [2 years], CLAIMS REPRESENTATIVE, Auto Insurance, 6789 Main Street, Beltsville, MD 20705, 40 hours per week, $41,908 per year, Chris Jones, may contact.

ANALYZED AND EVALUATED MORE THAN 120 COMPLEX VEHICLE CLAIMS EACH MONTH in accordance with accident investigation reports and customer policy limitations. Assessed damage, decided liability, and determined coverage. Negotiated settlements in damage, theft, forced entry, and vehicular death claims. Determined approaches to claims, based on an understanding of company's overall priorities. Coordinated with others to solve unique or highly complex claims. Evaluated total losses; arranged for salvage and disposal of lost vehicles. Made repair/replace decisions.

RESEARCHED AND PREPARED DAMAGE ESTIMATES on vehicles being repaired in affiliated shops. Ensured estimates were accurate and reflected best use of resources and options available to repair vehicles in a timely manner. Estimates include unibody, steering, mechanical, electrical, and other major structural damage. Monitored progress of repairs; intervened between customer and shop when required to facilitate timely and quality repairs.

PLANNED AND CONDUCTED INVESTIGATIONS of complex motor vehicle accidents, theft, and forced entry. Investigations included on-scene investigation, examination of the vehicle, extensive and detailed interviews of witnesses and participants, collection of evidence, review of medical records, analysis of soft tissue injuries, and related issues. Prepared mock diagrams to illustrate circumstances. Used established analytical and investigative techniques to conduct investigations. Determined liability and loss; evaluated claims for on-going medical treatment. Coordinated with state and local law enforcement as appropriate.

NEGOTIATED AGREED PRICE with shop manager and established timeframes for job completion. Monitored and tracked job progress; reviewed and authorized supplemental work. Negotiated settlements with customers, consistent with company policy.

DEMONSTRATED EXCEPTIONAL SERVICE ORIENTATION, INTERPERSONAL AND ORAL COMMUNICATION SKILLS. Interacted with a diverse range of internal and external customers including shop managers, repair personnel, company clients, employees, law enforcement, and attorneys. Consistently provided timely, accurate, and responsive service. Appropriately represented company to external customers. Demonstrated tact and courtesy on all occasions, even when under pressure.

ORGANIZED CLAIMS WORK AND ENSURED QUALITY PRODUCTION in affiliate shops. Monitored repair progress, capacity, and availability. Influenced repair process progression. Tracked facility performance on timeliness and repair quality; identified problems and recommended approaches to solve quality issues. Influenced decisions regarding affiliate suspension, elimination, and new shop development.

KEY ACCOMPLISHMENT: Selected to participate in resolute of a Texas hailstorm claim; the largest catastrophe in company history.

08/20xx to 02/20xx, MANAGER TRAINEE, Enterprise Rent-a-Car, 1234 Baltimore Avenue, Gaithersburg, MD, 40 hours per week, $32,000 per year, Greg Andrews, 301-345-6789, may contact.

PARTICIPATED IN THE FULL RANGE of facility management including business-to-business accounts, contracts, and accounts receivable. Coordinated communications between insurance companies and auto body repair shops to facilitate repair to damaged vehicles.

DEMONSTRATED EXCELLENT COMMUNICATION AND INTERPERSONAL SKILLS; interacted with individual and corporate customers on a daily basis; provided outstanding service by identifying and addressing needs. Prepared and presented a wide range of written numerical and narrative reports that analyzed trends, reported status, and made recommendations for enhancing operational efficiency. Utilized Word, Excel, Outlook, and proprietary software to analyze information and prepare reports.

PROFESSIONAL TRAINING

Investigative Report Writing, 20xx
Interviewing for Investigations, 20xx
Investigative Skills, 20xx

EDUCATION

20xx, Bachelor of Arts, Temple University, Philadelphia, PA, major: Criminal Justice, 120 semester hours.

19xx, Diploma, Haddonfield High School, Haddonfield, NJ

# JOHN WALLSTONE

**SOUS CHEF LANDS POSITION AS PROGRAM ANALYST**
**GENERAL ADMINISTRATIVE, CLERICAL, AND OFFICE SERVICES GROUP, GS-0300**

## Administration and Program Management
#4 in professional fields for projected government hiring in FY 2007 - 2009
14,305 projected to be hired in 2009

Includes human resources, equal employment opportunity, management/program analysis, telecommunications, and a variety of clerical support activities

| Top Ten Hiring Agencies | No. of Employees | Projected Hires |
|---|---|---|
| Department of Defense | 13,113 | 3,188 |
| Department of Justice | 8,513 | 2,908 |
| Department of Housing and Urban Development | 2,705 | 1,213 |
| Department of Health and Human Services | 4,571 | 789 |
| National Aeronautics and Space Administration | 3,239 | 665 |
| Department of Commerce | 1,122 | 552 |
| Department of Agriculture | 3,873 | 525 |
| General Services Administration | 2,000 | 474 |
| Department of Veterans Affairs | 1,527 | 418 |
| Department of Transportation | 595 | 360 |
| Total (all agencies) | | 14,305 |

Partnership for Public Service, *Where the Jobs Are: Mission Critical Opportunities for America*, July 2007, http://ourpublicservice.org/OPS/publications/viewcontentdetails.php?id=118

## Facts

**Past Position:** Sous Chef, Executive Chef, Annapolis, MD
**Past Salary**: $60,000
**Target Federal Job:** Program Analyst, GS-0343-9/12

## Qualifications

John demonstrates in his résumé that he has one year specialized experience at or equivalent to the GS-11 level. John has actually changed jobs since his first position in government. He is currently at FEMA in a GS-12 position.

## Starting Salary

$48,000 to $90,000 USD per year

## Promotion/Promotional Potential

Promotion to GS-12

## Results

John interviewed with the Secret Service and FEMA, and was offered a job at FEMA as a Program Analyst, GS-11, in a four-year appointment. After 17 months of federal employment, John was promoted to Program Analyst, GS-12, in a permanent position.

# Target Job Announcement

## Program Analyst, GS 9/11/12

| | |
|---|---|
| SALARY RANGE:<br>45,911.00 – 90,698.00 USD per year | OPEN PERIOD:<br>Wednesday, October 15, 20xx to Tuesday, October 28, 20xx |
| SERIES & GRADE: GS-0343-09/12 | POSITION INFORMATION:<br>Excepted Service Permanent Full-Time |
| PROMOTION POTENTIAL: 12 | DUTY LOCATIONS:   One position, Washington, D.C. |

DUTIES FOR THIS POSITION MAY INCLUDE ALL OR PART OF THE FOLLOWING:

- **Conducts needs assessment surveys** using complex methods for assigned program(s). Collects, analyzes, and maintains data required to manage assigned programs (i.e. historical, statistical, etc). Researches and **investigates best practices** for applications to organization/agency programs or operations.  Incumbent conducts studies of efficiency and productivity.  Incumbent conducts studies and **analysis of operations, procedures and policies, and analyzes staff strengths and weaknesses**, to determine if more efficient or cost effective methods/practices can be achieved or if **customer satisfaction** can be improved.

- **Identifies resources required** to support varied levels of program operations. **Compiles budget information and performs cost and price comparative analysis** to determine fiscal resources for implementing changes in pricing and practices.

- Develops management and/or program evaluation plans, procedures, and methodology.  Recommends changes or improvements to **achieve the highest efficiency** in programs and **ensures efficient business processes**. **Manages operations** by **directing staff** to implement recommended changes. **Creates a timeline of implementation** and monitors the development of and evaluates the execution of project(s) and program(s).  Incumbent will **develop new pricing and cost accounting procedures** based on analysis of findings. **Oversees vendor contracts** to **ensure efficiency, security, and reduce waste**.

QUALIFICATIONS REQUIRED:
Qualifications for the GS 11: Applicants must possess one (1) full year of SE equivalent to the GS 9 in the Federal service. This experience must be characterized by at least three (3) of the following:

- Performing research and analysis of management/program analyses functions for the development of proposed activities.
- Comparing existing and proposed systems and/or procedures.
  Organizing and documenting findings, including suggestions for improvement.
- Assisting with the budget administration process.
- Reviewing results of study segments for compliance with objectives, policies and plans.

Qualifications for the GS 12:  Applicants must possess one (1) year of SE equivalent to the GS 11 level in the Federal service. This experience must be characterized by three (3) of the following:

- Performing analyses to determine the nature of requirements, logical work and information flows.
- Analyzing and evaluating the impact of objectives, operations, and resources on the feasibility of implementing new projects and programs.
- Researching and analyzing existing reports, files, guidelines, directives, laws, etc. in order to obtain accurate and relevant information.
- Formulating and analyzing the budget for particular appropriations.
- Verifying and maintaining financial records relating to administrative/program operations.

# Resume Writing Tips

Use these tips to help you transform your private industry resume into a targeted federal resume. The BEFORE and AFTER resumes are featured on the following pages.

## BEFORE – Private Industry Resume

### Resume Problem

This is clearly a career change campaign. The resume needs to emphasize the transferrable skills now to the new federal career in program analysis. His private industry resume includes too many words that have to do with cooking such as, kitchen, culinary, restaurant, food and beverage, grocery, frozen, menus, and sanitation. Our goal for the resume was to feature project management, supply and inventory management, supervision, teamwork, purchasing, and problem solving.

## AFTER – Federal Resume Focused Toward Target Position

### Resume Solution

The resume solution was to feature such keywords as Operations, Project Management, Budget, Purchasing, Supervision, and the skills that can be transferrable to another position outside of a kitchen. John is obviously responsible, dedicated, and analytical in managing a large kitchen services program. The new resume also includes accomplishments and specifics, leaving out most of the "kitchen/cooking" terminology.

# BEFORE : Private Industry Resume

**John Wallstone**
123 Dewberry Way
Baltimore, MD 21243
Home Phone (410) 123-4567
jwallstonecraft@gmail.com

## EDUCATION
20xx-present   Computer Programming Degree, Anne Arundel Community College
20xx   A.A. Degree, Restaurant Cooking Skills, Baltimore International College
19xx   B.S. Business Administration, Shepherd University

## EMPLOYMENT
20xx-Present [8 years]   Sous Chef, Government House
- Logistical kitchen planner for food and beverage events for the Governor of Maryland.
- Plan, purchase, and execute specific menus. Coordinate meeting and convention service requests. Inventory, inspect, and rotate fresh, frozen, and grocery stocks.
- Coordinate and communicate relevant information with the Governor's office, Maryland State Police, and other state agencies.
- Provide and deliver personal needs of the first family.
- Protect privacy of the first family, as well as proprietary information pertaining to Government House. Provide information to the media as needed.
- Direct usage of Department of Corrections trustees.
- Develop, implement, and insure sanitation programs.
- Maintain and reconcile departmental petty cash funds.
- Successful implementation of private sector ideas and technologies to a public sector environment.

19xx-19xx [1 year]      Banquet Chef, Hyatt Regency, Bethesda
- Designed and executed high-end food operations for exclusive catered events.
- Led production team by communication of specific customer directed protocols regarding national and international clients.
- Implemented quality assurance and cost control measures.
- Made purchasing, cost, and quality recommendations to upper management.
- Was recognized by management for innovative ideas that improved operational effectiveness.

19xx-19xx [1 year]      Food and Beverage Director; Executive Chef, Quality Food Service Corporation
Food and Beverage Director: Executive Dining Room at BellSouth headquarters.
- Supervised staff of 8 employees, both front and back of the house.
- Designed and directed production of breakfast and lunch menus for service 5 days a week.
- Increased new catering sales, while maintaining repeat customer clients.
- Developed and led employee training sessions for customer service, food production, and sanitation.
- Updated computer technology to modernize purchasing and just in time inventory systems.
- Developed marketing and advertising campaigns to grow business. Installed thorough accounting and customer service tracking systems.
- Introduced and maintained hazardous area critical control points program to promote safe food handling.
- Managed of all vending operations.

- Served as the customer service agent.

5/19xx-5/19xx [1 year]  Executive Chef, Spirit of Washington
- 450-passenger vessel serving lunch, dinner, and catered events.
- Over saw all menu design, purchasing, inventory control, and training involved with menu execution.
- Increased efficiencies in areas of purchasing, inventory, and scheduling by fully realizing existing computer technology.
- Developed and implemented new sanitation and food safety training programs.
- Recognized by management for improvements to product quality, cost effectiveness, and employee morale.

**JOHN WALLSTONE**
123 Dewberry Way • Baltimore, MD 21243
Residence: 410-123-4567 • Office: 202-123-4567
Email: jwallstonecraft@gmail.com

---

SSN: 123-45-6789
Citizenship: U.S.

Veteran's Preference: N/A
Candidate Source: External

**PROFILE:** Over 12 years of management experience in state government and corporate settings. Demonstrated expertise in project management, team building, budget management, and improving operations. Able to assess needs, processes, and performance and recommend and implement improvements. Strong skills in customer service, as well as interpersonal, written and verbal communications. Excellent ability to establish priorities, multi-task, and meet strict deadlines. Proven proficiency in developing innovative solutions to problems and achieving results.

## PROFESSIONAL EMPLOYMENT

**Government House, State of Maryland**
SOUS CHEF
110 State Circle Salary: $60,000 per annum
Annapolis, MD 21401
Supervisor: Susan B. Arnold, 410-333-4444, May be contacted.

06/19xx to Present [8 years]

40 hours/week

Serve as second in command of kitchen staff for First Family of Maryland. Manage kitchen operations and direct staff to ensure efficient business processes and customer satisfaction.

- Operations Management: Direct daily operations of full-service kitchen, planning, coordinating, and preparing formal and informal meals and events for up to 3,000 people, both planned in advance and last minute, with range of guests from international dignitaries to constituents. Continually analyze operations, procedures, and policies to achieve highest efficiency and best practices. Recommend and implement range of process improvement initiatives. Implement, apply, and interpret policies, regulations, and directives. Work with senior management to establish goals and objectives.

- Project Management: Conduct needs assessment surveys and determine needs based on event specifications and labor demands. Plan event with consideration to protocol, preferences, caliber of event, attendees, and lead time. Create project timeline and assign, monitor, and adjust tasks according to staff strengths/weaknesses to fulfill deadline completion. Review progress and make production and priority adjustments as needed. Manage multiple task lists to complete projects with adjacent deadlines. Resolve problems and issues, including crisis situations. Conduct post-event assessment to identify successes and areas for improvement.

- Supply Management: Take inventory and plan orders to regulate flow of product and ensure stock levels meet event and daily needs. Research best products and vendors to comply with state purchasing regulations; establish delivery protocols and resolve delivery problems. Rotate stock, monitor usage and storage to ensure efficiency, sanitation, and security, and reduce waste. Negotiate, administer, and oversee vendor and service contracts. Maintain documentation, verify invoices, and assure prompt payment.

- Budgeting / Funds Management: Develop pricing and cost accounting procedures. Analyze and forecast product and labor costs estimates. Apply due diligence to projects to ensure feasibility and cost effectiveness, as well as conduct after-action reviews. Compile budget information and apply generally accepted accounting procedures and state regulations to track expenditures, including petty cash. Perform cost and price and comparative analyses. Develop and implement pricing and marketing information for clients. Identify and resolve budget issues and develop cost-cutting solutions to ensure budget adherence. Brief management and recommend cost control improvements and budget adjustments.

- Logistics Management: Integrate logistics of event planning, including manpower and personnel, supply, training, storage, and facilities. Research and plan manpower, equipment, and fiscal resources.

- Personnel Management: Direct kitchen and wait staff, promoting teamwork and communication. Provide continual training and coaching to improve employee performance, job knowledge, and career advancement; also, serve as point of contact for benefit information. Write position descriptions and assist in hiring process. Resolve employee issues and provide employee input and feedback to management. Assist in background checks for auxiliary employees and vendors. Train others in security and privacy protection.

- Customer Service: Serve as personal and administrative assistant to First Family. Anticipate and respond to needs, maintaining flexible and service-oriented attitude. Purchase personal and business related goods, including supplies, as extension of house staff. Assist in managing schedule and making travel arrangements and appointment reservations, as needed. Protect privacy of First Family and work with Maryland State Police to ensure security precautions are followed at all times.

- Communications: Build rapport with internal staff and external departments to improve operations and flow of information. Respond to written and verbal inquires from the public and the media, adhering to strict communication standards. Represent First Family at charity and press events.

- Information Management: Develop and utilize spreadsheets, databases, and professional documents to improve operational readiness, manage projects, and research information. Maintain records on events, including menus, demographics, and after-action reports. Assist in establishing database for mailing list.

*Key Accomplishments:*

- Plan, coordinate, and execute breakfast, lunch, dinner for First Family and other events, including seated dinners and open houses for up to 4,000, with usually 3-5 events per week, as many as 2 per day.
- Instituted process changes to increase efficiency and change mind-set from reactive to proactive. Created plan to work one meal ahead, allowing time to respond to last minute requests, changes, and events.
- Received letter of appreciation from the White House for organizing luncheon attended by President Bill Clinton with less than 24-hour notice.
- Implemented industrial production system, automated systems and information management for production, scheduling, and cost control.
- Actively built team mindset and morale and implemented employee incentive program, stressing interdepartmental cooperation and employees' role in organizational success. Resulted in improved attendance and performance.

**Quality Food Service Corporation**                                    07/19xx – 05/19xx [1 year]
FOOD AND BEVERAGE DIRECTOR; EXECUTIVE CHEF
789 Jefferson Ave.                                                      Salary: $28,000 per annum
Silver Spring, MD 21045                                                 40 hours/week
Supervisor: Alice B. Toklas, 800-333-0000. May be contacted.

*Held two positions with this international food and facilities management company. Hired as Executive Chef for Spirit of Washington; promoted to Food and Beverage Director in May 19xx.*

- <u>Food and Beverage Director</u>, Executive Dining Room: BellSouth Network Services. Designed and directed production of breakfast and lunch menus for service 5 days a week, for 100 employees. Supervised staff of 8. Served as point of contact for BellSouth management. Increased new catering sales and established new client services. Developed and led employee customer service and food production and sanitation training sessions. Updated computer technology to modernize purchasing and just in time inventory systems. Developed marketing and advertising campaigns to increase business. Installed accounting and customer service tracking systems. Introduced and maintained hazardous area critical control points program to promote safe food handling. Managed a 70-machine vending operation.

- <u>Executive Chef</u>, Spirit of Washington: Oversaw menu design, coordination, and execution for lunch, dinner, and catered events on 450-passenger vessel. Led galley team of 20 employees and 2 supervisors. Employed commercial and banquet- style food production methods to achieve time and product management. Directed purchasing, inventory control, and training involved with menu execution. Achieved increased efficiencies in purchasing, inventory, and scheduling using computer technology. Developed and trained employees in new sanitation and food safety training programs. Recognized by management for improvements to product quality, cost effectiveness, and employee morale.

## Information Technology

#5 in professional fields for projected government hiring in FY 2007 - 2009
11,562 projected to be hired in 2009

Includes systems analysis, security, applicationsoftware, data management, and network services.

| Top Ten Hiring Agencies | No. of Employees | Projected Hires |
|---|---|---|
| Department of Defense | 27,539 | 7,419 |
| Department of Treasury | 6,226 | 930 |
| Department of Commerce | 3,353 | 607 |
| Department of Justice | 2,726 | 532 |
| Departmetn of Agriculture | 3,493 | 407 |
| Department of Homeland Security | 1,670 | 406 |
| Department of Helath and Human Services | 2,358 | 318 |
| Department of Transportation | 2,004 | 180 |
| General Services Administration | 1,025 | 162 |
| Government Accountability Office | 297 | 118 |
| Total (all agencies) | | 11,562 |

Partnership for Public Service, *Where the Jobs Are: Mission Critical Opportunities for America*, July 2007, http://ourpublicservice.org/OPS/publications/viewcontentdetails.php?id=118

## Facts

**Past Position:** Senior IT Consultant, Fortune 500 Company
**Past Salary:** $108,000
**Target Federal Job:** Supervisory IT Specialist (Product Assurance), GS-2210-14

## Qualifications

Tom demonstrates in his resume that he has one year specialized experience at or equivalent to the GS-13 level. He actually has 20 years of experience and a B.S. degree and easily met all of the specialized experience requirements.

## Starting Salary

$91,407 - $118,828 USD per year

## Promotion/Promotional Potential

GS-14

## Results

Tom had 20+ years in the private sector, beginning as a network/system administrator and finally working more on the programmatic side, capturing and developing IT-related business opportunities with a range of federal clients for Fortune 500 level corporations in the Washington, DC area. He translated e-Government requirements into solid enterprise architecture solutions for his clients. He was highly experienced in both the emerging technologies with application to federal initiatives and well versed in the government-wide procurement strategies.

Tom wanted to move into Government service to get out of the Beltway contractor realm and apply his program and IT experience in designing and implementing standards-based IT infrastructures for a federal agency. He applied to several agencies over the course of about six months and was offered a position as a GS-14, Step 5, Supervisory IT Specialist. His starting federal salary was $5K lower than his private sector salary, but with added value of the federal benefits package and guaranteed cost of living adjustments, he actually came out ahead by going federal. Tom said:

> " I was hired as a GS-14, Step 5, at a starting salary of $103, which was slightly lower than my private sector salary of $108K. However, the non-monetary benefits of my new job, like the public transportation incentive, made the decision to transition to federal an easy decision. Now, just two years after accepting my new position as a Supervisory IT Specialist with the Department of Homeland Security, I am now making more than I ever made in the private sector AND I am on track to a secure retirement and a truck load of job satisfaction."

# Target Job Announcement

This was a perfect announcement for Tom because he met all of the necessary qualifications and specialized experience, and his private sector salary was in the middle of the proposed salary range.

Supervisory IT Specialist (Product Assurance)

| | |
|---|---|
| SALARY RANGE:<br>91,407.00 - 118,828.00 USD per year | OPEN PERIOD:<br>Thursday, May 11, 20xx to Thursday, June 08, 20xx |
| SERIES & GRADE: GS-2210-14/14 | POSITION INFORMATION: Full-Time Permanent |
| PROMOTION POTENTIAL: 14 | DUTY LOCATIONS: 1 vacancy - Washington DC Metro Area, DC |

**JOB SUMMARY:**
This position is located in the Office of the Chief Information Officer (OCIO). The purpose of this position is to support the Mission of the organization in providing state of the art application development, information management, quality and repeatable work products, and operational support services to complement the United States Treasury Department's business processes.

**Qualifications:**
If you are qualifying based on experience, you must have served at least one year working in a job that required specialized experience. This experience must be equivalent to at least the GS-13 level. Specialized experience includes experience serving as a **supervisor, team lead, or project manager over an IT staff, engaged in supporting the business operations (applications software and network) of an organization**.

Business functions supported must include **identifying information technology requirements** and acquiring IT commodities and/or **support services** to meet those needs; AND ensuring **cyber security** requirements/compliance is met; AND include at least one of the following: 1)**managing contracts/delivery orders to support business systems**; 2)**conducting systems analysis**; or 3)**managing software life cycle processes** (quality assurance, configuration management, testing products).

# Resume Writing Tips

Use these tips to help you transform your private industry resume into a targeted federal resume. The BEFORE and AFTER resumes are featured on the following pages.

## BEFORE – Private Industry Resume

### Resume Problem

Tom's resume did not include detailed information about his scope of work or accomplishments. There was too much detail about education and training at the top. This resume was missing many of the keywords from above. The descriptions did not include enough details on the projects that he was leading.

## AFTER – Federal Resume Focused Toward Target Position

### Resume Solution

Tom's new resume summarizes his IT experience and incorporates keywords from the specialized experience. His education and the long training list were moved to the end of the resume. The new resume focuses on his extensive project management experience with concise summaries of his key projects.

The specialized experience in the announcement was an excellence source of keywords for this resume:

- supervisor, team lead, or project manager over an IT staff
- supporting the business operations (applications software and network) of an organization
- managing contracts/delivery orders to support business systems
- conducting systems analysis
- managing software life cycle processes (quality assurance, configuration management, testing products)

Tom Danson

SSN: xxx-xx-xxxx
Citizenship: United States
Federal Civilian Status: Not Applicable
Veteran's Status: Not Applicable

8000 Memory Lane, Vienna, VA 22182
Email: tomd@aol.com
Home: (704) 888-8888
Work: (704) 888-8888
Mobile: (704) 888-8888

## Work Summary

Eighteen years of progressive and intensive experience in IT operations management, design, and implementation of multi-platform network computing solutions for technical and non-technical clients. Fourteen years of project management experience and direct supervision of technical staff. Ten years of custom database programming at the workgroup and enterprise level.

## Education

University of Miami, Miami, FL 55555
        Bachelor of Science, Psychology, 19xx

## Continuing Education and Training

[expo training]
[date] How to Prepare a Quality IT Offer 0.1 Credits
[date] GSA Vendor Payment Update 0.1 Credits
[date] e-Authentication 0.1 Credits
[date] Secure Wireless Technology 0.1 Credits
[date] Proper Use of Non-DoD Contracts 1.0 Credit
[date] GWAC Direct Order Direct Bill Authority 0.1 Credits
[date] Marketing Strategies and Techniques for Small Business 0 Credits
[date] The 1102 Contract Specialist as a Business Manager 0.1 Credits
[date] GSA Governmentwide Acquisition Contracts (GWACs), Part 2 0.1 Credits
[date] GSA Governmentwide Acquisition Contracts (GWACs), Part 1 0.1 Credits
[date] Steps for Success: Teaming for Success 0.1 Credits

## Experience

Sentry Corp, Vienna, VA, November 20xx – Present [3 years]
*Senior Consultant*
700 Park Dr., Vienna, VA 22222
40 hours per week / $108,000, Supervisor:

- Analyzes the competition, briefs capabilities to the customer, gathers requirements, designs win themes, coordinates teaming, writes technical proposals, and informs pricing and staffing. Develops process and procedures for the program management office.

- Project Manager for Department of Education Financial Management System (FMS) Archiving Independent Verification and Validation (IV&V).

- Technical Lead for Energy Dept. Re-engineering and Implementation Support initiative to replace its aging financial management system with a modern, Joint Financial Management Improvement Program (JFMIP)-compliant commercial off-the-shelf (COTS) Enterprise Resource Planning (ERP) solution. Analyzed and documented support systems as part of the re-engineering study and development of target system requirements.

- Provided security analysis of the Federal Technical Data Solution (FedTeDS) compliance with DoD Information Technology Security Certification and Accreditation Process (DITSCAP), National Information Assurance Certification and Accreditation Process (NIACAP), National Institute of Standards and Technology (NIST) security standards, and other Federal agency directives to enhance cyber security documentation.

**Tom Danson**
8000 Memory Lane, Vienna, VA 22182
Home: (704) 888-8888
Work: (704) 888-8888
Mobile: (704) 888-8888
tomd@aol.com

## PROFILE

Information Technology Director with an outstanding record of success delivering enterprise applications and architectures for federal and commercial organizations. Extensive experience developing short and long term Information Technology (IT) strategies, practices, policies, and metrics for highly technical and agile organizations in the public and private sectors. Experienced in all phases of the Software Development Life Cycle (SDLC) from requirements analysis through user acceptance and operational support. Combines results-oriented project management skills with expert technical knowledge of network and IT service offerings to deliver best value solutions for the customer. A decisive and participatory leader with keen business acumen, motivating leadership skills, and extensive knowledge of emerging trends in the information age.

**CLEARANCE:** Secret

## EXPERTISE

- **Project Management:** Applies industry best practices in Project Management to ensure the success of mission critical initiatives.

- **System Development Life Cycle (SDLC):** Leads full life cycle software development projects for federal and commercial applications.

- **IT Operations Management:** Directs enterprise data, computing, and networking operations to meet evolving organizational needs.

- **Federal Acquisitions:** Applies expertise with federal procurement processes and regulations to negotiate win-win solutions in a tough, competitive market.

## PROFESSIONAL EXPERIENCE

**SENTRY CORPORATION**
700 Park Drive, Fairfax, VA 22222
20xx – Present [3 years]

**Senior** Consultant [3 years]
Public Sector, Business Consulting Services
Full-Time: 40+ hours/week
Base Salary: $108,000
Supervisor:

*Introduction*

As Sentry's lead for the competition and pricing strategy for the upcoming Alliant business development opportunity, develop partnering and technical approaches to win new IT business opportunities. Serve as an authority on emerging information technologies, eGovernment initiatives, and technical solutions. Ensure the performance and delivery of high profile IT programs with national scope and impact. Develop new business through an in-depth understanding of customer needs, a detailed knowledge of IT products and technologies, and a broad-based knowledge of federal government procurement rules and regulations.

### *Responsibilities*

- Lead business development capture activities for the federal sector. Establish Customer Relationship Management (CRM) strategies. Research and contact prospective clients, brief corporate capabilities, identify customer and agency requirements, and recommend standards-based IT architecture solutions for their current and future business needs.
- Lead proposal development activities for technical products and services. Analyze the competition, design win themes, coordinate teaming agreements, write technical proposals, and develop pricing and staffing models.
- Serve as program manager for key customer accounts with the Department of Education (DE) and the National Gallery of Art (NGA). Develop program management processes, meet with technical and management personnel from client agencies to determine customer satisfaction, provide advice, counsel, and recommendations to project teams, provide contract management support, and identify, communicate, and resolve program issues.
- Representative at national-level conferences, meetings, and expositions. Attend the annual GSA Expo to identify opportunities for upcoming federal business and potential teaming arrangements. Serve as the representative to cross-functional working groups including the Coalition for Government Procurement, the Association for Federal Information Resources Management (AFFIRM), and the Industry Association Counsel (IAC).
- Serve as the IT Subject Matter Expert (SME) during the evaluation of potential business partnerships. Research partner technologies and corporate financial health to determine viable teaming relationships for upcoming Requests for Proposals (RFPs).
- Maintain a working knowledge of Sentry's technical solutions and emerging information technologies. Analyze the technical and economic feasibility of various IT solutions.

### *Key Accomplishments*

- **Alliant GWAC:** Competition and pricing strategist for Sentry's bid for the Alliant GWAC for the GSA. Regarded as the premier next generation GWACs for GSA, this broad, ten-year, multiple-award, indefinite Delivery/Indefinite Quantity (MAIDIQ) contract for IT solutions for federal departments and agencies is due for award in FY0x and will represent a $50 billion opportunity (20xx – Present).
- **Trusted Foundry:** IT Subject Matter Expert for expansion of the Trusted Foundry contract. Completed a three-month gap analysis for two facilities to recommend personnel, facilities, and procedural changes to conduct chip design processes in a classified (Secret/Top Secret) environment. Applied National Industrial Security Program Operating Manual (NISPOM) and Director of Central Intelligence Directives (DCID) standards to assess physical, personnel, and IT security (20xx).
- **FMS Archiving Project:** Project Manager for the Department of Education Financial Management System (FMS) Archiving Independent Verification and Validation (IV&V) program. Led a six-month effort to provide independent verification of the Software Development Life Cycle (SDLC) processes for the FMS Archiving Project. Updated security documentation and processes in compliance with Federal Information Security Management Act (FISMA) and Plan of Action and Milestones (POA&M) compliance reporting (20xx).
- **NGA ERP Solution**: Technical Lead and on-site project coordinator for the NGA Re-engineering and Implementation Support Initiative. Analyzed the legacy system infrastructure and developed engineering requirements for a Commercial-of-the-Shelf (COTS) Enterprise Resource Planning (ERP) solution, fully compliant with the Joint Financial Management Improvement Program (JFMIP) (20xx).
- **FedTeDs**: Completed a security analysis of the Federal Technical Data Solution (FedTeDS) to determine its compliance with federal security directives, including the DOD Information Technology Security Certification and Accreditation Process (DITSCAP), the National Information Assurance Certification and Accreditation Process (NIACAP), and the National Institute of Standards and Technology (NIST) security standards (20xx-20xx).

# MARGARET CHAPLIN

## Business and Industry

#6 in professional fields for projected government hiring in FY 2007 - 2009
11,407 projected to be hired in 2009

Includes contracting, property management, trade specialist, loan specialist, and realty specialist.

| Top Ten Hiring Agencies | No. of Employees | Projected Hires |
|---|---|---|
| Department of Defense | 18,677 | 6,841 |
| General Services Administration | 4,382 | 1,119 |
| Department of Agriculture | 8,182 | 1,064 |
| Department of Homeland Security | 822 | 1,000 |
| Department of Commerce | 817 | 305 |
| Department of Housing and Urban Development | 3,452 | 303 |
| Department of Treasury | 459 | 195 |
| Department of Energy | 402 | 175 |
| National Aeronautics and Space Administration | 696 | 160 |
| Environmental Protection Agency | 490 | 90 |
| Total (all agencies) | | 11,407 |

Partnership for Public Service, *Where the Jobs Are: Mission Critical Opportunities for America*, July 2007, http://ourpublicservice.org/OPS/publications/viewcontentdetails.php?id=118

# Facts

**Past Position:** Warehouse Supervisor
**Past Salary:** $58,000
**Target Federal Job:** Energy Management Specialist, GS-1101-9/12

## Qualifications

Margaret demonstrates in her resume that she has one year specialized experience at or equivalent to the GS 9-12 levels. She actually has 20 years of experience, an associate's degree, and hundreds of hours of specialized training.

## Starting Salary

Margaret accepted a cut in pay, as a GS-9 with promotion potential to $84,559 within two years (GS-1101-9/12). Margaret was promoted to GS-11 on her one year mark and expects to be promoted to GS-12 at her two-year anniversary.

Margaret was seeking a job with stability, day shift hours, and long-term benefits. She was interested in improving her qualify of life; she believes that even though she took an initial pay cut, the benefits and quality of life improvement more than made up for the difference in salary. She said, "This is the best move that I could ever have done!!"

## Promotion/Promotional Potential

This position offered promotion potential to a GS-12. Margaret was told by her hiring manager that she would most likely be promoted from a GS-9 to a GS-11 within one year.

## Results

Margaret worked in several similar positions in industry for various companies. With some 20 years of specialized experience, she was the top candidate for the position posting.

# Target Job Announcement

Although this is not the actual announcement to which Margaret applied, it is the same title, grade, and series. Margaret applied for this announcement; she qualified for the position, interviewed, received an offer, and started employment in less than four months of the closing date.

## Energy Management Specialist, Department of Defense

| | |
|---|---|
| SALARY RANGE:<br>$36,671.00 - $84,559 USD per year | OPEN PERIOD:<br>Wednesday October 4, 20xx to Wednesday October 25, 20xx |
| SERIES & GRADE: GS-1101-9/12 | POSITION INFORMATION:<br>Full-Time Career / Career Conditional |
| PROMOTION POTENTIAL: 12 | DUTY LOCATIONS:<br>Few Vacancies – Ft. Belvoir, Fairfax, Manassas |

### Major Duties:

The incumbent serves as a **Supply Specialist Team Leader**. As such, provides day-to-day guidance and **operational oversight** for professional subordinates and technical employees that deal with Worldwide Operation. The incumbent **plans, directs, and coordinates supply operations** including functions such as **inventory management, acquisition, warehouse, traffic management, utilization, and disposal.** Acts as a **supply logistics expert** and interprets Department of Defense policy in all support areas for **materials management;** responsible for DLA **material management, implementation, and operation of the supply program, stock record control,** requirements requisition processing, micro purchase, simplified acquisition, research/catalog. **Establishes guidelines**, interprets directives, and general policies issued by higher authority. Renders **technical advice** to management staff and subordinates in solving **material management problems**. Acts as the **focal point** between the agency and source(s) of supply (government and commercial), and activities providing **logistics support and services**. Write policy and procedures on **material management** and related topics for inclusion into agency regulations and manuals. Independently **plans, schedules, coordinates, and monitors the effectiveness of supply operations.** The incumbent **assigns work** based on priorities, **reviews and evaluates work**; **advises subordinates** on work and administrative matters; assures that **production requirements are met.**

**KNOWLEDGE, SKILLS, AND ABILITIES REQUIRED FOR THE POSITION:** Address these KSAs with your answers under Occupational Questionnaire:

1. **Experience as a Supply/Logistics Specialist with a comprehensive knowledge of DoD Supply Experience to support activities geographically separated from the parent organization.**
2. **Experience which has led to a thorough knowledge of DoD, GSA, DLA, and materials management systems, applicable regulations, and procedures as well as trends and methods used in private industry.**
3. **Experience and an in-depth knowledge of the principles of DoD programming, planning, and budget systems to interpret, analyze, develop, and evaluate fiscal programs.**
4. **Experience and a thorough knowledge of various logistical functions which interface with the activities supported, e.g., procurement, transportation, inventory management, warehouse services, and accounting/finance.**
5. **Experience leading diverse working groups under pressure, with short suspenses and emergency deadlines.**

# Resume Writing Tips

Use these tips to help you transform your private industry resume into a targeted federal resume. The BEFORE and AFTER resumes are featured on the following pages.

## BEFORE – Private Industry Resume

### Resume Problem

The client tried to submit applications using a corporate-style formatted resume. However, the application required an online federally formatted resume with essay responses to several Knowledge, Skills, and Abilities statements. Even though the corporate resume included many specific results, it lacked in Challenge and Action statements to fully incorporate keywords and competencies required in the announcement. For instance the words "Material Management" are not in this resume.

## AFTER – Federal Resume Focused Toward Target Position

### Resume Solution

Margaret's new federally formatted outline resume includes keywords and core competencies taken from the major duties and the KSA statements to highlight her actual accomplishments. She also wrote KSA essays using specific examples in the CCAR format to describe her scope of work and tie the stories to the accomplishments.

MARGARET CHAPLIN
2980 Thunder Hill Road • Columbia, MD 55555
555.555.5555 • mchaplin@aol.com

## EXECUTIVE-LEVEL MANAGEMENT: Operations, Logistics, Sales

Award-winning team leader and business planner with more than 17 years of combined experience impacting corporate performance through skillful operational development and dynamic personnel management in retail and logistics industries. Expertly align organizational quality standards and profitability objectives through strategic start-ups, turnarounds, team building, and guidance.

---

Inventory/Loss Prevention/Quality Control and Assurance • Shipping/Receiving • Audits • Reporting
Client Relations • Product Launch • Sales Forecasting • Distribution • Logistics • Warehousing
Risk Management • Internal Controls • Communications • Customer Service • Event Planning
Budget Forecasting • Strategic Planning • Cost/Benefit Analysis • Expense Control • Payroll
Operational Streamlining • P&L • Policy Development • Staff Management • Startup Ops
Cost Reduction • Operations Management • Turnarounds • Training/Development
Demographic Analysis/Utilization • Regulatory Compliance • Human Resource

---

## PROFESSIONAL EXPERIENCE

**BEVERAGE ENTERPRISES, Columbia, MD • 20xx-Present**
Leading international provider of non-alcoholic beverages. Annual sales revenues total $19.2B. Organization is comprised of 73,000 employees.

**Warehouse Supervisor**
Command alignment of warehouse productivity levels with organizational objectives, spearheading a talented team of 30 members. Oversee daily warehouse activities and product loss control. Maintain suitable inventory levels, managing and allotting incoming/outgoing shipments, safeguarding company assets, and managing P&L.

**Operational Highlights:**
- Boosted productivity from 110 to 178 cases per hour in 90 days through implementation of an expert training program.
- Slashed overtime by 51% through efficient training reforms, resulting in the decrease of average monthly overtime from 37% to 18.8%.
- Restructured warehouse and trucking operations to increase output efficiency.
- Served an instrumental role in maintaining unit revenues at $30M.

**HOME IMPROVEMENT CORP, Baltimore, MD • 20xx-20xx**
Nation-wide home improvement retail organization with annual sales of $46.7B.

**General Store Manager**
Aligned integral operational norms and standards with budgeted company objectives, policies, and procedures. Assembled all in-store functions and activities while providing satisfactory customer service, merchandising, safety, and security standards. Endorsed organizational merchandising standards by ensuring quality merchandise resets and displays, daily inventory replenishment, promotional and seasonal sets, zone recovery freight flow, product communications, and overall store presentation.

**Financial/Operational Highlights:**
- Maintained constant sales increase of 14%, augmenting annual sales from $4.2M in 20xx to $4.9M in 20xx.
- Implemented a Servant Leadership Process that promoted internal communications to develop team dynamics and company culture.
- Elevated company ranking from 312 to 92, maximizing profitability.
- Sustained unit revenues at $59M through key management strategies.
- Obtained top District and Regional Rankings including #1 Lowest Shrink Percentage of 0.51%, Top 3 for Overall Spring and Summer Sales, and many more.

MARGARET CHAPLIN
2980 Thunder Hill Road • Columbia, MD 55555
555.555.5555 • mchaplin@aol.com

EXPERIENCE
11/20xx-Present. 55 hours per week. WAREHOUSE SUPERVISOR, Salary: $58K. Beverage Enterprises, Columbia, MD. Supervisor: Mike Miles. Phone: 555-555-5555. No, may not contact current employer.

Beverage Enterprises is a leading international provider of non-alcoholic beverages with annual sales revenues totaling $19.2B. The organization is comprised of 73,000 employees.

OPERATIONAL MANAGEMENT: Align warehouse productivity levels with organizational objectives. Lead a team of 30. Oversee daily warehouse activities and product loss control. Maintain suitable inventory levels, manage and allot incoming/outgoing shipments, safeguard company assets, and manage Profit and Loss. Plan, direct, and coordinate supply operations. Effectively allocate resources providing quality logistical and supply requirements. Manage QA/QC inspections.

PROPERTY ACCOUNTING: Oversee and control property accounting procedures involving Requisitions, Stock Records, Storage, Distribution, Audits, Supply Locator System, Supply Safety and Security Operations, POL, and Authorized Stockage List. Evaluate programs, constantly analyze data and systems, identify and report trends, and recommend specific courses of action to resolve logistical supply or technical problems. Monitor stock record control and render technical advice to management and subordinates in resolving materials management problems.

CUSTOMER SERVICE: Determine stock levels, conduct inventories, and project trends/demands based on changing customer needs, specialized supply items usage, and projected depletion. Maintain specialized Property Book Accounts and records and update databases. Offer exceptional customer service and assist customers, storage depots, and other organizational representatives.

OPERATIONS PLANS AND TRANSPORTATION CONTRACTS: Develop, implement, and monitor operational plans and procedures. Provide assistance in reviewing training and transportation contracts, and recommend changes as required to maintain high operations tempo in the warehouse.

PERSONNEL ADMINISTRATION: Coordinate work schedules, determine priorities, distribute workload, and train personnel. Ensure the timely completion of taskings. Assist employees in resolving a myriad of supply issues and complaints. Technical knowledge of supply regulations, policies, procedures, techniques, and methods to guide staff. Ensure supply support.

OPERATIONAL HIGHLIGHTS
PRODUCTIVITY: Boosted productivity from 110 to 178 cases per hour, in 90 days, through implementation of a targeted training program.

FINANCIAL SAVINGS: Slashed overtime by 51% through efficient training reforms, resulting in the decrease of average monthly overtime from 37% to 18.8%.

TRANSPORTATION: Restructured warehouse and trucking operations to increase output efficiency. Monitor inventory and seasonal trends and forecast transport of large seasonal orders, i.e., water in the hot summer months.

REVENUE: Served an instrumental role in maintaining unit revenues at $30M.

OTHER / ADDITIONAL INFORMATION

MILITARY EXPERIENCE
[dates], U.S. Army Reserves 3521 - Motor Transport Mechanic, Supply Chain and Logistics Management / Transport Mechanic, Washington, DC.

Supervised supply unit operations and managed inventory of field equipment, personnel equipment, and weapons and ammunition. Attended monthly logistics meetings.

PROFESSIONAL TRAINING
CompUSA/IACET-NASBA/CPE Sponsored Microsoft Certification Training:
Intermediate/advanced
Word, Excel, Access

PROFILE
Proactive, award-winning team leader and business planner with more than 17 years of combined experience positively affecting corporate performance through skillful operational development and dynamic personnel management in retail and logistics industries. Expertly align organizational quality standards and profitability objectives through strategic start-ups, turnarounds, team building, and guidance. Planned and organized large-scale operations, managed large staffs (up to 100+) and multi-million dollar budgets, and communicate as a refined, polished professional in oral presentations and meetings, and via written communications and reports.

Conducted management, operational, and customer service studies and analyses to facilitate new processes and functions, streamlining and standardizing operations in retail operations as a Store Manager for large operations and in inventory supply chain management operations for major companies. Employed new technologies and managed change in a positive, forward-thinking and innovative manner. Rallied the consensus of staff and management to change operations, processes, or procedures to redesign customer service requirements or inventory ramps. Excellent problem solver.

Areas of expertise include Inventory / Loss Prevention / Quality Control and Assurance, Audits, Reporting, Client Relations, Product Launch, Sales Forecasting, Distribution, Logistics, Warehousing, Risk Management, Internal Controls, Communications, Customer Service, Event Planning, Budget Forecasting, Strategic Planning, Cost/Benefit Analysis, Process Analysis, Expense Control, Payroll, Operational Streamlining, P&L, Policy Development, Staff Management, Startup Ops, Cost Reduction, Operations Management, Turnarounds, Procedures Development, Oral and Written Communications, Problem Solving, Conflict Resolution, Training/Development, Demographic Analysis/Utilization, Regulatory Compliance, Shipping / Receiving, and Human Resources Management.

COMPUTER SKILLS: Word, Excel, PowerPoint, Access, and inventory control for inbound and outbound: IMS, SAP, PEOPLESOFT

# JANNA JOHNSON

## Engineering

#7 in professional fields for projected government hiring in FY 2007 - 2009
10,712 projected to be hired in 2009

Includes all disciplines of engineering and architecture.

| Top Ten Hiring Agencies | No. of Employees | Projected Hires |
|---|---|---|
| Department of Defense | 36,786 | 7,652 |
| Department of Transportation | 5,434 | 900 |
| National Aeronautics and Space Administration | 9,014 | 807 |
| Department of Energy | 2,819 | 403 |
| Environmental Protection Agency | 1,898 | 120 |
| Department of Homeland Security | 857 | 87 |
| Department of Commerce | 328 | 65 |
| Department of Labor | 226 | 42 |
| Department of Interior | 963 | 36 |
| Federal Communications Commission | 266 | 33 |
| Total (all agencies) | | 10,712 |

Partnership for Public Service, *Where the Jobs Are: Mission Critical Opportunities for America*, July 2007, http://ourpublicservice.org/OPS/publications/viewcontentdetails.php?id=118

## Facts

**Past Position:** Vice President of Risk Management
**Past Salary:** $120,000
**Target Federal Job:** Engineer, YC-0801-3/3

## Qualifications

Janna had outstanding experience and the advantage of reinstatement eligibility that allowed her to apply as a status candidate. She was able to demonstrate her experience using federal language and get referred. Her interview further reinforced her qualifications as an excellent candidate.

REINSTATEMENT ELIGIBILITY: Yes

Reinstatement eligibility comes from prior federal service. Applicants who have three or more years in the competitive service, no matter how long ago, may compete for positions as a status candidate. Applicants with one to three years of former competitive service experience may compete as a status candidate for three years following their separation.

## Starting Salary

$91,728.00 to $148,740.00 USD per year, Pay Band YC-343-3. This position is under the NSPS, the Department of Defense's new National Security Personnel System, and is equivalent to a GS-14/15 supervisor. Janna successfully negotiated a matching salary of $120K.

## Promotion/Promotional Potential

Although this federal position did not offer promotion potential within this same position, Janna feels she is still way ahead of the curve with her federal job versus her former private sector position. She had turned down a position with the government previously because the salary was not high enough. But, through negotiating her salary and having a resume that demonstrated a higher level of experience, Janna was able to get the job she wanted. Not having to market services all the time and the chance to make a difference were a big plus for Janna. Additional fringe benefits such as transit subsidies, flex time, telecommuting, and the potential of NSPS add to the value of her new position. She really liked the pay for performance aspect of the NSPS; since she was coming from the private sector, she was very comfortable with being held accountable for her results.

## Results

Janna was rated best qualified for two positions she applied for, using her reinstatement eligibility. She was rated best qualified based on her specialized experience in environmental engineering and remediation. Her federal job search was limited to the two positions she applied for; she started her job less than four months after her first application.

# Target Job Announcement

## Engineer

| | |
|---|---|
| SALARY RANGE: 91,728.00 - 148,740.00 USD per year | OPEN PERIOD: January 09, 20xx to February 07, 20xx |
| SERIES & GRADE: YC-801-3/3 | POSITION INFORMATION: Permanent position. -- Full Time |
| PROMOTION POTENTIAL: n/a | DUTY LOCATIONS: 1 vacancy - AL – Huntsville |

### Qualifications:

Applicants will be rated using CATEGORY Rating & Selection Procedures. Individual numerical scores will not be assigned. Category rating is the process of establishing quality categories based on job related criteria, evaluating qualified applicants against the criteria and placing them in the appropriate category.

The incumbent of this position will be required to provide management and oversight for highly technical programs requiring an **understanding of technical requirements** across programmatic lines. Extensive **knowledge of management concepts, principles, and practices** as well as a general knowledge of the methods, practices, and processes of technical disciplines. Typical programs and projects include, but are not limited to <u>**ordnance investigation and removal, design and remediation of environmental hazards and toxic waste,**</u> and <u>**military munitions cleanup.**</u> Experience must be equivalent to the YC-2 payband in Federal service and have provided the following knowledge, skills, and abilities: Knowledge of a **wide spectrum of environmental sciences associated with hazardous and toxic waste and environmental restoration** coupled with **a host of interrelated construction disciplines**; Knowledge and understanding **military munitions program, policies, and procedures**. Skill in **strategic project planning and direction; control, allocation; and Knowledge of utilization of allocated resources**; manpower, facilities, and equipment planning.

**TIP:** This CPOL Resume includes "KSAs in the Resume". The announcement states the KSAs required, but also that the KSA information should be included in the resume. The CPOL Resume is a 12,000 character section for the Work Experiences.

# Resume Writing Tips

Use these tips to help you transform your private industry resume into a targeted federal resume. The BEFORE and AFTER resumes are featured on the following pages.

## BEFORE – Private Industry Resume

### Resume Problem

Janna was clearly qualified for this job and had great experience. However, Janna's resume was hard to read and was not really directed toward the target position. It did not demonstrate enough detail and did not show off her skills and abilities to her best advantage. Keywords from the Duties section from the announcement were clearly missing from her private industry resume, including: "**ordnance investigation and removal, design and remediation of environmental hazards and toxic waste,** and **military munitions cleanup** and wide spectrum of environmental sciences associated with hazardous and toxic waste and environmental restoration."

## AFTER – Federal Resume Focused Toward Target Position

### Resume Solution

The Outline Format with Headlines clearly presents the skills and keywords from the announcement in an easy to read format. It was important to reframe Janna's experience in federal language. She was clearly qualified and had a lot of outstanding and relevant experience although she was a bit weak in munitions remediation. We emphasized munitions to the extent that we could and highlighted her knowledge of relevant federal laws, used the key words of the announcement, and made sure there was no question about her qualifications.

This Outline Format resume includes Headlines which are similar to the Knowledge, Skills, and Abilities required for this position. The keywords from the announcement Duties section and the KSAs are in bold in the following resume. The boldtype would not appear in the CPOL resume.

**TIP:** Janna's Professional Profile was put in the Additional Information box at the end of the resume builder. This is a great place to add information to further support your application and another opportunity to use the target words of the announcement.

Janna Johnson, P.E.
104 Mulberry Lane
Monroe, MS

Evening Phone: 555-xxx-xxxx
Day Phone: 555-xxx-xxxx
Contact Email: janna@hmail.com

**VP Risk Management**
Major Projects:
Successful implementation of site redevelopment projects (Brownfield projects) in RI, MS, and PA
$2,000,000 CERCLA project from initial site assessment, Remedial Investigation and Feasibility Study to ongoing in situ remediation
$12,000,000 comprehensive environmental site assessment and rehabilitation program to comply with the Quebec Environmental Policy Act
Negotiated multiple permits for Title V air permits, wastewater, storm water, and RCRA in TN, AL, MS, NC, and OK.
Led due diligence for new operations in Mexico and Portugal
Instituted Health and Safety Management system that reduced company wide safety losses by more than 75% over 6 years (from $2,200,000 to $408,000 in 2008).
Provide senior organization leadership on all aspects of environmental, health, and safety programs and risk management for a $1 billion multinational corporation.
Work with executive management team to establish and manage $19,000,000 environmental remediation budget, ongoing facilities operational and project budgets, and $5,000,000 risk management program. Evaluate, prioritize, and approve capital projects to assure compliance with environmental standards.
Developed and implemented environmental, health, and safety program covering 3,000 employees and 15 facilities in 8 states and 3 foreign countries
Direct facility managers in all areas of operational compliance. Establish and validate EHS improvement goals. Perform loss control audits.
Lead multidisciplinary teams on technical, environmental, safety, and legal issue. Team members include management (senior and executive), engineers, financial, human resources, attorneys, hourly employees, and contractors.
Provide compliance and technological expertise and direction to all facilities. Direct interface with state and federal EPA and OSHA on major issues. Conduct compliance audits, establish resolution tracking system, and incident investigation system to assure compliance.
Evaluate needs for new environmental programs; set goals, objectives, and budget; manage schedules using MS Project; track costs and comply with financial reporting requirements.
Managed 4 direct reports and 15 engineering, safety, and human resource professional in a distributed matrix organization. Leveraged the strengths of a multi-cultural and multinational organization to achieve stated goals.
Prepare and deliver written, power point, and oral presentations for the executive management team, board of directors, and outside groups. Interface with the media.
Led successful public relations campaign to build and open a manufacturing facility in Portugal - including participating in a national press conference.
Oversaw design, specifications, and contract negotiations for wastewater treatment systems for three facilities. Led environmental impact analysis and permitting for a $40 million capital expansion program.

Janna Johnson, P.E.
104 Mulberry Lane
Monroe, MS

Evening Phone: 555-xxx-xxxx
Day Phone: 555-xxx-xxxx
Contact Email: janna@hmail.com

US Citizen
Social Security Number: xxx-xx-xxxx
Veteran's Preference: N/A
Highest Previous Grade: GS-801-12, 12/1985-06/1990; Reinstatement eligible
Security Clearance: Secret/CNWDI (inactive)

RELEVANT PROFESSIONAL EXPERIENCE

04/19xx to present, VICE PRESIDENT, RISK MANAGEMENT, ABC Corporation, Inc. Corporate
Headquarters, Gulfport, MS, 50 hours per week, $120,000 per year, John Smith, 601-xxx-xxxx,
please contact me first.

OVERSEE SUCCESSFUL, IMPLEMENTATION AND MANAGEMENT OF COMPLEX SITE
**ENVIRONMENTAL AND REDEVELOPMENT PROJECTS** for $1 billion multinational
corporation. **Analyze and evaluate project risk** and direct the planning, programming,
budgeting, and direction of environmental remediation. Projects include brownfields,
wastewater, RCRA, CERCLA, and other **environmental hazards and toxic waste**. Evaluate,
prioritize, and approve capital projects, ensuring **compliance with environment regulations**,
policies, procedures, and standards.

UTILIZE KNOWLEDGE OF ENVIRONMENTAL SCIENCES TO PLAN AND CONDUCT **SITE
ASSESSMENTS, LOSS CONTROL AUDITS, FEASIBILITY STUDIES**, and other activities.
Analyze environmental programs and projects from initial **site assessment** through remedial
investigation to ongoing in situ remediation. **Lead multidisciplinary teams** of engineers,
financial, attorneys, and contractors on technical, environmental, safety, and legal issues.
Develop plans for **remediation of environmental hazards;** develop budgets, monitor
implementation, and assess project success. Make adjustments to address changing conditions
and new information.

USING KNOWLEDGE OF MANAGEMENT CONCEPTS, PRINCIPLES, AND PRACTICES,
PROVIDE LEADERSHIP, DIRECTION, AND **SUPERVISION FOR 4 DIRECT REPORTS** AND
15 OTHER PROFESSIONALS IN MATRIX ORGANIZATION; mentor them to provide
outstanding service and exceed organizational goals, offering advice and instruction as needed.
Delegate authority to oversee **planning, direction, and timely execution** of various programs.
Assign and evaluate work, with eye toward continual improvements in efficiency and
effectiveness. Promote diversity; engage in proactive recruitment to ensure equitable
representation of minorities and women. Interview candidates for vacancies, evaluate
qualifications, and make hiring decisions. Recognize performance and other contributions
through honorary and monetary awards. Provide disciplinary actions when warranted, and
handle the rare employee complaints. Ensure employees are fully briefed on goals, strategies,
and policies. Provide briefings and recommendations to senior company executives.

**SKILLFULLY DEVELOP AND MANAGE $19 MILLION BUDGET FOR ENVIRONMENTAL REMEDIATION, PLUS $5 MILLION ANNUAL RISK MANAGEMENT PROGRAM;** make decisions regarding resource allocation; ensure effective use of resources. Develop and implement project budgets. PERFORM STRATEGIC PLANNING, develop work plans, evaluate and prioritize projects. Establish INTERNAL AND EXTERNAL METRICS, goals, and strategies to achieve objectives and further mission. Identify and implement midcourse corrections.

PREPARE COMPLEX WRITTEN DOCUMENTS including highly technical project plans, multi-million dollar budgets, studies, environmental audits, and other documents. Develop, implement, monitor, and track complex, technical action plans; update as needed. Develop technical manuals and instructions on regulations, policies, and environmental technology. Utilize Word, Excel, PowerPoint, Access, Project, and proprietary software for written communications.

RESEARCH AND ANALYZE properties of various hazardous materials, including solvents, VOCs, heavy metals, and other environmental contaminants to provide expert advice and guidance on alternative techniques to remediation and restoration. Support **environmental stewardship** to anticipate and prevent the **exacerbation of environmental contamination** and promote **sustainability**.

ASSESS, EVALUATE, AND MANAGE IMPLEMENTATION of **remedial designs, actions**, and operations and long-term management of multiple sites. Monitor complex and highly technical projects, and ensure compliance with applicable federal, state, local and sometimes international regulations. Leverage resources to ensure timely, cost-efficient, and effective restoration and remediation.

ENGAGE IN PROACTIVE ORAL COMMUNICATIONS WITH A WIDE VARIETY OF INTERNAL AND EXTERNAL STAKEHOLDERS including contractors, colleagues, and federal and state regulatory agencies including the Environmental Protection Agency, to brief them on activities and project progress. Negotiate with stakeholders on matters related to environmental technology. Prepare and present technical training and briefings to corporate executives on effective environmental remediation and restoration. **Serve as technical expert on techniques, technologies; theories and practices of environmental cleanup;** or science and technology relative to chemical contaminants or hazardous materials. Represent the Company in high level meetings related to environmental program activities worldwide; routinely interact with the media. Demonstrate professionalism, tact, and courtesy on all occasions.

**ANALYZE AND INTERPRET COMPLEX, TECHNICAL, ENVIRONMENTAL, AND RELATED REGULATIONS, including the National Contingency Plan, CERCLA** as amended by Superfund Amendments and Reauthorization Act (SARA), Resource Conservation Recovery Act (RCRA), Clean Air Act Amendments of 1990, and other federal, state, and international regulations, policies, and procedures. Ensure compliance in all activities. Authoritative source of information on these regulations for internal and external stakeholders.

MAINTAIN CURRENCY in field through attendance at professional conferences, active membership in professional organizations, review of professional journals, and best practices. Share knowledge with colleagues.

KEY ACCOMPLISHMENTS: Successfully led **multi-million dollar projects on environmental remediation for VOC groundwater contamination, petroleum products,** chlorinated solvents, heavy metals, PCBs, industrial wastewater, air pollution, and related issues. Oversaw environmental remediation projects at military bases to address groundwater contamination in munitions areas. Developed and implemented effective environmental health and safety program covering 3,000 employees across the globe.

Characters: 7077 with spaces

ADDITIONAL INFORMATION

PROFESSIONAL PROFILE

Expert licensed and experienced environmental engineer with a Master's degree and demonstrated ability to remediate environmental concerns caused by a wide range of environmental hazards and toxic waste. Extensive experience as a **Project Manager** overseeing complex **environmental remediation worldwide;** knowledgeable of federal laws, regulations, policies, and procedures regarding **environmental cleanup**. Proven track record for meeting targets, developing and implementing effective **policies**, managing diverse programs, and providing excellent service to internal and external customers. Demonstrated success at forging collaborations with all constituencies. Highly developed organizational and supervisory abilities coupled with superb communication skills support an ability to achieve quantifiable program results. Polished, professional presentation.

# FRANK MASON

FORMER WALL STREET PROFESSIONAL AND SMALL BUSINESS OWNER LANDS GS-13
FINANCIAL POSITION WITHIN FOUR MONTHS OF STARTING HIS FEDERAL JOB SEARCH
ACCOUNTING AND BUDGET GROUP, GS-0500

## Accounting and Budget

#8 in professional fields for projected government hiring in FY 2007 - 2009
9,841 projected to be hired in 2009

Includes financial management/administration, accounting, auditing, revenue agent, tax specialist, and budget analysis.

| Top Ten Hiring Agencies | No. of Employees | Projected Hires |
|---|---|---|
| Department of Treasury | 29,279 | 8,096 |
| Department of Transportation | 780 | 300 |
| Securities and Exchange Commission | 896 | 266 |
| Department of Homeland Security | 741 | 260 |
| General Services Administration | 1,060 | 249 |
| Federal Deposit Insurance Corporation | 2,195 | 150 |
| Government Accountability Office | 240 | 119 |
| National Aeronautics and Space Administration | 745 | 104 |
| Department of Energy | 317 | 94 |
| Department of Housing and Urban Development | 393 | 78 |
| Total (all agencies) | | 9,841 |

Partnership for Public Service, *Where the Jobs Are: Mission Critical Opportunities for America,* July 2007, http://ourpublicservice.org/OPS/publications/viewcontentdetails.php?id=118

## Facts
**Past Position:** Small business owner and Wall Street Financial Consultant
**Past Salary:** $75,000
**Target Federal Job:** Budget Analyst, GS-0560 and Financial Management Analyst, GS-0501

## Qualifications
Frank clearly demonstrates in his resume that he has 15+ years of financial and budget analysis experience equivalent to the GS-13 level. His experience exceeds the one year specialized experience specified in the announcement. Frank is a veteran with 5 veteran's preference points, but he can apply to Status positions through VEOA programs.

VETERAN'S PREFERENCE: 5 points

## Starting Salary
$69,764 – $107,854 USD per year

## Promotion/Promotional Potential
Within four months of sending out his first application, Frank was hired as a GS-13, Step 10 Financial Manager on the White House staff. His starting salary was $107K, an increase of $32K over his current salary. After three years, he was selected for a GS-14 level financial position with a different federal agency.

## Results
This candidate was laid off from his position as a financial consultant with a top Wall Street firm following the downturn in the financial industry post-9/11. He worked in the private sector financial industry for over 15 years. After leaving Wall Street he owned a small business franchise before deciding to go federal.

# Target Job Announcement

## Financial Specialist

| SALARY RANGE:<br>69,764.00 - 107,854.00 USD per year | OPEN PERIOD:<br>Wednesday, July 16, 20xx to Tuesday, October 14, 20xx |
| --- | --- |
| SERIES & GRADE: GS-0501-12/13 | POSITION INFORMATION: Full Time Career/Career Conditional |
| PROMOTION POTENTIAL: 13 | DUTY LOCATIONS:<br>few vacancies - Arlington 'Ballston Area', VA |

MAJOR DUTIES:
Performs a variety of top level bureau functions, such as: Participating in **decision-making** sessions with top bureau management officials. **Advises** program managers on regulatory requirements. **Accounting and financial policies**. Planning, developing, and coordinating accounting and **financial management improvements**. Coordinating the resolution of accounting system problems. **Providing interpretive guidance** to other accounting and financial management staff and functional representatives;

**Preparing organization comments** on GAO, OMB, and Treasury proposals preparing policies, procedures, and **guidelines on accounting** functions for use by program staff and technical personnel;

**Planning, analyzing, and determining programmatic/financial relationships**;
Providing authoritative policy interpretations and functional recommendations
Developing systems and procedures for bureau-wide implementation of laws, standards, regulations, and policies;

**Advising management on changes** to function/program workflow practices
Preparing, or overseeing the preparation of, the bureau's **annual financial statements**. Providing staff direction and guidance in the design, development, and implementation of automated systems;

**Developing and performing ongoing analyses** and interpretation of financial data
Performing analyses to ensure that the general ledger is maintained to provide the quality and reliability of information sufficient to preclude audit qualifications on the bureau's Chief Financial Office (CFO) financial statements;

Analyzing the requirements of the governmentwide **Standard General Ledger** (SGL) Board. Developing and maintaining a complex of automated subsystems to produce accounting and financial information, and define system specifications.

QUALIFICATIONS REQUIRED:
**Specialized Experience Required (GS-13)**: Applicants for the GS-13 grade level you must have at least 52 weeks of specialized experience equivalent to the GS-12 grade level in federal service. Specialized experience is described as experience that is directly related to the position to be filled and has equipped the candidate with the particular knowledge, skills, and abilities to successfully perform the duties of the position. For this job, specialized experience is experience that includes the following: **expert knowledge of financial management concepts, principles and practices; financial management and accounting techniques and procedures; reviewing and analyzing financial plans and summaries, ensuring effective management and accountability of funds, applying analytical methods and techniques to identify and resolve accounting issues, advising on complex financial management issues.**

# Resume Writing Tips

Use these tips to help you transform your private industry resume into a targeted federal resume. The BEFORE and AFTER resumes are featured on the following pages.

## BEFORE – Private Industry Resume

### Resume Problem

1) The keywords are used incorrectly. The private industry resume focused on keywords for the private industry, rather than utilizing federal resume keywords for the financial management specialist. 2) The work experience description is not detailed enough to demonstrate specialized experience or descriptive enough about past performance to prove ability to perform the duties of this position. 3) The small business experience should be moved to the ADDITIONAL INFORMATION section (for the USAJOBS version) because it is not as relevant as other financial management positions.

### Keywords For Private Sector Resume

Start-Ups, Turnarounds, Strategic Planning, B2B, B2C, e-Commerce, Cost Containment, Project Management, Budgeting, Treasury, Bank Relationship Management, Logistics, Process Automation, Contract Negotiations, Training & Development, Productivity, Organizational Development, Risk Management, Cash Management & Control, P&L, Vendor Relations, Credit & Collections, Shareholder Relations

## AFTER – Federal Resume Focused Toward Target Position

### Resume Solution

The target federal announcement was used to form the outline for Frank's new federal resume. His qualifications summary was totally revamped to showcase the critical skills he would bring to the job such as budget formulation, justification, execution, and performance cycle management. Because his experience as a small business owner was not as relevant to the federal job he was seeking as his previous financial career, his Wall Street position was listed first on the resume, even though it was not his current job.

### Keywords For Federal Resume

Advise program managers, Accounting and financial policies, Develop financial management improvements, Resolve accounting systems problems, Provide interpretive guidance to financial management staff, Guidelines on accounting functions, Plan financial relationships, Provide authoritative policy interpretations, Advise manager on changes in program workflow practices, Analyze and interpret financial data, Provide quality and reliability of information

**FRANK MASON**

511 Manor Road                                   914.999.9999 (c)

Albany, NY 10000         E-MAIL: fm4222@aol.com         914.999.9999 (f)

## DYNAMIC, FOCUSED OPERATIONS MANAGEMENT SPECIALIST & LEADER

Start-Ups • Turnarounds • Strategic Planning • B2B • B2C • *e*-Commerce • Cost Containment
Project Management • Budgeting • Treasury • Bank Relationship Management • Logistics
Process Automation • Contract Negotiations • Training & Development • Productivity
Organizational Development • Risk Management • Cash Management & Control
P&L • Vendor Relations • Credit & Collections • Shareholder Relations

High-impact, results-oriented financial industry professional dedicated to profitability and growth through excellence and customer service. Valued for leadership in leveraging broad background in Banking, Finance, Capital Markets, and Brokerage with Internet technology and *e*-Commerce. Prized for recruiting, training and motivating productive, cohesive teams that build the next generation of profits. A leader in conceptualizing the corporate vision, obtaining buy-in and attaining mutually held goals.

## CAREER HISTORY

**THE SHIPPING STORE**, Scarsdale, New York               20xx – Present [2 years]

A holding company for family owned and operated franchises. The Shipping Store primarily does business as part of the largest express carrier and largest package carrier in the world.

### *Owner*

Manage the day-to-day operation of this retail company. Offer businesses and consumers a wide range of products and services available in one convenient location, i.e., packing, shipping, copying, and print services, notary, mail services, and computer services, just to name a few. Centers are start-up businesses that are clearly customer focused with gross sales growing 2.5% monthly.

**FINANCIAL SERVICES GROUP**, New York, NY             20xx – 20xx [2 years]

Providers of services in six lines of business in 150 countries: Audit, Assurance and Business Advisory; Business Process Outsourcing; Financial Advisory; Global HR Solutions; Global Tax Services; and Management Consulting.

### *Principal Consultant*

- Managed an engagement to identify derivative systems and software products for a global management advisor. Scope involved identifying rules-based, *"expert systems"* prompted and driven by artificial intelligence. Gathered competitive intelligence for this client.

- Provided expertise to the SIA's Interoperability and Standards/Code of Practices {CoP} project. This project, awarded to FSG by the SIA, focused on current and future process flows and their message, data, time, and control components.

- Managed large financial service-related projects for the largest U.S. Stock Transfer Agency with 27 full-time internal associates. Headed the six-month Nominee Partnerships Project that streamlined the current need for and use of Nominee Partnerships. Designed risk management guidelines, policies and procedures. Managed client relationships with senior managers, directors, and internal counsel.

- Worked with a team to create a proposal for a global foreign bank to enhance and control their Global Equity Research Content Management; the project was awarded.

**SECURITY FINANCIAL GROUP**, Blue Ridge, PA                              19xx – 20xx [2 years]

A multi-bank holding company, that provides financial products and services in both domestic and international markets.

*VP, Chief Domestic Operations Manager*

Restructured, turned around, revitalized, and provided direction to Capital Markets Domestic Operations. Identified and managed security settlement risk. Reorganized and re-engineered Securities Clearance Operation, which included both debt and equity, some of which utilized Internet technology, which had a direct impact on Broker/Dealer achieving Tier II, enabling growth and incremental revenue for the Division. Worked closely with integrator community. Directed mid-management staff: Cash Management and Control, Safekeeping, Receive & Deliver, and Data Entry.

Frank Mason
511 Manor Road
Albany, New York 10000
Day/Evening: 914-999-9999
fm4222@aol.com

## PROFESSIONAL EXPERIENCE

05/20xx to 02/20xx [2 years], PRINCIPAL FINANCIAL CONSULTANT; Financial Services Group; Salary $120,000; 60 hours per week; 230 Madison Ave., New York, NY 10000. Supervisor:

**FINANCIAL CONSULTANT**: Recruited to lead complex FINANCIAL, OPERATIONAL, and technology-related projects and programs. Analyzed and evaluated the effectiveness of a broad range of **programs, procedures, systems, and operations, and developed solutions** for improving organizational performance, operating program effectiveness, and efficiency.

**FINANCIAL, ANALYTICAL TEAM-MEMBER**: Worked independently and as part of **team** to **evaluate internal controls,** resource allocations, automated systems, and budgetary and financial issues, and to **develop policies** and financial programs goals for improving the organization and its processes.

**PRIMARY LIAISON** to external entities including the Security Industry Association ( SIA), Federal and State Banking officials, auditors, accountants, attorneys, and other senior-level financial professionals. **Advisor** for difficult accounting system and operation problems. **Researched, identified, and developed data** for use in the oversight and direction of management and program efforts.

PROJECTS AND ACHIEVEMENTS: Collaborated with Operations Managers at major banks and brokerage houses to streamline the clearance and settlement processes. **Orchestrated dramatic improvements in operational efficiency, productivity,** and internal communications by automating job functions, and by **promoting teamwork and collaboration among employees** through hands-on teaching, coaching, counseling, and mentoring.

**TEAM LEADER AND SUBJECT MATTER EXPERT** to the Security Industry Association for a successful project that improved and expedited the securities clearance process.

**MANAGED LARGE, MULTI-TEAM FINANCIAL-SERVICES PROJECTS** with the U.S. Stock Transfer Agency and a staff of 27 full-time associates, including **leadership** of the six-month Nominee Partnership Project. Designed risk management guidelines, policies and procedures; and managed relationships with senior managers, directors, attorneys, and staff. Successfully completed the project on time and within budget, streamlining the need for and use of Nominee Partnerships.

February 02/20xx to 05/20xx [2 years], VICE PRESIDENT, CHIEF DOMESTIC OPERATIONS MANAGER; Salary, $100,000; 60 hours per week; Security Financial Corporation, Financial Center, Blue Ridge, PA 15222; Supervisor: (name/phone number)

**DIRECTED CAPITAL MARKETS DOMESTIC OPERATIONS** for this multi-bank holding company. Directed 52 mid-management staff in four departments. Reported to President/CEO. Managed a $9 million budget. Identified and managed security settlement risk. Worked closely with integrator community. Prepared monthly presentations on departmental goals, status, and results to top executives.

Led the **upgrade and reengineering of automated systems to improve operating efficiencies.** Worked with departments throughout the organization to analyze work processes and develop and implement productivity and efficiency improvements. Teamed with Human Resources and Compensation departments to rewrite job descriptions. Upgraded staff and salary grades.

ACHIEVEMENTS: Within nine months after joining the company, orchestrated the revitalization of Capital Market Operations, enabling SFC to achieve recognition by the Federal Reserve as full-fledged securities Broker/Dealer (Tier II Review). Effectively managed relationships at all levels of the organization to facilitate the following measurable process, productivity, and profit improvements:

U.S. MILITARY EXPERIENCE: United States Navy, 19xx to 19xx; Active/Reserves, 19xx to Present. Honorably discharged veteran with Top Secret clearance.

JOB RELATED CERTIFICATIONS AND LICENSES: New York State Official, Notary Public; Member, Franchise Industry Association

## ADDITIONAL INFORMATION

**SUMMARY OF SIGNIFICANT SKILLS AND EXPERIENCE:**

**CRITICAL SKILLS:** Budget Formulation; Justification and Execution; Project and Program Management; Strategic Planning and Performance Measurement; Financial and Operational analyses; Fiscal Risk, Change Management; Developing and Implementing Internal Controls; Relationship Management; Cash Management & Control; Training & Organizational Development; Profit and Loss; Productivity and Efficiency Improvement; Information Technology Management. Strong critical thinking, problem solving, analytical, team building, mentoring, and leadership skills.

**PLANNING, BUDGETING, and PERFORMANCE CYCLE MANAGEMENT EXPERIENC**E. Devise creative solutions to achieve organizational missions through budget planning, resource management, and negotiating requirements. Develop and implement effective business performance outcome measures. Reengineer processes and procedures. Formulate strategic business and fiscal management plans. Expertise writing and presenting business operating plans, budget and financial reports and narratives, and program development plans.

# LIONEL TIMMONS

**ATTORNEY-ADVISOR / GENERAL ATTORNEY / SUPERVISORY ATTORNEY**
**LEGAL AND KINDRED GROUP, GS-0900**

## Legal

#9 in professional fields for projected government hiring in FY 2007 - 2009
9,691 projected to be hired in 2009

Includes attorney, contact representative, paralegal, passport/visa examining, and claims examining/assistance.

| Top Ten Hiring Agencies | No. of Employees | Projected Hires |
|---|---|---|
| Department of Treasury | 15,154 | 4,152 |
| Social Security Administration | 12,569 | 3,000 |
| Department of Justice | 13,117 | 2,680 |
| Department of Veterans Affairs | 6,495 | 850 |
| Department of Homeland Security | 1,363 | 505 |
| Deparmtent of Labor | 1,667 | 447 |
| Securities and Exchange Commission | 1,350 | 258 |
| Department of Transportation | 696 | 180 |
| Department of Commerce | 872 | 172 |
| Federal Communications Commission | 476 | 75 |
| Total (all agencies) | | **9,691** |

Partnership for Public Service, *Where the Jobs Are: Mission Critical Opportunities for America*, July 2007, http://ourpublicservice.org/OPS/publications/viewcontentdetails.php?id=118

# Facts

**Past Position:** Private Practice Attorney (Solo Practitioner)
**Past Salary:** $85,000
**Target Federal Job:** Attorney-Advisor and General Attorney, GS-905-14/15

## Qualifications

Lionel was planning to relocate from Florida to Colorado for personal reasons. A career-long attorney, Lionel was not licensed to practice in Colorado, which made government employment the best option. To be a federal attorney, one must only be licensed in one of the fifty states or the District of Columbia. Lionel demonstrates a high level of experience as an attorney, with over 20 years experience handling complex cases. He has practiced in county government and in private practice, in all areas of the law. He developed a specialty in resource and land use law, which makes Department of the Interior jobs a great match. He also has firm administrator experience, making supervisory jobs an option, too.

## Starting Salary

$115,000 - $149,000 USD per year. Lionel can negotiate within this range, and this would be a significant increase over his previous solo practice job. As a federal employee, he will not have to worry about the overhead of having his own firm or the pressure of constantly generating new clients. His income will remain stable despite changes in the economy. Although at a senior level in his career, Lionel plans to work for many more years and can benefit from federal retirement, as well as other excellent benefits such as paid time off and health insurance.

## Promotion/Promotional Potential

Lionel is qualified at the GS-15 level, but is open to GS-14 jobs as an entrée into a federal career. Future promotion potential includes Senior Executive Service and Administrative Law Judge positions, which would give him more responsibility and more autonomy in his work. He is well qualified for these promotions and will be well positioned after one to two years in a GS-15 job.

## Results

This was Lionel's first application for a federal job, and he was referred to the selecting official. He applied to several positions in the 905 series at the GS-14 and GS-15 levels, and was rated best qualified and referred for this GS-15 Supervisory Attorney at the Department of the Interior. He is still awaiting news on selection.

# Target Job Announcement

## Supervisory Attorney-Adviser (General)

| | |
|---|---|
| SALARY RANGE:<br>115,451.00 - 149,000.00 USD per year | OPEN PERIOD:<br>Monday, April 14, 20xx to Wednesday, May 14, 20xx |
| SERIES & GRADE: GS-0905-15 | POSITION INFORMATION:<br>Full Time Excepted Service Permanent |
| PROMOTION POTENTIAL: 15 | DUTY LOCATIONS: 1 vacancy - Lakewood, CO |

This is the actual job Lionel applied for and was referred to the selecting official. It requires a resume, questionnaire, and KSA narratives. It is a lengthy application and has a lot of instructions that must be followed exactly. Attorney positions have a positive education requirement (JD or LLM required) so transcripts must be presented. Also, federal attorneys must be a member in good standing of the bar association of any of the 50 states or the District of Columbia. Other than those two minimum requirements, each announcement will state whether experience practicing law is required and if so, for how long.

While this announcement is very specialized, we also analyzed other attorney announcements and made sure to include key words required for jobs pertaining to the specific tasks and duties of a legal professional. Some of the critical key words for attorneys, in general, are: research, legal analysis, legal writing, oral communication, provide advice, statutory interpretation, litigation, and solving problems.

EXCEPTED SERVICE POSITIONS: Some positions—and even all positions in some agencies—are specifically excepted from the competitive service by law, the president, or OPM. Excepted service positions are filled without the use of OPM's competitive examining procedures. Many excepted service positions require certification or licensing beyond the Government's control that it is not practicable to hold a competitive examination for them or to apply the usual competitive examining procedures to them. For example, attorney positions are excepted from the competitive examining process. For all practical purposes, the bar exam replaces competitive examining. Even so, agencies are required to adhere to the principle of merit in filling these positions, and agencies may devise their own processes to identify highly qualified applicants.

## Major Duties:

This position is a supervisory attorney in the Denver Regional Office of the Rocky Mountain Region. The incumbent assists the Regional Solicitor in the oversight and management of the Rocky Mountain Region and is the **direct supervisor** of the support staff and attorney-advisors in the Denver Regional Office. Major duties include, but are not limited, to the following:

- Provides **legal advice and counsel** on matters which may include **general law, resource law, environmental law** or other areas of law performed by the Department.
- May provide legal services under such laws as the **National Environmental Policy Act, the Mineral Leasing Act, Federal Land Policy and Management Act, Endangered Species Act,** and other **public land, mining, oil and gas, water,** and **environmental** laws that might apply to the Department's activities.
- May provide legal services in **employment law** matters including representing the Department **administrative hearings** before the **EEOC, MSPB,** and/or **FLRA.** Also oversees assigned duties related to **FOIA, the Privacy Act, contracts, tort claims,** or other legal matters.
- Appears before **Administrative tribunals** as Department Counsel with ultimate responsibility for assigned cases such as adverse actions and contract **appeals.**
- Performs and supervises highly **technical** and **exhaustive legal research** relative to any of the above legal activities involving **complex** and **difficult facts** and legal situations, and **prepares legal briefs** and **opinions,** both **oral** and **written,** relative to any legal questions presented.
- Works closely with the Department of Justice and U.S. Attorneys Office on **judicial litigation** involving the above-described matters.
- **Supervises attorneys and support staff** which includes **assigning problems, cases** or matters to staff, **initiating overall work plans,** and **dictating priorities.** Also includes hiring staff and managing employee performance.
- Assists Regional Solicitor in **management tasks,** and coordinates with field offices reporting to the Region. **Analyzes workload** and personnel available, reviews **budgetary demands** involved in Regional operations, and **analyzes costs** related to new programs and projects in order to determine and justify expenditures.

## Qualifications:

Minimum Qualifications:

4. Applicants must have a **law degree** from a law school accredited by the American Bar Association;
5. **Be a member in good standing** of a state, territory of the United States, District of Columbia, or Commonwealth of Puerto Rico **bar**; and have

**Six (6) years of professional legal experience** following law school graduation.

# Resume Writing Tips

Use these tips to help you transform your private industry resume into a targeted federal resume. The BEFORE and AFTER resumes are featured on the following pages.

## BEFORE – Private Industry Resume

### Resume Problem

Lionel's previous private resume was not organized in a way that made it easy for a human resources specialist with no legal training to find the top skills and key words; it also did not contain all the information necessary for a federal application. Like many attorneys' resumes, there was little detail about daily duties and responsibilities, with limited usage of keywords. While Lionel had a lot of experience with environmental law, the issues were different in Florida and Colorado. He had challenges finding ways of working the particular Colorado land use laws into his application materials.

## AFTER – Federal Resume Focused Toward Target Position

### Resume Solution

The Resume Place writer provided more description on the top skills of the job, featured knowledge of the specialized statutes, rewrote the accomplishments to use keywords, and focused the resume to be targeted and relevant. By reorganizing Lionel's resume so that we divided the paragraphs by skill sets rather than by particular accomplishments or cases, it better matches the crediting plan that the HR specialist will be following to rate the resume. We featured his accomplishments at the end of each job and gave special treatment to his reported cases (which are not shown here for privacy reasons). We capitalized on local government experience from years earlier, supervisory/administrative experience from private practice, and knowledge of the specialized area of the law. In addition, we made direct comparisons to Lionel's work in Florida and showed how it aligned with particular land use and resource laws in Colorado. This was a winning combination and will be successful for any legal jobs that focus on administrative or general law.

### TIP:

Making direct, parallel comparisons in the resume between your experience and the specialized experience of the target job can help the HR Specialist see how your skills match up.

# LIONEL TIMMONS, ESQ.

500 Clearlake Avenue
St. Augustine, Florida 32080

Primary: 555-555-5555
Email: lioneltimmons@yahoo.com

---

## PROFESSIONAL EXPERIENCE

**LIONEL TIMMONS (ST. AUGUSTINE, FLORIDA)** MARCH 19XX TO DATE     **[12 YEARS]**

- ◆ **Practiced land development**, construction, eminent domain, real property, and land use law
- ◆ **Represented numerous governmental entities** such as the Supervisor of Elections, County Fire District, County Water District, County Construction Industry Licensing Board, City of St. Augustine's Boards of Adjustment and Appeals (requested on conflict cases), et *al.* In the capacity of their advisor, I would analyze and assist the administration on the various issues or cases to be brought before the government and advise the government in an impartial way so that it would have the latitude to make a decision as it sees fit. Many times the issues involved many disciplines or professions and a team approach to planning , organizing, and directing a presentation was involved. In the capacity as their attorney, when they were sued I have successfully represented them in a court of law. E.g. *See* Appendix – Cases, *infra.*
- ◆ **Represented numerous private entities** (e.g. Esso Oil) on land development and land use issues including rezonings, conditional uses (special exceptions), variances, planned unit developments, developments of regional impact, and code enforcement at both the administrative and court hearing levels. Prior to any hearing for a development order, rezoning, or conditional use, information was obtained from the owner, his engineers and planners, and the government's building and zoning officials. Based upon the information obtained, I developed a plan for an organized presentation, which I directed and controlled to a successful outcome. I always kept an open mind and sought a team approach. This approach has resulted in many unique solutions.
- ◆ **Established various principles** of land use and development law. *See* Appendix-Cases, *infra.*
- ◆ **Designed a process** for a shopping center to understand the maze of leases it had executed and determine the parameters of its ability to expand with additional leases.
- ◆ **Negotiated, drafted, and reviewed purchase agreements and commercial leases** including residential (multifamily and single family), office, warehouse, and shopping center developments.
- ◆ **Law Firm Administrator**. I administrated and ran this small business.

**ROBINS, ELLIOTT AND ASNER, LLC (ST. AUGUSTINE, FLORIDA)** AUGUST 19XX TO MARCH 19XX
**[14 YEARS]**

- ◆ **Vice-President**, Secretary and Treasurer of AV rated law firm. The firm dissolved in 19xx.
- ◆ **Represented numerous governmental and private entities** in the manner previously stated above.
- ◆ **Law Firm Administrator.** This firm consisted of approximately 30 persons of which 14 were lawyers. When forced to move the office to another location, financial and administrative issues arose. I was part of a three-person team to solve this problem. I was instrumental in planning, organizing, and persuading the team to adopt a unique approach to budgeting and administrating the law firm. The new system required the preparation of an overall and individual budget, monitoring progress in relationship to both budgets, and an evaluation of employee performances and the organizations' productivity. I was then selected to implement this new approach and administrate the law firm for its first year at the new location.
- ◆ **County Bar Association.** President, Vice-President, Secretary, Treasurer. For five years I was actively involved as an officer of the Bar Association. Like any organization, this required budgeting, planning and organizing functions, and the overseeing of the business of running a bar association.

Lionel Timmons, Esq.
500 Clearlake Avenue
St. Augustine, Florida 32080
Primary: xxx-xxx-xxxx
Email: lioneltimmons@yahoo.com

U.S.Citizen
SSN: xxx-xx-xxxx
Veteran's preference: N/A

## PROFESSIONAL EXPERIENCE

**ATTORNEY AT LAW**
Lionel Timmons
P.O. Box 444 St. Augustine, FL, 32080
Supervisor: N/A; self-employed.

March 19xx – Present [12 years]
50+ hours per week (average)
Salary: $85,000 per year

**ATTORNEY** AND **FIRM ADMINISTRATOR** in this small business. Supervise **legal support personnel** and manage 20-25 simultaneous cases.

PRACTICE **LAND DEVELOPMENT, ENVIRONMENTAL, REAL PROPERTY, LAND USE, eminent domain,** and **construction law**. **Interpret** and **apply statutes**, regulations, directives, case law, administrative rulings, legal precedents, and court decisions.

**LEGAL REPRESENTATIVE** TO **GOVERNMENT** AND PRIVATE ENTITIES; a sampling of clients includes Esso Oil, Supervisor of Elections, County Fire District, County Water District, County Construction Industry Licensing Board, and the City of St. Augustine's Boards of Adjustment and Appeals (requested on conflict cases).

**ANALYZE ISSUES** AND **ADVISE CLIENTS** on various issues or cases brought before the government. Provide impartial advice to government entities to allow latitude in further actions as it sees fit. **Render legal opinions**, both written and oral.

**RESEARCH** AND **ANALYSIS**: Conducted **legal research** on **complex factual, legal,** and **policy** issues. Assemble, correlate, and **analyze** voluminous material. **Draw logical conclusions** and **formulate opinions** based on sound legal positions. Review and/or request documentary evidence. Use computer-aided legal research tools such as LexisNexis and Westlaw, among other sources. **Prepare briefs** and other legal documents including comprehensive citations of cases, opinions, and legal precedents.

ISSUES OFTEN CROSS MULTIPLE DISCIPLINES or professions (engineering, architecture, etc.); use team approach to plan, organize, and direct legal presentations. Examples include **land development** and **land use** issues including rezonings, conditional uses (special exceptions), variances, planned unit developments, developments of regional impact, and code enforcement at both the **administrative** and **court hearing** levels. Prior to any hearing for a development order, rezoning or conditional use, information is obtained from the owner, his engineers and planners, and the government's building and zoning officials. Based upon the information obtained, I develop a plan for an organized presentation which I direct and control to a successful outcome. Results have included numerous innovative solutions.

**ORAL COMMUNICATION** AND PUBLIC PRESENTATIONS: Prepare and deliver persuasive communication; **present complex arguments** in real time before mediators, arbitrators, the judiciary, government officials, and other professionals. **Provide advice** to clients via **oral briefings**. Interview parties and witnesses; conduct depositions. Communicate effectively orally and in writing to convey legal positions and their basis to a wide range of audiences with diverse backgrounds and varied levels of expertise or understanding.

MAKE **PUBLIC PRESENTATIONS** BEFORE GOVERNMENT BODIES including the State Administrative Law Judges, the County, the Cities, construction boards, zoning boards of appeals, and more. Speak from talking points and extemporaneously; respond to questions. Provide unrehearsed information in a manner as to not preclude unduly influenced board decisions. **Represent the government** and private entities.

**WRITING** / DRAFTING RECOMMENDATIONS: Draft recommendations regarding settlement, compromise or adjustment of claims, or termination of litigation; provide advice in legal memoranda. Use computer-aided word processing and presentation software including MS Word and Word Perfect.

**LITIGATION STRATEGY** AND MANAGEMENT: Successfully represent clients in a court of law when suits are deemed necessary. Provide legal advice and guidance on **litigation strategy**, **discovery** and evidentiary issues; prepare **motions**, **interrogatories**, and **appellate briefs**; **attend depositions, hearings,** and **trials** involving a broad scope of matters; experienced in the application of rules of civil, criminal, and appellate procedure and evidence; draft litigation reports, settlement memoranda, and appeal recommendations; **prepare and present cases at trial**, settle claims, and participate in alternative dispute resolution.

KEY ACCOMPLISHMENTS:
+ Designed a process for a shopping center to understand the maze of leases it had executed and determine the parameters of its ability to expand with additional leases.
+ Negotiated, drafted, and reviewed purchase agreements and commercial leases including residential (multifamily and single family), office, warehouse, and shopping center developments.

# CHAD JONES

STATE VOCATIONAL REHABILITATION SPECIALIST SUPERVISOR TO FEDERAL VOCATIONAL REHABILITATION SPECIALIST SUPERVISOR RECEIVES A $21K RAISE AND USES SCHEDULE A APPOINTMENT PERSON WITH DISABILITIES HIRING AUTHORITY SOCIAL SCIENCE, PSYCHOLOGY, AND WELFARE GROUP GS-0100

## SOCIAL SCIENCES
#10 in professional fields for projected government hiring in FY 2007 - 2009
4,151 projected to be hired in 2009

Includes economics, workforce training/development, social work, recreation activities, and public welfare and insurance programs (e.g., unemployment insurance). Also includes intelligence analysis which this study lists under security and protection.

| Top Ten Hiring Agencies | No. of Employees | Projected Hires |
|---|---|---|
| Social Security Administration | 38,637 | 3,000 |
| Department of Labor | 1,960 | 408 |
| Department of Justice | 1,807 | 225 |
| Department of Treasury | 462 | 189 |
| Court Services and Offender Supervision Agency | 795 | 150 |
| Department of Commerce | 516 | 146 |
| Federal Trade Commission | 77 | 18 |
| Office of Personnel Management | 43 | 7 |
| Federal Deposit Insurance Corporation | 60 | 5 |
| Federal Communications Commission | 57 | 3 |
| Total (all agencies) | | 4,151 |

Partnership for Public Service, *Where the Jobs Are: Mission Critical Opportunities for America*, July 2007, http://ourpublicservice.org/OPS/publications/viewcontentdetails.php?id=118

## Facts

**Past Position:** State Of Maryland Vocational Rehabilitation Specialist Supervisor
**Past Salary:** $56,000
**Target Federal Job:** Vocational Rehabilitation Program Specialist (VRPS), Department Of Education, GS-0101-13

## Qualifications

Chad clearly demonstrates in his resume that he has 16 years of experience equivalent to the GS-12 level. His experience actually exceeds the one year of specialized experience specified in the announcement. Even though he was a Schedule A candidate, he still had to have the necessary qualifications and specialized experience for the job. Federal agencies have direct hire authority for Schedule A appointments, but Chad still had to prove in his resume that he was qualified for the job. He had to accumulate enough points to make the "best qualified" list to be selected for an interview.

Chad utilized the Schedule A Certification Letter from the Vocational Rehabilitation agency as indicated on the USAJOBS website. Networking with federal employees, an HR specialist, and supervisors really paid off for Chad.

## Starting Salary

77,353 - $100,554 USD per year. Chad was initially hired at $77,353 USD per year, GS-0101-13.

## Promotion/Promotional Potential

This position can grow to the GS-13 level with a salary of $100,554.

## Federal Job Networking

Chad did not rely solely on the submission of his application package to land his new job. He was proactive in his federal job search. He followed up on his application with the HR contact listed in the announcement after two weeks by email and phone. He researched the agency's mission and networked with current federal employees, former colleagues, and federal hiring managers at the target agency to reinforce his interest in the job. He did an informal site visit to the federal agency to see where the building was located and met different people at the work site, including the federal manager.

## Results

This candidate worked for over 16 years in a state government position very similar to the federal position he was targeting. As a Schedule A applicant (a candidate with a significant disability), he was eligible to apply under two different hiring categories: status and non-status candidate. He qualified for the position based on his specialized experience and was offered the job within three months of beginning his federal job search.

# Target Job Announcement

Vocational Rehabilitation Program Specialist, GS-0101-13

Salary Range: 82,961.00 - 107,854.00 USD per year

Open Period: Thursday, September 11, 20xx to Thursday, October 09, 20xx

Series & Grade: GS-0101-13/13

Position Information: Full-time Permanent

Promotion Potential: 13

Duty Locations: 4 vacancies - Washington DC Metro Area, DC

## Qualifications:

**GS-13: 52 weeks of specialized experience, that equipped the applicant with the particular knowledge, skills, and abilities to perform successfully the duties of the position, and that is typically in or related to the work of the position to be filled. To be creditable, specialized experience must have been equivalent to at least the GS-12 level.**

**Examples of specialized experience** would include a comprehensive knowledge of work with **program planning and development** in areas of **social welfare, health and rehabilitation**; or research work in organizations concerned with social, psychological, vocational or economic aspects of programmed services; and demonstrated knowledge of laws, regulations and policies governing Vocational Rehabilitation programs.

## SELECTIVE FACTOR

The candidate must have experience with **policy development** and **evaluating program effectiveness** for programs authorized under Titles I or V of the Rehabilitation Act of 1973, as amended, obtained through work in a state vocational rehabilitation agency, a Client Assistance Program or protection and advocacy system, or participation on a State Rehabilitation Council.

CANDIDATES WHO DO NOT MEET THE SELECTIVE FACTOR WILL AUTOMATICALLY BE FOUND INELIGIBLE FOR THIS POSITION.

Note: Applicants who met the basic requirements and selective factor, were also rated on their responses to an online questionnaire.

## Tips

- The Questionnaire is critical to any federal application. Chad was able to rate himself as a high candidate on the Self-Assessment Questionnaire. The questionnaire should be reflected on his resume so there is consistency of experience in both Resume and questionnaire).

- The Selective Factor is a "screen out" factor. If you cannot prove this knowledge in your resume, you will not get the job. This entire paragraph is a keyword paragraph.

- Chad had 16 years experience to support this Selective Factor. He also had the required 52 weeks of specialized experience (as described above). He was clearly qualified, but needed his resume to include the specialized experience.

# Resume Writing Tips

Use these tips to help you transform your private industry resume into a targeted federal resume. The BEFORE and AFTER resumes are featured on the following pages.

## BEFORE – Private Industry Resume

### Resume Problem
The client tried to write a federal resume in the Outline Format, but since he held the position for SO long, he could not adequately describe the accomplishments, cases, and technical knowledge. Important keywords such as case review, service delivery system, policy development, and evaluating program effectiveness were missing.

## AFTER – Federal Resume Focused Toward Target Position

### Resume Solution
EXPANDED THE DESCRIPTION AND USED TWO JOB BLOCKS FOR ONE JOB THAT SPANS MANY YEARS. Since Chad's description of his supervisory position of five years was very detailed, it exceeded the 3,000 characters allowed in the USAJOBS Builder. His current position was divided into two Job Blocks so the position could be described in more detail while complying with character limits. Please see Job Block 2, where his current supervisory position description from Job Block 1, including accomplishments, was continued.

Chad Jones
6790 Glen Road
Philadelphia, PA 21117
Evening Phone: 410-555-5555
Day Phone: 410-555-5555
Email: cjones@hotmail.com

WORK EXPERIENCE
Pennsylvania Department of Education-Division of Rehabilitation Services (DORS) 9/19xx - Present
Philadelphia, PA 21111, United States US Salary: 56,616.00 USD Per Year
Hours per week: 40

Vocational Rehabilitation Specialist Supervisor
Knowledge and expertise in area vocational rehabilitation. Plan, develop, implement, and maintain a comprehensive service delivery system for over 16 years.
Areas of expertise include:
Knowledge and expertise in area vocational rehabilitation. Plan, develop, implement, and maintain a comprehensive service delivery system. Handle multiple tasks and make most of available resources. Review and approve eligibility decisions, Plan for Employment, authorization for purchase of training needs, and utilize comparable benefits and resources.

SUPERVISION
Supervise Five Vocational Rehabilitation Counselors. Write performance evaluations on a six-month basis. Design corrective measures as necessary to achieve standards in compliance with Division of Rehabilitation Services and State policies. Ensure that staff are in compliance with eligibility within guidelines. Analyze cases and provide direction for case decisions and management plan for five Vocational Rehabilitation Counselors. Counsel persons with disabilities concerning careers vocations, etc.

DIRECT AND LEAD MANAGEMENT OF CASES
Demonstrate knowledge and ability to interpret complex medical information and diagnostics in order to determine employability and independent living potential. Provide leadership and guidance to assist staff in reaching their outcome goals.

Review and approve eligibility decisions, Plan for Employment, authorization for purchase of training needs, and utilize comparable benefits and resources. Provide technical assistance to staff on policy interpretation and administration of vocational rehabilitation services.

OFFICE MANAGER, PHILADELPHIA OPERATIONS
Facilitate communication, information, and activities between management and staff regarding recruiting efforts and placement procedures with various partnering community agencies, community rehabilitation programs, long-term support agencies, local schools, colleges, and local One Stop Career Center.

Model excellent customer service as a priority by providing follow-up, research, and attention to detail to resolve and address problems within one business day, ensuring customer satisfaction. Provide accurate information pertaining to policy and procedures regarding client inquiries and complaints. Handle multiple tasks and make most of available resources

Demonstrate knowledge and ability to interpret complex medical information and diagnostics in order to determine employability and independent living potential. Provide leadership and guidance to assist staff in reaching their outcome goals.

ADVOCATE
Serve as a spokesperson for subordinates and people with disabilities. Work successfully under deadlines.

COMMUNITY RELATIONSHIPS
Knowledge of techniques in determining program effectiveness, and recommending courses of action for improved performance. Facilitate working relationships with community resources through motivation, encouragement, and empowerment. Facilitate strong and consistent working relationships with employers, private and non-for-profit agencies, businesses, organizations, and federal and state agencies. Achieve and/or exceed the federal and state performance standards.

PERSONS WITH DISABILITIES EMPLOYMENT CONSULTING
Identify and implement reasonable accommodations and architectural barriers to allow people with disabilities to become gainfully employed. Serve on various committees on technical and programmatic issues to enhance and improve service delivery. Provide follow-up services to ensure all individuals with disabilities, including the mental health population, maintain their jobs.

SPECIALIZED KNOWLEDGE
Stays current on vocational rehabilitation trends by attending on-going professional development. Facilitate communication, information, and activities between staff/vendors.

**CHAD JONES**
6790 Glen Road
Philadelphia, PA 21117
Home: 410-555-5555
Work: 410-555-5555
Email: cjones@hotmail.com

**PROFESSIONAL EXPERIENCE**

Job Block 1
VOCATIONAL REHABILITATION SPECIALIST SUPERVISOR, 9/19xx to Present,
Pennsylvania State Department of Education, Division of Rehabilitation Services, DORS
Philadelphia, PA MD 21111
Salary: $56,616/year; 40 hours/week Supervisor: (name/phone)

OFFICE MANAGER, PHILADELPHIA OPERATIONS: **Plan, develop, implement, and manage a comprehensive vocational rehabilitation service delivery system for individuals with physical and mental disabilities.** Oversee daily office operations, provided budgetary oversight, and manage staff of five rehabilitation counselors. **Ensure the quality and delivery of program services** through effective case management, client advocacy, dedication to customer service, and by **fostering partnerships** with community agencies to fully develop client opportunities for quality employment, education, training, medical care, and rehabilitation.

**MANAGE VOCATIONAL REHABILITATION SERVICES policy development** and **evaluate program effectiveness** for programs authorized under Titles I or V of the Rehabilitation Act of 1973, as amended.

OPERATIONS MANAGEMENT: Supervise all daily operations and manage $500,000 client services budget. Review and approve eligibility decisions and Plans for Employment. Direct case service allocations, and authorize expenditures and payments for diagnostics services, such as psychological and medical evaluations, career assessments, vocational training, and job placement.

CONDUCT PERFORMANCE BENCHMARKING: **Evaluate program effectiveness and performance metrics** daily to pinpoint areas for improvement. Interpret and apply knowledge of vocational rehabilitation laws, rules, and regulations to assure compliance. **Develop solutions to strengthen and improve delivery of services to disabled individuals.**

CUSTOMER SERVICE: First point of contact for client inquiries and services issues. Promote the highest standards of performance and customer service. Strive to address, research, and resolve all problems within one business day to ensure customer satisfaction.

CASE REVIEW AND MANAGEMENT: Review and analyze all staff caseload and provide direction for case decisions and management. Review and oversee as many as 15 cases per week. Ensure case documentation complies with state and federal policies and deadlines. Monitor performance standards, timelines, case movement, and expenditures to ensure clients become successful in employment. Interpret complex medical information and diagnostics to determine employability and independent living potential.

MENTOR AND MOTIVATE STAFF: Provide technical assistance and guidance on policy interpretation and the administration of vocational rehabilitation services. Lead and guide staff with reaching target outcome goals for eligibility determination, IPE development, adherence to policies and procedures, and successful employment outcomes. Encourage independent problem solving, teamwork, and innovation; and the importance of delivering services promised to clients. Lead brainstorming sessions to develop creative solutions to challenging client placements. Write performance evaluations on a six-month basis.

Characters: 2870 total characters with spaces.

**Job Block 2**
VOCATIONAL REHABILITATION SPECIALIST SUPERVISOR, 9/19xx to Present, Pennsylvania State Department of Education, Division of Rehabilitation Services, DORS
Salary: $56,616/year; 40 hours/week

Continued from Job Block 1
FOSTER STRONG COMMUNITY PARTNERSHIPS: Facilitate productive, consistent working relationships between employers, private and not-for-profit agencies, and federal and state agencies through motivation, encouragement, and empowerment. Communicate daily, both orally and in writing, with community partners to maximize use of available resources and to fully develop client opportunities for quality employment, education, training, medical care, and rehabilitation.

DISABILITY ADVOCATE: Serve as an **advocate and spokesperson for the disabled** by supporting the removal of physical and attitudinal barriers and by promoting their abilities and accomplishments in the community. Lead presentations for community groups and employers to promote disability awareness, hiring, and education on how to work with people with disabilities. Clearly communicate information on the Americans with Disabilities Act (ADA) and other key regulations.

COMMUNITY LEADERSHIP, **DISABILITIES EMPLOYMENT CONSULTING**: Identify and implement reasonable accommodations and architectural barriers to allow people with disabilities to become gainfully employed. Assemble teams of experts, as needed to identify the best means of accessibility at a work site or client home. Serve on agency committees to address technical and programmatic issues, improve and strengthen service delivery to clients, and develop collaborative partnership opportunities to assist clients to become competitively employed.

ACCOMPLISHMENTS:
++ Instrumental in achieving a placement success rate of 70% and a customer service satisfaction rate of 86%. Achieved or exceeded federal and state performance standards throughout 16-year career.

++ Orchestrated and led a successful vocational rehabilitation placement for a challenging client with immediate employment needs. Assembled a team to expedite assessment and training, and arranged employer interviews and community resources. By expediting the case management process, client was able to secure a new temporary job within weeks and subsequently secured a permanent position.

++ Drove increases in employment outcomes for the disabled through networking, teamwork, and positive, open communication with community groups and employers.

Characters: 2263 characters with spaces

309

**ADDITIONAL INFORMATION**

*Tip: You can review your top qualifications in this section in USAJOBS to ensure your qualifications are clear!*

QUALIFICATIONS SUMMARY

Results-oriented Vocational Rehabilitation Specialist / Supervisor with more than **16 years of successful performance in vocational rehabilitation counseling**. Combines sound staff leadership and business-management abilities with a professional, hands-on administrative style that inspires goal-oriented work and enhances the quality of services and case management for individuals with disabilities. Professional, and articulates with well-developed interpersonal and counseling skills. Team player, team builder, and effective community liaison.

VOCATIONAL REHABILITATION EXPERTISE AND KNOWLEDGE:

++ **Extensive knowledge of vocational rehabilitation counseling**, case management techniques, and diagnostic assessment processes and placement testing.

++ Exceptional record of performance providing vocational rehabilitation plans, guidance and counseling services to a diverse population. Compassionate, empathetic, and an excellent listener. Excels in motivating and empowering individuals with disabilities and helping them to become stable, employed, and integrated in society.

++ Keen ability to establish mutual trust with others and communicate with people from diverse cultural, educational, and economic backgrounds.

++ Comprehensive **knowledge of federal and state vocational rehabilitation laws, rules, and regulations** and One-Stop Delivery Systems gained through career experience and extensive professional development.

# MICHAEL DRUMMER

## Administration and Program Management

#4 in professional fields for projected government hiring in FY 2007 - 2009
14,305 projected to be hired in 2009

Includes human resources, equal employment opportunity, management/program analysis, telecommunications and a variety of clerical support activities

| Top Ten Hiring Agencies | No. of Employees | Projected Hires |
|---|---|---|
| Department of Defense | 13,113 | 3,188 |
| Department of Justice | 8,513 | 2,908 |
| Department of Housing and Urban Development | 2,705 | 1,213 |
| Department of Health and Human Services | 4,571 | 789 |
| National Aeronautics and Space Administration | 3,239 | 665 |
| Department of Commerce | 1,122 | 552 |
| Department of Agriculture | 3,873 | 525 |
| General Services Administration | 2,000 | 474 |
| Department of Veterans Affairs | 1,527 | 418 |
| Department of Transportation | 595 | 360 |
| Total (all agencies) | | 14,305 |

Partnership for Public Service, *Where the Jobs Are: Mission Critical Opportunities for America*, July 2007, http://ourpublicservice.org/OPS/publications/viewcontentdetails.php?id=118

## Facts

**Past Position:** Semi-Retired, Real Estate Developer
**Past Salary:** $200,000
**Target Federal Job:** Administrative and Program Management, GS-0301, Iraq Jobs

## Qualifications

Mr. Drummer demonstrated in his resume that he has outstanding entrepreneurial experience, having started several of his own companies. He shows that he can serve as a Senior Economic Advisor to those who would revitalize the economy of Iraq by providing a broad range of expert technical and advisory services in support of the U.S. mission. He demonstrates that he has already served as an overseas Station Chief in a developing country with the Peace Corps. He also demonstrates through his experience that he could work actively with Team Leaders and representatives of various U.S. Agencies and the military, as well as aid organizations and the Iraqi government to build capacity and self-reliance. His experience is sufficient to qualify him for this position and it appears to be a "good fit."

## Starting Salary

$93,822 - $143,471 USD per year. Michael presented W-2s from the highest salary position he has held (Peace Corps about 10 years ago) at $150K. He was offered the $150K to match, plus 35% incentive pay for the Iraq Assignment totaling approximately $225K.

## Promotion/Promotional Potential

This position is a one-year temporary position, to be extended and offered based on experience, budget, and opportunity. Promotion potential and incentives will depend on budget and performance.

## Results

Michael was serious and put a lot of time in researching and writing new information to transition the writing for private industry real estate owner / developer to federal positions in finance, operations, and senior level positions. We worked on the federal job campaign for four months and produced and submitted various applications with a federal resume, CHART RESUMIX (Navy system), KSAs, Private Industry (www.opsladders.com), and a www.fedbizopps.gov application. JOB OFFER: After four months, Michael was offered and accepted a position with the U.S. Department of State. He will be sworn into the Department of State mid-February and will fly to Iraq two days later. Michael is very thrilled about this opportunity. He negotiated a GS 15/15 salary of $150K plus a 70% differential, which is about $230K. He will deserve it in Iraq.

Michael found his announcement on www.fedbizopps.gov (early December) and passed clearance, medical, and all examinations. He really wanted to do something important with his life and is very pleased. He will begin three weeks of intensive training in Arabic language and cultural training.

# Target Job Announcement

This is a great announcement for Mr. Drummer because it emphasizes the kinds of international business challenges that fit his particular skill set. The "Job Summary" on the first page of the announcement says: "The U.S. Department of State is the lead U.S. foreign affairs agency. Our mission in Iraq is to support the sovereign, democratic rights of the Iraqi people to govern themselves, defend their country, and rebuild their economy. The Iraq Reconstruction Management Office (IRMO) was established by National Security Presidential Directive (NSPD) 36 to facilitate this mission. Join IRMO and help shape a freer, more secure and prosperous Iraq."

To be considered for this position, the candidate had to respond online to these Screening Questions in a narrative or essay AND demonstrate these competencies in his resume. Screening questions are on the CD-ROM.

## PRT Senior Economic Advisor

| | |
|---|---|
| SALARY RANGE:<br>93,822.00 - 143,471.00 USD per year | OPEN PERIOD:<br>Monday, May 21, 20xx to Wednesday, November 14, 20xx |
| SERIES & GRADE: AD-0301-05/05 | POSITION INFORMATION:<br>Full Time Temporary Excepted Appointment NTE 13 months |
| PROMOTION POTENTIAL: 05 | DUTY LOCATIONS:<br>Few vacancies - Washington DC/TDY to Iraq |

JOB SUMMARY:
The U.S. Department of State is the lead U.S. foreign affairs agency. Our mission in Iraq is to support the sovereign, democratic rights of the Iraqi people to govern themselves, defend their country, and rebuild their economy. The Iraq Reconstruction Management Office (IRMO) was established by National Security Presidential Directive (NSPD) 36 to facilitate this mission. Join IRMO and help shape a freer, more secure and prosperous Iraq.

This position is located in one of 20 Provincial Reconstruction Teams (PRT) in Iraq. PRTs directly support U.S. policy priorities by shaping the provincial and municipal political environment and supporting Iraqi moderates, maintaining provincial-level capacity development efforts, and facilitating transition of capacity development activities from U.S. Government to Iraqi Government funds.

The incumbent serves as a PRT Senior Economic Advisor with responsibility for providing a broad range of expert technical and advisory services in support of the U.S. mission in Iraq. The Senior Economic Advisor is a key member of the PRT, working actively with PRT Team Leader and representatives of various US Agencies and the military, as well as aid organizations and the Iraqi government, to build capacity and self-reliance.

THIS POSITION IS BASED IN IRAQ.

KEY REQUIREMENTS:
* Must be able to obtain and maintain a Secret security clearance
* TEMPORARILY ASSIGNED TO IRAQ
* Must be able to obtain a medical clearance
* Must be able to obtain an ethics clearance
* U.S. Citizenship required

# Resume Writing Tips

Use these tips to help you transform your private industry resume into a targeted federal resume. The BEFORE and AFTER resumes are featured on the following pages.

## BEFORE – Private Industry Resume

### Resume Problem

This was Michael's private industry resume from Ladders.com, which did not include any of the keywords from the target international announcement. The private industry resume did focus on project management, senior management, and operations. The real estate-specific experience was toned down due to the downturn in real estate development and the real estate economy at that time. Keywords for his resume were researched on ladders.com and the profile was changed based on his interests.

## AFTER – Federal Resume Focused Toward Target Position

### Resume Solution

OUR MATCHING STRATEGY: Mr. Drummer's background in real estate development, negotiations, and problem-solving in communities will support the skills required by the Provincial Reconstruction Team in Iraq. The goal was to match the economic development experience in Connecticut and Denver with economic development in Iraq.

The target State Department announcement was analyzed for keywords and a new federal resume was produced featuring the Outline Format with keywords in ALL CAPS. This format is readable and provides emphasis on international experience, leadership, and technical experience for the TRP economic development work. High-level decision-making and negotiations were also emphasized.

**MICHAEL C. DRUMMER**
*500 Brumfield*
*Williamsburg, Virginia 23188*
*Phone: (757) 555.5557*
mcdrummer@gmail.com

**Operations Manager / Strategic Planner / Growing or Start-up**

TARGET INDUSTRIES (flexible): Transportation, distribution, facilities, manufacturing, small business (growth), and start-up.

STRATEGIC PLANNER AND BUSINESS DEVELOPMENT: Proven expertise in business development, contract management, negotiation, marketing and analyzing potential for profitable business directions. SUCCESSFUL TRACK RECORD.

OPERATIONS AND PROJECT MANAGER: More than 25 years of experience in project management, successfully meeting deadlines, time and budget objectives. CLIENT SATISFACTION is primary consideration!

INTERNATIONAL DEVELOPMENT: Former Peace Core Country Director for Kyrgyzstan. Global perspective. Readily adaptable to various cultures having lived in Kyrgyzstan, Morocco, Turkey, and France and traveled extensively throughout 37 other countries.

EXECUTIVE COMPETENCIES: Leading people, entrepreneurial, creative, initiative, and highly skilled in public relations and opportunity development.

**EXPERIENCE:** 25 Years
**HIGHEST EDUCATION:** Bachelor

**JOB GOAL**
SENIOR MANAGER / PROJECT MANAGER - OPERATIONS AND MARKETING
**COMMUTE:** Within 2500 miles of 23188  Willing to consider any other location

**WORK EXPERIENCE**
**FOUNDER AND CEO AT PALMETTO GROUP, INC. PARK CITY, UTAH**
1-100 Employees, Real Estate Development Company
January 19xx — December 20xx (13 years, 11 months) Comp: $125k-$150k

**FOUNDER, CEO, and OPERATIONS MANAGER** of this Management Consulting firm. Grew the business into a leading construction management firm for multi-million dollar properties in Park City, Utah. Networked, developed relationships, and grew business and contracts through quality service, meeting time and cost deadlines, and outstanding public relations. Obtained a B100 unlimited General Contractors license and created new construction division.

**LEADERSHIP SKILLS:**

**OPERATIONS MANAGER.** Hands-on manager, overseeing all business aspects (estimating and bidding, contract management, project management, labor laws, lien laws, financial management, risk management, critical path management and safety), built and managed more than $25 million worth of new construction over a three-year period. Also improved internal operations to improve efficiency and cost control:

- Reorganized accounting policies and reduced delinquent accounts receivable by 70%.
- Achieved maximum operational efficiency by streamlining communication systems, office procedures, and eliminating excess waste.
- Established consistency in operating standards by reorganizing and integrating multiple business entities.

**STRATEGIC PLANNER**. Developed strategic plan to expand Palmetto Group into residential and resort properties. Increased sales 450% in three years.

- Developed capital plans for the company to ensure valuable resources were fully utilized resulting in savings of $1,500,000; increased revenue of more than $600,000 annually and increased net worth of properties held by the company by $6,000,000.

**CONSULTANT AND OUTSTANDING CLIENT SERVICES:**

- Managed more than 1,000,000 sq ft of industrial space and 600,000 sq ft of commercial space. Negotiated leases, addressed deferred maintenance issues, and worked directly with architects, engineers, and design contractors.

**PRESIDENT AT THE WESTON GROUP, MIDDLETOWN, CT**
1-100 Employees, Real Estate and Construction Company
January 19xx — January 19xx (8 years) Comp: $100k-$125k

**FOUNDER, PROPERTY DEVELOPMENT FIRM AND COMMUNITY DEVELOPMENT.**
Performed every phase of real estate development and project management, from acquiring sites to coordinating the professional team; obtained local government approvals, market analysis, pre-construction planning, design, construction, marketing, and management. Coordinated private equity financing, joint ventures and syndications, and direct participation programs to provide equity capital and raise external loan financing. Provided investment advisory services and functioned as securities broker/dealer.

**MICHAEL C. DRUMMER**
*500 Brumfield*
*Williamsburg, Virginia 23188*
*Phone: (757) 555.5557*
mcdrummer@gmail.com

Citizenship: US
Highest Civilian Grade: GS-15 Equivalent (US Peace Corps)
Current Civilian Grade: N/A
Veterans Status: Coast Guard Veteran
Security Clearance: Top Secret-Peace Corps (Not Current)

OBJECTIVE: ANNOUNCMENT NUMBER: IRMO-2007-0170
POSITION TITLE: PRT Senior Economic Advisor- (Iraq)
PERIOD OF PERFORMANCE: 13 months
ORGANIZATIONAL LOCATION OF POSITION: Washington DC / TDY to Iraq
AREA OF CONSIDERATION: All US Citizens

**PROFESSIONAL PROFILE:**

- BUSINESS DEVELOPMENT: **Experienced business developer with outstanding strategic, technical, and organizational leadership skills**. Comfortable advising others who are interested in tackling new business start-up challenges. Known for the ability to collaborate with individuals and teams to develop business strategies and manage specific components of strategies to meet measurable performance benchmarks. Recognized as an expert in private sector development, including host-country economic development programs and policies, having served as a Country Director (GS-15) in the Peace Corps, in Kyrgyzstan.

- BUSINESS ACUMEN: Excellent business instincts, including **financial and human resource allocation, and leveraging technological resources**. Demonstrated ability to provide exceptional customer services by assessing customer needs, meeting quality standards, and evaluating customer satisfaction.

- LEADER OF CHANGE: Accomplished at leading change, starting new companies and taking them from conceptualization through to completion, and also reorganizing existing companies. **Skilled at evaluating, negotiating, planning, budgeting, and administering projects and proposals with an emphasis on dollar productive activities**. Ability to convince others of the value of a specific course of action.

- **GOVERNMENT ISSUES**: Intensely curious about how things work in politics, the world of investing, community affairs, business, and governmental issues. Always willing to seek the advice of experts in various fields before coming to a conclusion or final decision.

**TECHNICAL SKILLS:**

- PRIVATE SECTOR DEVELOPMENT: Knowledgeable in all phases of business start-up/turnaround projects, construction and land use, property development, redevelopment, interaction with government and elected officials, attorneys, engineers, and architects, management of complex and varied development operations, and recruitment, training, supervising, and motivation of personnel at all levels of an organization.

- CONSTRUCTION MANAGEMENT: More than 25 years of experience in construction management, real estate development, sales and marketing, real estate securitization, lending, investment advisory services, and start-up/turn around projects. Experienced at design/build and fixed bid contracts. Managed multiple multi-million dollar construction projects and related activities simultaneously.

- INTERNATIONAL DEVELOPMENT: Former Peace Corps Country Director for Kyrgyzstan. Readily adaptable to various cultures having lived in Kyrgyzstan, Morocco, Turkey, and France for more than eight years, and traveled extensively throughout 37 other countries.

## PROFESSIONAL EXPERIENCE

**FOUNDER AND CEO**  
Palmetto Group Inc  
Park City, Utah  
Palmetto Group, LLC, Williamsburg, Virginia  
Supervisor: N/A

19xx – 20xx  
40 + Hrs per week  
Salary: $200,000.00 per yr (average)

**BUSINESS DEVELOPMENT**: Founded and functioned as CEO of the Princeton Group, Inc., and Princeton Group, LLC specializing in management consulting, construction management, real estate development, and lending. Analyzed operations to evaluate performance of a company and its staff in meeting objectives and to determine areas of potential cost reduction, program improvement, or policy change. Effectively managed the company's overall vision, mission, strategy, goals, and objectives, and worked with employees to support these plans in order to achieve profit targets and maximized dollar productive activities.

**BUSINESS AND FINANCIAL MANAGEMENT:** Branched off into property development/new construction by obtaining a B100 unlimited General Contractors license and creating a new construction management division of the company. Deeply involved in all phases of the business organization including estimating and bidding, contract management, project management, labor laws, lien laws, financial management, risk management, critical path management, and safety. Over a three year period, built and managed more than $25 million worth of new construction. Also expanded the company into sales and marketing residential and resort properties. Increased sales 450% in three years.

_Significant Accomplishments_:

Of all major accomplishments, the most significant were achieved during a single consulting engagement over a 15-month period, as outlined below:

- Reorganized accounting policies and reduced delinquent accounts receivable by 70%.

- Achieved maximum operational efficiency by streamlining communication systems, office procedures, and eliminating excess waste.

- Established consistency in operating standards by reorganizing and integrating multiple business entities.

- Managed more than 1,000,000 sq ft of industrial space and 600,000 sq ft of commercial space. Negotiated leases, addressed deferred maintenance issues, and worked directly with architects, engineers, and design contractors.

- Developed capital plans for the company to ensure valuable resources were fully utilized resulting in savings of $1,500,000; increased revenue of more than $600,000 annually and increased net worth of properties held by the company by $6,000,000.

**COUNTRY DIRECTOR**                                                          19xx
Peace Corps of the United States                             40 + Hours per week
Washington, DC and Bishkek, Kyrgyzstan GS-15 (Step 7)

**OVERSEAS/MULTI-CULTURAL:** Independently, and with freedom to act on behalf of the United States Government, established the initial Peace Corps program in Kyrgyzstan, a republic of the former Soviet Union. Exercised complete responsibility for analyzing, implementing, managing, and directing all aspects of this Peace Corps program in a highly challenging environment. This was a start-up operation in a country where few Americans had ever been. Personally developed the vision for the country program and created the plan for achieving that vision. Established temporary office space.

**VISITING FELLOW, MCF, WOODROW WILSON SCHOOL**             19xx – 19xx
Princeton University                                         40 + Hours per week
Princeton, New Jersey                                               Salary: N/A
Supervisor: Not Available
ADVANCED ACADEMIC: Following an intense and highly competitive selection process, was honored by being invited to participate in this rigorous and intensive one-year program. The program was designed to afford an exclusive group of Federal Senior Executives, visiting foreign scholars, and mid-career professionals in international and domestic public policy, and private sector professionals with an opportunity to broaden their economic, policy, and leadership skills.

# Index

# STILL NEED ASSISTANCE WITH YOUR FEDERAL JOB APPLICATION?

Trust your job application to the experts.

Try our professional federal resume and KSA writing services, career consulting, and USAJOBS training!

Kathryn Troutman, Author and president of The Resume Place, Inc. and the team of Certified Federal Resume Writers who wrote the successful federal resumes in this book can help you put your very best foot forward in your federal job search.

The Resume Place has been in the business of advising federal job seekers for over 30 years, and we have trained many of our competition.

We can assist you with every step of your federal job search:
✪ Creating your own Outline Format USAJOBS Federal Resume
✪ Finding the right vacancy announcements
✪ Identifying your keywords
✪ Showcasing your accomplishments
✪ Using the proper formatting techniques
✪ Writing effective KSAs and questionnaire answers
✪ Applying online
✪ Interviewing

"Kathryn Troutman is helping applicants learn to be concise and reinvention-minded when they get ready to market themselves to federal agencies."
✪ Brian Friel, Government Executive Magazine

"When it comes to getting a federal job, few people know more than Kathryn Kraemer Troutman."
✪ Mike Causey, former columnist, Washington Post

"This was the best investment I ever made. The results were fantastic and it landed me my permanent job!"
✪ Mathew K.

Professional federal job search consulting and writing services are available to you a la carte or as packages to accommodate your job objectives and budget. Our personalized, expert services are tailored to your needs. For a complete listing and description of our services, check our website at www.resume-place.com.

| Professional Service | Hours |
|---|---|
| Start-up Consult – Federal Job Search Discussion<br>*Starting point: professional review of your job search* | 1 |
| Finding Job Announcements—USAJOBS Orientation<br>*Become a skilled announcement searcher on USAJOBS*<br>*Prerequisite: Start-up Consult* | 1 |
| Resume Critique<br>*Get a certified resume writer's critique of your resume draft*<br>*Prerequisite: Start-up Consult* | 1 |
| Federal Resume Writing<br>*See our packages for your every writing need*<br>*Prerequisite: Start-up Consult* | 2-8 |
| KSA/Questionnaire Consult<br>*Learn the keys to an effective KSA*<br>*Lessons in completing Questionnaires correctly* | 1 |
| KSA/Questionnaire Critique<br>*Get input on the KSAs you have already written*<br>*Prerequisite: KSA/Questionnaire Consult* | 1 |
| KSA/Questionnaire Writing<br>*For help with writing KSAs*<br>*Priced per application depending on scope* | 2-4 |
| Keyword Analysis<br>*Find out the keywords in an announcement* | 1 |
| Interview Prep | 1-3 |
| Salary Negotiation | 1 |
| SES – see our SES page | |

**Fees:** *Professional Certified Resume Writers and Coaches: $125-150/hour*

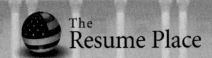

The
Resume Place

89 Mellor Avenue  Baltimore, MD 21228
(888) 480-8265
www.resume-place.com
Email: resume@resume-place.com

*Photo: Emily Troutman*

# Kathryn K. Troutman

Kathryn K. Troutman is the founder and president of The Resume Place, Inc., a service business located in Baltimore, MD, specializing in writing and designing professional federal and private-sector resumes, as well as coaching and education in the federal hiring process. For over 30 years, Ms. Troutman has managed a professional writing and consulting practice, a publishing and federal career training business, and a team of certified federal resume writers. The Resume Place currently assists hundreds of federal, military, and private industry clients worldwide per month.

Internationally recognized as the "Federal Resume Guru" by federal jobseekers and human resources specialists, Ms. Troutman created the format and name for the new "federal resume" that became the industry standard when the SF-171 form was eliminated in 1995. She outlined her pioneering design and is the author of The Federal Resume Guidebook, now in its 4th printing.

Ms. Troutman is an in-demand, government-contract career trainer, who has trained thousands of federal employees in writing federal resumes, KSAs, Resumix, USAJOBS, and Quickhire resumes for more than 200 federal agencies in the United States and Europe. Her federal career training courses and publications are listed on the GSA Schedule for government agency purchase.

Ms. Troutman created the Certified Federal Job Search Trainer program–the first federal career train-the-trainer program ever–to instruct federal and military career counselors in the federal hiring process. The course is based on her award-winning and popular book, Ten Steps to a Federal Job™. Since 2002, more than 350 career counselors and workshop leaders have been licensed to teach the Ten Steps™ curriculum.

In addition, the 62 U.S. Navy Fleet and Family Support Centers worldwide teach this program to separating and retiring military personnel and family members as part of the Transition Assistance Program (TAP). The U.S. Air Force, Coast Guard, and Army military transition centers use the Ten Steps Jobseeker's Guide™ to help military personnel write federal resumes for submission to Resumix databases. Recently, Ms. Troutman modified her successful Ten Steps™ training program to address the needs of University career counselors nationwide, and offers the Certified Federal Career Counselor program.

Ms. Troutman's additional federal career publications include the award-winning The Student's Federal Career Guide and Military to Federal Career Guide, used in every Navy and Marine Corps base, and most Air Force career transition centers in the world.

A dynamic radio, TV, and online guest, Ms. Troutman answers questions about federal careers, resume writing, and job search techniques. She currently serves as Monster.com's Federal Career Coach and writes a monthly column. She has been quoted and published hundreds of times on the topic of federal resume writing and job search through syndicated news articles by Joyce Lain Kennedy and numerous career columnists. She is a frequent guest on www.washingtonpost.com's Federal Diary Live On-Line and www.federalnewsradio.com. Ms. Troutman is a member of Career Master's Institute, Professional Resume Writing Association, National Resume Writer's Association, Publisher's Marketing Association, and the Association of Women's Business Owners.

Her popular website, www.resume-place.com, receives tens of thousands of visitors per month, and provides online tools to assist jobseekers worldwide.